Second Language Learning and Language Teaching

Vivian Cook

Edward Arnold
A division of Hodder & Stoughton
LONDON NEW YORK MELBOURNE AUCKLAND

©1991 Vivian Cook

First published in Great Britain 1991

Distributed in the USA by Routledge, Chapman and Hall, Inc.
29 West 35th Street, New York, NY 10001

British Library Cataloguing in Publication Data
Cook, Vivian.
    Second language learning and language teaching / Vivian Cook.
        p. cm.
    Includes bibliographical references (p.) and index.
    ISBN 0–340–52626–2 : $15.95
    1. Second language acquisition. 2. Language and languages—
Study and teaching.   I. Title.
P118.2.C67   1991
418′.007—dc20   91–8543
                                                           CIP

Typeset in Times by Anneset, Weston-super-Mare, Avon
Printed and bound in Great Britain for Edward Arnold,
a division of Hodder and Stoughton Limited,
Mill Road, Dunton Green, Sevenoaks, Kent TN13 2YA
by Biddles Limited, Guildford and King's Lynn

Contents

Acknowledgements

This book arose out of the complaints of language teachers that books on L2 learning were too academic and insufficiently linked to the classroom. It benefits from discussions and examples given by teachers, students, colleagues and friends throughout, particularly Bernard Spolsky, David Singleton, Hans Dechert, Patsy Lightbown and Leslie Dickinson. It would never have been finished without the influence of David Murray, Mike Osborne, Ornette Coleman, and Steve Williamson, and of Sam, prince of black cats.

'The really important thing is less the destruction of bad old methods than a positive indication of the new ways to be followed if we are to have thoroughly efficient teaching in modern languages.'

Otto Jespersen 1904

1

Second Language Learning and Language Teaching

Language is at the centre of human life. It is one of the most important ways of expressing our love or our hatred for people; it is vital to achieving many of our goals and our careers; it is a source of artistic satisfaction or simple pleasure. We use language for planning our lives and remembering our past; we exchange ideas and experiences through language; we identify ourselves with people who speak the same language. Some people are able to do this in more than one language. Knowing another language may mean: getting a job; a chance to get educated; the ability to take a fuller part in the life of one's own country or the opportunity to emigrate to another; an expansion of one's literary and cultural horizons; the expression of one's political opinions or religious beliefs. It affects people's careers and possible futures, their lives and very identities. In a world where probably more people speak two languages than speak one, language learning and language teaching are vital to the everyday lives of millions.

A new academic subject has recently emerged, called *second language (L2) learning research* or *second language acquisition research (SLA)*, which looks at second and foreign language learning from a scientific perspective. Though still in its early stages of development, it has already produced insights from many perspectives. Most teachers have been trained to teach, not to think about second language learning. Yet everything that is achieved in the classroom depends eventually upon what goes on in the students' minds. Whether they know it or not, all teachers assume something about L2 learning. Without an understanding of why people need to learn other languages and of how knowledge of other languages is stored and learnt, teachers will always be less effective than they could be. Knowledge about L2 learning is a valuable complement to the teacher's other skills and knowledge.

1. The scope of this book

This book tries to convey why the development of L2 learning research is exciting for language teaching. Its main aim is to inform those concerned with language teaching about L2 learning research. It is not a guide to L2 research methodology or to the merits and failings of particular research techniques, which are covered in other books (Ellis, 1985; McLaughlin, 1987). L2 learning research provides valuable insights into teaching that will help teachers whatever their methodological slant. Partly this is at the general level of understanding; knowing what language learning consists of colours the teacher's awareness of everything that happens in the classroom and heightens the teacher's empathy with the student. Partly it is at the more specific level of the choice of teaching methods, the construction of teaching materials, or the design and execution of teaching techniques. The links between L2 learning and language teaching that are made are mostly suggestions of what can be done rather than accounts of what has been done. Some ideas presented here are based on a solid agreed foundation; others are more controversial or speculative.

The book gradually widens its scope from particular aspects of language to broader contexts and more general ideas. The first two chapters look at how people learn particular aspects of language, grammar in chapter 2, pronunciation, vocabulary, and conversational discourse in chapter 3. The next two chapters treat learners as individuals, chapter 4 looking at how individuals process language by listening, reading, and so on, and chapter 5 describing how learners vary in terms of factors such as motivation and age. Next come aspects of the learning situation: chapter 6 examines the characteristics of language teaching in classrooms, chapter 7 puts L2 learning in the wider context of society. Finally the research is integrated into more general ideas: chapter 8 describes overall models of L2 learning in relationship to teaching, chapter 9 relates teaching methods to L2 learning.

Much of the discussion concerns the L2 learning and teaching of English, mainly because it is the chief language that has been investigated. English is, however, the language used here for exemplification rather than the subject matter itself. The teaching and learning of other modern languages is discussed when appropriate. Most sections of each chapter start with a display defining keywords and end with a boxed summary of the L2 learning area in question.

The contact with the language teaching classroom is maintained in this book chiefly through the discussion of published EFL coursebooks. These provide a window into the classroom, even if good teachers use them only as a jumping-off point. The textbooks and syllabuses cited are taken from countries ranging from Germany to Hungary to the United States, though inevitably for reasons of accessibility the bias is towards those published in England.

2. What the teacher can expect from L2 learning research

Let us take three examples of the contribution L2 learning research can make to language teaching: understanding the students' contribution to learning, understanding how teaching techniques and methods work, and understanding the overall goals of language teaching.

Understanding the student's contribution to learning

All successful teaching depends upon learning; there is no point in providing entertaining, lively, well-constructed, language lessons if students
do not learn. The proof of the teaching is in the learning. One crucial aspect of L2 learning is what the students bring with them into the
classroom. With the exception of young bilingual children, L2 learners
have fully-formed personalities and minds when they start learning the
L2, which have profound effects on their ways of learning and on how
successful they are. L2 learning research for example has established that
the students' diverse motivations for learning the L2 affect them powerfully.
Some see learning the L2 as extending the repertoire of what they can do,
others see it as a threat to their very identities. The different ways in which
students tackle learning also affect their success. For instance those who
rely on getting the overall gist while listening do better than those who
try to make out every word. What is happening in the class is not equally
productive for all the students because their minds work in different ways.
The variations between individuals do not disappear when students come in
the classroom door.

Students base what they do on previous experience of learning and of
using language. They do not start from scratch with no backgrounds or
predispositions to learn language in one way or another. Students also
have much in common by virtue of possessing the same human minds. For
instance L2 learning research predicts that, however advanced they are,
students will find that their memory works less well in the new language,
whether they are trying to remember a phone number or the contents of an
article.

On the one hand L2 learning research helps in understanding how apparently similar students react differently to the same teaching technique. On
the other it reveals the problems that all students share.

Understanding how teaching methods and techniques work

Teaching methods usually incorporate a view of L2 learning, whether
implicitly or explicitly. Grammar-translation teaching emphasizes explanations of grammatical points because this fits in with its view that L2
learning is the acquisition of conscious knowledge. Communicative teaching
methods make the students talk to each other because they see L2 learning
as growing out of communication. For the most part teaching methods
have developed these ideas independently from L2 learning research. They
are not based, say, on L2 research into how learners use grammatical
explanations or how they learn by talking to each other. More information
about how learners actually learn helps the teacher to make *any* method
more effective.

The reason why a teaching technique works or does not work depends
on several factors. A teacher who wants to use a particular technique will
benefit by knowing what it implies in terms of language learning and
language processing, the type of student for whom it is most appropriate,
and the ways in which it fits into the classroom situation. Suppose the

teacher wants to use a communicative game in the classroom, in which the students spontaneously exchange information. This implies that students are learning by communicating, that they are prepared to speak out in the classroom, and that the educational context in the country allows for learning from fellow students rather than from the teacher alone. L2 learning research has something to say about all of these, as we shall see.

Understanding the goals of language teaching

The reasons why the second language is being taught depend upon overall educational goals, which vary from one country to another and from one period to another. One avowed goal of language teaching is to help people to think better — brain-training and logical thinking; another is appreciation of serious literature; another the student's increased self-awareness and maturity; another appreciation of other cultures and races; another communication with people in other countries, and so on. Most of these have been explored in particular L2 learning research. For example the goal of brain-training is supported by evidence that people who know two languages think more flexibly than monolinguals (Landry, 1974). Or, to take the communicative goals, it is crucial to L2 learning how the group to which the L2 learner belongs regards the group that speak the L2 (Schumann, 1978). This information is vital when considering the viability and teaching implementation of communicative goals for a particular group of students. L2 learning research can help define the goals of language teaching, assess how achievable they may be, and contribute to their achievement.

   L2 learning research is a scientific discipline that tries to describe how people learn language. It cannot decide issues that are outside its domain. While it may contribute to the understanding of teaching goals, it is itself neutral between them. It is not for the teacher, the methodologist, or any other outsider to dictate whether a language should be taught for communication, for brain-training, or whatever, but for the society or the individual student to decide. One country specifies that groupwork must be used in the classroom because it encourages democracy. Another country bans any reference to English-speaking culture in textbooks because English is for international communication rather than for developing relationships with England or the USA. A third sees language teaching as a way of developing honesty and the values of good citizenship. L2 learning research as a discipline neither commends or denies the value of these goals, since they depend on morality or politics rather than science. But it provides guidelines how these goals may best be achieved and what their costs may be, particularly in balancing the needs of society and of the individual.

   Teachers also need to see the classroom from many angles, not just from that of L2 learning research. The choice of what to do in a particular lesson depends upon the teacher's assessment of all the factors involved in teaching *those* students in *that* situation. L2 learning research shows some of the strengths and weaknesses of a particular teaching method or technique and it provides information that can influence and guide teaching. It does not provide a magic solution to all teaching problems such as a patented method with an attractive new brand-name.

3. The independence of L2 learning research

Keywords

> *second language*: "A language acquired by a person in addition to his mother tongue"
>
> *interlanguage*: the language of the L2 learner considered as a system of language in its own right rather than as a defective version of the target language

The establishment of L2 learning research as an independent discipline had several broad implications, which underlie much of the research to be discussed later.

L2 learning is distinct from from language teaching

Earlier approaches to L2 learning often started from language teaching and asked the question: which teaching methods give the best results? Is an oral method better than a translation method? A communicative method better than a situational one? Putting the question in this form accepts the status quo of what already happens in teaching rather than looking at underlying principles of learning. A more logical sequence is to start by investigating how people learn language and then to turn to the evaluation of teaching methods in the light of what has been discovered, the order followed in this book. The first step in L2 learning research is to study learning itself and only later move on to see how teaching relates to learning.

The new field did not blindly take over the concepts previously used for talking about L2 learning. Language teachers for example often contrast *second* language teaching — that takes place in a country where the L2 is widely used, say the teaching of French to immigrants in France — with *foreign* language teaching — that takes place in a country where it is not an everyday medium, say the teaching of French in England. While this distinction is often convenient, it cannot be taken for granted that learners in these two situations necessarily learn in two different ways, without proper research evidence. Indeed we shall later look at many other dimensions to the learning situation.

So the term 'L2 learning' is used in this book to include all learning of languages other than the first in whatever situation or for whatever purpose. This is the sense of 'second language' defined by UNESCO — "A language acquired by a person in addition to his mother tongue". Nor does this book make a distinction between language 'acquisition' and language 'learning', as some writers do (e.g. Krashen, 1981a).

L2 learning is not necessarily the same as L1 acquisition

Teaching methods have often been justified in terms of how children learn their first language (L1) without investigating L2 learning directly. The 'audiolingual' method of teaching and the 'direct' method, to take two instances, were based primarily on particular views of L1 learning rather than on research into L2 learning, different as the methods were in themselves.

But there is no intrinsic reason why learning a second language should be the same as learning a first. Learning a first language for example is, in Halliday's phrase, 'learning how to mean' (Halliday, 1975) — discovering that language is used for relating to other people and for communicating ideas. People learning a second language already know how to mean. L2 learning is inevitably different in this respect from L1 learning. The similarities between learning the first and second languages have to be established by research rather than taken for granted. In some respects the two forms of learning may well be rather similar, in others quite different. Evidence about how the child learns a first language has to be interpreted with caution in L2 learning and seldom in itself provides a basis for language teaching.

L2 learning is more than the transfer of the L1

One view of L2 learning sees the crucial element in L2 learning as the transfer of aspects of the L1 language onto the L2. The first language helps learners when it has elements in common with the second language and hinders them when they differ. Spanish speakers may leave out the subject of the sentence when speaking English, saying "Is raining" rather than "It's raining", while French speakers do not. The explanation is that subjects may be omitted in Spanish, but they may not be left out in French. Nor is it usually difficult to decide from accent alone whether a foreigner speaking English comes from France, from Brazil, or from Japan.

But the importance of such transfer has to be looked at with an open mind. Varied aspects of L2 learning need to be investigated before it can be decided how and when the first language is involved in the learning of the second. Though transfer from the L1 indeed turns out to be important, often in unexpected ways, its role needs to be established through properly balanced research rather than being taken for granted.

Learners have language systems of their own

Suppose a student learning English says "Me go no school". Many teachers would see it as equivalent to the native sentence, "I am not going to school", even if they would not draw the student's attention to it overtly. In other words this is what the student might say if he or she were a native speaker. So what the current student is 'really' trying to produce is a present continuous tense "am going", a first person subject "I", a negative "not", and an adverbial "to school", ending up with the native version "I am not going to school". But something has gone drastically wrong. Perhaps the student has not yet encountered the appropriate forms in English or perhaps he or she is transferring constructions from the first language. The assumption is that the student's sentence should be compared to one produced by a native speaker. In a way this comparison is justified as native-like speech is often a goal for the student.

But this is where many students want to be, not where they are at the moment. It is judging the students by what they are *not* — native speakers. L2 learning research insists that learners should be judged by the standards appropriate for *them*, not by those used for natives. "Me go no school" is an example of learner language that shows what is going in their minds. "Me" shows that they do not distinguish "I" and "me", unlike native English; "no" that negation consists for them of adding a negative word after the verb, unlike its usual position before the verb in English; "go" that they have no grammatical endings such as "-ing"; and so on. All of these apparent 'mistakes' conform to regular rules in the students' own knowledge of English; they are only wrong when measured against native speech. Their sentences relate to their own temporary language systems at the moment when they produce the sentence, rather than to the native's version of English.

However peculiar and limited they may be, learners' sentences can be seen as the product of those learners' own language systems; their speech shows rules and patterns of its own. At each stage learners have their own language systems. The nature of these learner systems may be very different from that of the target language. While they are idiosyncratic and constantly changing, they are nonetheless systematic. The starting point for L2 learning research is the learner's own language system, christened *interlanguage* by Larry Selinker (1972). Learners are not wilfully distorting the native system; they are inventing a system of their own. No-one is claiming that the learner's interlanguage takes precedence over the version of the native speaker. That after all is where the learners are in a sense heading. But finding out how they learn means starting from the curious rules and structures which they invent for themselves as they go along — their interlanguage.

The interlanguage assumption had a major impact on teaching techniques in the 1970s. Teaching methods that used drills and grammatical explanations had insisted on the seriousness of the students' mistakes. A mistake in an audiolingual drill meant the student had not properly learnt the 'habit' of speaking; a mistake in a grammatical exercise meant the student had not understood the rule. The concept of interlanguage liberated the classroom and in part paved the way for the communicative language teaching methods of the 1970s and 1980s. Learners' sentences reflect their temporary language systems rather than an imperfect grasp of the target language. If a student makes a 'mistake', it is not the fault of the teacher or the materials or even of the student, but an inevitable and natural part of the learning process. Teachers could now use teaching activities in which students talked to each other rather than to the teacher because the students did not need the teacher's vigilant eye to spot what they were doing wrong. Their mistakes were minor irritants rather than major hazards. Hence groupwork and pairwork were now possible as the teacher did not have to continuously supervise the students' speech to pinpoint their mistakes.

The controversy about the uniqueness of language

A further issue that needs to be mentioned is the dispute between those who think language is a unique property of the human mind and those who think it is the same as other aspects of the mind. Those who believe in its uniqueness take the view that the types of structures that are found in language, the kinds of meaning that they have, and the ways in which they are used are different from anything else in human beings, or indeed in animals. This means that language is learnt in unique ways. Hence research into language learning always needs to provide evidence of its own rather than generalizing from the learning of other skills.

The opposing view is that L2 learning is a special case of general principles that apply to everything people do; there is nothing unique to it, apart from its sheer complexity. Hence it is learnt in the same way as skills such as learning to ride a bicycle, or as cognitive processes such as learning to do multiplication. If this is accepted, L2 learning research can draw on research into all forms of learning, not just language learning. The advocates of uniqueness are mostly applied linguists, those who support non-uniqueness mostly psychologists. The argument between them is unresolved as it involves different conceptions of language, of learning, and of research methods.

But the controversy has strong implications for teaching. Uniqueness advocates insist that language teaching is unlike other school subjects and must therefore be taught in ways that are peculiar to it, differently from teaching someone physics or how to drive a car. Supporters of non-uniqueness emphasize that language teaching is the same in principle as other forms of training, and so language teaching can use methods employed for teaching other subjects.

Background reading

Good technical introductions to L2 learning can be found in Ellis, R. (1985). *Understanding Second Language Acquisition*, Oxford University Press, and Romaine, S. (1989), *Bilingualism*. Blackwell.

2

Learning different types of grammar

Language has patterns and regularities which are used to convey meaning, some of which make up its grammar. Part of grammar is the order of words. Any speaker of English knows that "Ernest Hemingway likes John" does not have the same meaning as "John likes Ernest Hemingway". Another part of grammar is changes in the forms of words (morphology) — "The cow is mad" means something different from "The cows were mad".

Knowledge of grammar is thought by many to be the central area of the language system. However important the other components of language, they relate to each other through grammar. Grammar is also the most distinctive aspect of language, having features many claim are unique to language and hence learnt in different ways from anything else that people learn. In some ways grammar is easy to study in L2 learners, because it is highly systematic and its effects are usually fairly obvious in their speech. For these reasons much of the L2 learning research of the 70s and 80s concentrated on grammar. Hence it is a useful starting point from which to look at L2 learning research. This chapter first looks at different types of grammar and then selects four areas of grammatical research into L2 learning to represent the main approaches.

1. What is grammar?

Keywords

prescriptive grammar: grammar that 'prescribes' what people should say

traditional grammar: 'school' grammar concerned with labelling sentences with parts of speech

structural grammar: grammar concerned with how words go into phrases, phrases into sentences

grammatical (linguistic) competence: the native speaker's knowledge of language

> ***communicative competence***: the speaker's ability to put language to communicative use
>
> ***pragmatic competence:*** the speaker's ability to use language for a range of public and private functions, including communication

To elucidate what the term "grammar" means in the context of L2 learning, it is easiest to start by eliminating what it does ***not*** mean.

Prescriptive grammar

One familiar type of grammar is the rules found in school-books, say the warnings against final prepositions in sentences, "This can't be put up with", or the diatribes in letters to the newspaper about split infinitives, "To boldly go where no man has gone before". This is called ***prescriptive grammar*** because it 'prescribes' what people ought to do. Modern grammarians have mostly avoided prescriptive grammar because they see their job as describing what the rules of language *are*, just as the physicist says what the laws of physics are. The grammarian has no more right to decree how people *should* speak than the physicist has to decree how electrons should move. Language is bound up with human lives in so many ways that it is easy to find reasons why some grammatical forms are 'better' than others, but these are based on criteria other than the grammar itself. The grammarian's first task is to decide what people actually say; after this has been done, then others may decide whether it would be better to change what they say.

Traditional grammar

A second popular meaning of "grammar" concerns the parts of speech — "a noun is the name of a person, place or thing". Analysing sentences means labelling the parts with their names and giving rules that explain verbally how they may be combined. This is often called ***traditional grammar***. While many grammarians today do not reject this type of grammar outright, they again feel it is unscientific. After reading the definition of a noun, we still do not know what a noun is in the way that we know what a chemical element is. And, while the concept of the parts of speech is indeed part of grammar, there are many other powerful concepts that also need to be taken into account.

Some language teaching uses forms of grammar that resemble a sophisticated form of traditional grammar. Typical grammar-books for language teaching, say the ***Penguin Students' Grammar of English*** (Bosewitz, 1987), rely on statements such as "When we want to say that a completed action took place at a definite time in the past we use the PAST SIMPLE (SIMPLE PAST)". Some textbooks rely on the students knowing traditional grammar terms. In the first lesson of an EFL course for complete beginners called ***Blueprint One*** (Abbs & Freebairn, 1990), the 'Grammar Focus' uses the technical terms in English "subject pronouns", "possessive adjective", and "genitive 's".

Structural grammar

Language teaching has also made use of *structural grammar* based on the concept of phrase structure, which shows how some words go together in the sentence and some do not. In a sentence such as "The man fed the dog" the word "the" seems somehow to go with "man" but "fed" does not seem to go with "the". Suppose we group the words that go together. If we put "the" with "man", we get one structure "(the man)", "the" with "dog" we get another "(the dog)". Then these structures can be combined with each other and with the remaining words. "Fed" belongs with "(the dog)" to get a new structure "(fed the dog)". Now the two structures "(the man)" and "(fed the dog)" go together to assemble the whole sentence. A typical way of representing this phrase structure is through tree diagrams that show how the words build up into phrases and the phrases build up into the whole sentence, such as:

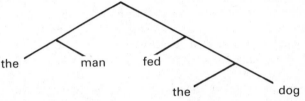

Structural grammar describes the sentence by fitting the parts together in more and more complicated ways.

Teachers have been using this directly in substitution tables since at least the 1920s. A typical example can be seen in the modern Bulgarian coursebook *English for the Fifth Class* (Despotova *et al*, 1988):

They I You	can	draw	a	black white red	dog cat rose

Students form sentences by choosing a word from each column: "I . . . can . . . draw . . . a . . . black . . . rose". They are substituting words within a constant grammatical structure. Such exercises have long been a staple of language teaching in one guise or another. Structure drills and pattern practice are based on the same idea. Substitution tables are still common in presentday course-books and grammar books, though today more as graphic displays of grammar than as teaching exercises. Much teaching simply uses structural grammar without realising that there are alternative approaches.

Grammar as knowledge.

But this chapter relies mainly on another meaning of "grammar" — the knowledge of language that the speaker possesses in the mind known as *linguistic* or **grammatical competence**. All speakers know the grammar of their language in this sense without benefit of study. A speaker of English knows that "Is John is the man who French?" is wrong without looking this up in any book — indeed few grammar-books would be of much assistance. A native speaker knows the system of the language. He or she may not be able to verbalise this knowledge clearly; it is 'implicit' knowledge. Nevertheless a single sentence of English could not be produced without knowing English grammar in this sense. A man who spontaneously says "The man fed the dog" shows that he knows the word order typical of English in which the Subject "The man" comes before the Verb "fed". He knows the ways of making irregular past tenses in English — "fed" rather than the regular "-ed" ("feeded"); he knows that "dog" requires an article "the" or "a"; and he knows that "the" is used to talk about a dog that the listener already knows about. This is a very different type of knowledge from the ability to describe the sentence he has produced in terms of grammar, something only people who have been taught explicit 'grammar' can do.

A parallel can be found in a teaching exercise that baffles EFL students — devising instructions for everyday actions such as, "Tell me how to put my coat on." Everyone knows how to put a coat on in one sense but is unable to verbalise this knowledge. There is one type of knowledge in our mind which we can talk about consciously, another which is far from conscious. This view of grammar as knowledge treats it as something stored unconsciously in the mind — the native speaker's competence. The point of sentence trees, structures, rules, and so on, is ultimately that they describe the competence in our minds. One of the great dilemmas in L2 learning is the nature of the relationship between such unconscious and conscious grammar, and how it can be exploited in language teaching.

As well as grammatical competence, native speakers also possess knowledge of how language is used. This is often called **communicative competence** by those who see public functions as crucial (Hymes, 1972). It is not just knowledge of the language that is important, it is how to use it appropriately for the activities in which speakers want to take part — complaining, arguing, persuading, declaring war, writing love letters, buying season tickets and so on. Others see language as having private functions as well as public — language for dreaming or planning a day out. Hence the more general term **pragmatic competence** reflects all the possible uses of language rather than restricting them to communication (Chomsky, 1986). This chapter concentrates on grammatical competence.

2. Grammatical morphemes

Keywords

> **morpheme**: the smallest unit of grammar, consisting either of a word ("toast") or part of a word ("'s" in "John's")

> **grammatical morpheme**: morphemes such as "-ing" and "the" that play a greater part in structure than content words such as "horse"

order of difficulty: how difficult particular aspects of grammar are for
L2 learners

Language teaching has often distinguished 'content' words from 'structure'
words. Content words have the kind of meaning that can be looked up in
a dictionary and they are numbered in thousands. "Beer" or "palimpsest"
are content words referring to definable things. A new content word can be
easily invented, advertisers try to do it all the time — "Contains the magic
new ingredient kryptonite". Structure words on the other hand are limited
in number; they consist of words like "the", "to", and "yet". A computer
program for teaching English needs about 220 structure words. It is easier
to look up structure words in a grammar book than in a dictionary. The
meaning of "the" or "despite" depends on the grammatical rules of the
language, not on dictionary definitions. It is virtually impossible to invent
a new structure word because it means changing the rules of the language
rather than adding an item to the stock of words of the language. Lewis
Carroll's *Jabberwocky* for instance uses invented content words such as
"tove" and "wabe" but combines them with familiar structure words and
endings such as "the", and "'s", to get:

> 'Twas brillig and the slithey toves
> Did gyre and gimble in the wabe.

The smallest unit of grammar is the 'morpheme'. When the sentence
is divided up in tree diagrams such as the one given earlier, the whole
sentence is at the top and the morphemes are at the bottom. Morphemes
are studied in a branch of grammar called 'morphology'. Some words
consist of a single morpheme — "to" or "book" or "like" or "black".
Some can have morphemes added to show their grammatical role in the
sentence, say "book*s*" or "lik*ing*" or "black*er*". Others can be split up into
several morphemes — "mini-supermarket" might be "mini-super-market";
"hamburger" is seen as "ham-burger" rather than "Hamburg-er" leading to
"vegeburger" or "cheeseburger" — whatever the inhabitants of Hamburg
may say. The word endings such as "-ing" are usually grouped together with
structure words such as "the" under the term 'grammatical morpheme'. In
many languages they are the essential clues to the structure of the sentence.

In the first language young children use content words more easily than
grammatical morphemes. Children commonly produce sentences such as
"Mummy go shop", meaning something like "Mummy is going to the
shops", where the adult sentence includes the 'missing' grammatical morphemes "is", "-ing", "to", "the", and "-s". It is as if the children know the
structure for the sentence and the content words, but either do not know
the grammatical morphemes or are incapable of using them.

In the early 1970s it was discovered that English children learn these
grammatical morphemes in a definite sequence (Brown, 1973). Dulay and
Burt (1973) decided to see what this meant for L2 learning. They made
Spanish-speaking children learning English describe pictures and checked
how often the children supplied eight grammatical morphemes in the appropriate places in the sentence. Suppose that at a rudimentary level L2
learners say "Girl go". How do they progress from this?

1. *plural "-s"*
The easiest morpheme for the learners was the plural "-s", getting "Girls go".

2. *progressive "-ing"*
Next easiest for the learners was the word ending "-ing" in present tense forms like "going".

3. *copula forms of "be"*
Next came the use of *be* as a copula, i.e. as a main verb in the sentence ("John is happy") rather than as an auxiliary used with another verb ("John is going"). Changing the sentence slightly gets "Girls *are* here".

4. *auxiliary form of "be"*
After this came the auxiliary forms of "be" with "-ing", yielding "Girls are going".

5. *definite and indefinite articles "the" and "a"*
Next in difficulty came the *definite and indefinite articles "the" and "a"*, enabling the learners to produce "*The* girls go" or "*A* girl go".

6. *irregular past tense*
The next morphemes were the irregular English past tenses, (those that do not have a form of "d" ending pronounced in the usual three ways /d/. /t/, or /id/) such as "came" and "went", as in "The girls *went*".

7. *third person "-s"*
The next in order of difficulty was the *third person "-s"* used with verbs, as in "The girl go*s*".

8. *possessive "'s"*
Most difficult was the "-s" ending used with nouns to show possession, as in "The girl*'s* book".

The order of difficulty for the L2 learners is then the sequence from 1 to 8. They have least difficulty with plural "-s", most difficulty with possessive "'s". The interesting discovery was the similarities between the L2 learners. This research with grammatical morphemes was the first to demonstrate the common factors of L2 learners so clearly. It was not just that Spanish-speaking children had a sequence of difficulty for the eight grammatical morphemes. Similar orders have been found for Japanese children, and for Korean adults (Makino, 1980; Lee, 1981) though not for one Japanese child (Hakuta, 1974). The first language does not seem to make a crucial difference: all L2 learners have much the same order. Nor does it matter if the learners are children or adults; adults have roughly the same order as children (Krashen *et al*, 1976). It did not even make much difference whether or not they were attending a language class (Larson-Freeman, 1976)! There was a strong similarity between all L2 learners of English, whatever the explanation may be. Later researchers such as Dulay, Burt, and Krashen (1982) tend to put the morphemes into groups rather than seeing them as separate items.

There has however been much controversy about these sequences of grammatical morphemes. The overall problem is that, while this research discovered a 'natural order' of difficulty, it did not find an explanation for this order. Without an explanation it can have only limited relevance to teaching. Another problem is over the interpretation of what a sequence is. Here we have been calling it an order of difficulty because it refers to how difficult a learner finds something at a particular moment. Sometimes however it has been interpreted as an order of acquisition — the sequence in which people actually acquire language. Researchers have come to realise that it is not necessarily true that things that are easy to use are learnt first and vice versa, even if in many cases this is true. An order of acquisition cannot be based solely on an order of difficulty. Lee (1981) for example showed that the lowest and highest groups of Korean learners found auxiliary forms the easiest but they were 8th out of 10 for the middle group. Patsy Lightbrown (1987) too found that the course of acquisition over time was far from smooth; accuracy on "-ing" for her French-speaking learners started at 69% in year 1, fell to 39% in year 2 and rose above 60% in year 3. For this and other methodological reasons researchers now have considerable reservations about the grammatical morpheme research.

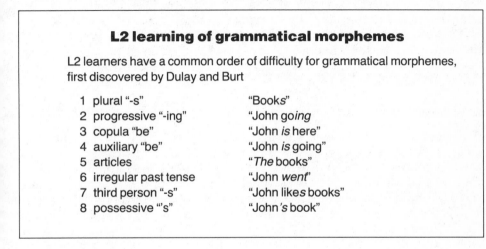

L2 learning of grammatical morphemes

L2 learners have a common order of difficulty for grammatical morphemes, first discovered by Dulay and Burt

1	plural "-s"	"Books"
2	progressive "-ing"	"John go*ing*
3	copula "be"	"John *is* here"
4	auxiliary "be"	"John *is* going"
5	articles	"*The* books"
6	irregular past tense	"John *went*"
7	third person "-s"	"John like*s* books"
8	possessive "'s"	"John*'s* book"

3. Negation

Keywords

> ***sentence-external*** versus ***sentence-internal*** negation: a negative element (e.g. "no") occurring outside the structure of the sentence is external, one occurring within its structure (e.g. "not") is internal

> ***anaphoric*** versus ***non-anaphoric*** negation: an anaphoric negative element stands for a whole negative sentence ("Do you like beer?" "No") while a non-anaphoric negative makes only a part of the sentence negative ("He doesn't like beer")

> ***sequence of acquisition***: the order in which L2 learners acquire different aspects of grammar as they develop

The question can be posed whether a common sequence can be found in areas of grammar other than grammatical morphemes. Much 1970s research tried to establish the sequence of acquisition for such aspects of structure as the formation of questions, the appearance of auxiliaries, and so on. The important thing was the actual appearance of items in the learner's language, just as it was for grammatical morphemes. The approach is not so much concerned with what the item means as with whether the learners actually use it. It is the presence or absence of the structure in their speech or writing that counts.

Negation in English has been intensively studied, notably by Henning Wode (1981). Three preliminary points need to be made:

Sentence-external and sentence-internal negation.

English, like many languages, has a negative form "no" that can be said on its own outside the sentence, as well as having other uses. The question "Do you like beer?" can have the answer "No" or "No, I don't"; "No" is here sentence-external negation. English also has negative form "not" and "n't" that occur *within* the sentence. If someone asks "Do you like it?", the answer is, "I don't like it" rather than "Not". This is sentence-internal negation. Other languages also have different words for these; in German "nein" versus "nicht", in French "non" versus "ne . . pas".

Anaphoric and non-anaphoric negation.

If you ask someone "Would you like some coffee?", they might reply "No milk" meaning either, "No I would like some milk instead" or, "Yes I would like some coffee but without any milk". Only the intonation pattern shows which is meant. "No" occurring by itself 'stands for' a whole sentence and so is called 'anaphoric'. Answering "No" to a question means you are denying the whole of the other person's sentence — "Do you like coffee?" "No" ("I don't like coffee"). "Not" or "n't" or "no" occurring inside the sentence means that negation is linked to the structure of the sentence and some part of it is denied rather than the whole, as in "I don't like it" and "There is no money". Sometimes there is genuine confusion between the anaphoric and non-anaphoric uses. As it stands "No milk" could mean either, "No I don't want milk" or "No I don't want whisky, I want milk".

Attachment to auxiliary verb

The "not" and "n't" forms in English are usually attached to an auxiliary verb such as "can" or to a form of "be" or "have", as in "He can't do it" or "He's not going", rather than occurring on their own. If none of these are present in the sentence, a 'dummy' auxiliary has to take their place in the shape of "do" — "I don't like it" or "He didn't come".

Wode (1981) kept a record of the sentences produced by his four German-speaking children aged 4–9 who were learning English in the United States. The children went through definite stages of acquisition:

1. *anaphoric sentence-external*

To begin with, the only negative they produced was the anaphoric sentence-external form "no", either at the end of the sentence as in "Kenny no", or at the beginning as in "No du mogelst ja". Wode claims that the sentence-external form is the first to be used by *all* learners of either L1 or L2. So French children start with "non" rather than "ne .. pas", as do English people learning French; German children or Japanese learning German start with "Nein" rather than "nicht". In discussions with EFL teachers with many first languages, I have never known this claim to be contradicted.

2. *non-anaphoric sentence-external*

Next came the use of "no" as sentence-external negation but with non-anaphoric meaning, as in "No finish" and "No sleep". In other words the children were starting to use non-anaphoric negation linked to part of the sentence but were putting the negative form at the beginning or end of the sentence rather than in its proper place in the middle. They still had only one negative form "no" rather than a range of forms.

3. *copula "be"*

The copula forms of "be" (i.e. those in which "be" is not an auxiliary) were learnt by the children next in combination with the rest of the sentence as in "That's no good"; the "not/n't" forms also start to be used at this stage.

4. *full verbs and imperatives with "don't"*

After this came the negatives "not" and "n't" used sentence-internally with full verbs as in "You have a not fish" and "I'm not missed it". The children did not use auxiliaries, except that they were starting to use "don't" sentence-externally with imperatives as in "Don't say something".

5. *"do" forms*

The last stage of their development recorded by Wode was the use of "don't" and "didn't" inside the sentence — "You didn't can throw it" and "I didn't have a snag". They had learnt that a 'dummy' auxiliary "do" is necessary, even if they were not completely sure of it.

Wode's research shows that anaphoric negation is learnt before non-anaphoric negation, and sentence-external negation before sentence-internal negation. The sequence of acquisition is: first negation with "be", then negation with full verbs, finally negation with auxiliaries. Similar sequences for negation have been found with other learners, though some of the details vary. "Not" occurred at the same time as "no" in the speech of a L2 Japanese child (Milon, 1974); Spanish speaking L2 learners used "He can't see" before "She didn't believe me", reversing stages 4 and 5 given here (Cancino *et al*, 1978); French learners used only "no" rather than "not" in stages 3 and 4 (Collin and Holec, 1985). Nevertheless Wode's research provides a clear and satisfying example of this type of grammar. Its aim is to find a universal sequence true in essentials of all learners of all languages, not just L2 learners of English.

How does negation research link to language teaching? It stresses that L2 learners have a series of interim grammars of English — interlanguages. Their first grammar has a pattern in which one form of negative "no" is independent of the structure of the sentence. In their next grammar negation still occurs in one place but is linked to the structure of the sentence; and so on through more complex and more inclusive interlanguage grammars. The final grammar reported is still not the same as the native speaker's, lacking for example the connection between negation and "any" familiar to EFL teachers — "I haven't got any sugar" rather than "I haven't got some sugar".

It is interesting to compare how EFL teaching materials present negation. The sequence in the **Cambridge English Course** (Swan & Walter, 1984) for instance is as follows, with the equivalent L2 stages given in brackets:

Lesson 1   *No I'm not*
(stage 1, sentence-external, anaphoric; plus 'reduced' sentences without main verb — past the 5 stages)

Lesson 6   *I don't like the Vermeer picture very much*
(stage 4, sentence-internal, non-imperative dummy "do", present tense)

Lesson 7   *There aren't any cows in this room*
(past the stages given here)

Lesson 8   *They didn't eat bananas*
(non-imperative dummy "do", past tense)

Lesson 14   *He can't cook* (stage 5, full verb negation with auxiliaries

Lesson 23   *Don't run after a meal* (stage 3, "don't" with imperatives)

The main differences between the L2 stages and the textbook sequence are then:

— the textbook sometimes divides an L2 stage into two, such as separating present tense "don't" from past tense "didn't"

— the textbook collapses two L2 stages into one, e.g. lesson 1 depends on stages 1 and 2, having both anaphoric and non-anaphoric negation

— the textbook goes against some aspects of the order, for example negative imperative coming late, "not .. any" coming early and 'reduced' "I'm not" coming in lesson 1.

— the textbook omits some stages, e.g. non-anaphoric external

The last point however leads to a general issue about language teaching. Learners' interlanguages contain rules that are different from the native speaker's competence. Hence the student may temporarily produce sentences that deviate from native correctness, say the stage 2 "No finish". Many teaching techniques however assume that the point of an exercise is to get the student to produce sentences from the first lesson on that are correct in terms of the target language, even if they are severely restricted in terms of grammar and vocabulary. The students are not supposed to be producing sentences like the stage 2 "no finish" in the classroom. Teaching materials also only present sentences that are possible in terms of the target language never letting learners hear sentences such as "no finish". Hence they can never fully reflect the stages that interlanguages go through. There is then an implicit contradiction between the pressure on students in many classrooms to produce well-formed sentences and the natural stages that students go through.

Negation has been used in this section partly as an interesting area in its own right but also as typical of the research into similar areas, such as questions. Time and again it shows that L2 learners go through similar sequences of acquisition whatever their first language. Dulay and Burt (1980) say that this discovery is 'surely one of the most exciting and significant outcomes of the last decade of second language research'. The negation research is looking at an order of acquisition and is not so controversial as the grammatical morphemes research. There does indeed seem to be an order of acquisition for certain aspects of grammar that is common to L2 learners regardless of their first language.

L2 learning of Negation

L2 learners go through a definite sequence of acquisition (Wode):

1 **anaphoric sentence external**: "no"
2 **non-anaphoric sentence external**: "No finish"
3 **copula "be"**: "That's no good"
4 **full verbs and imperatives with "don't"**: "You have a not fish", "Don't say something"
5 **"do" forms**: "You didn't can throw it"

---

4. Language universals; relative clauses

Keywords

> *accessibility hierarchy*: the ease with which different types of relative clause can be formed, based upon the role of the relative element in the clause, e.g. "The man who left was John" versus "The man than whom I am taller is John"
> *statistical universals of language*: aspects of grammar that are common to many, sometimes all, languages

So far in this chapter grammar has described the sentences of a single language. But grammar can also tell us what languages have in common. These common features are known as 'statistical' universals since they are established statistically by looking at as many languages as possible. An example is relative clauses such as that in "The man *who came to tea* was Jim". These sentences are usually seen as the combination of a main clause "The man . . . was Jim" with a relative clause ". . . who came to tea . . .". It was discovered by Keenan and Comrie (1977) that there were interesting similarities in how languages combine main and relative clauses together. These depended on the kind of word in the relative clause that was used as a link to the main clause. This concept was called the Accessibility Hierarchy, since some words could be 'accessed' for making relative clauses more readily than others.

Six types of relative clause make up the Accessibility Hierarchy. They can be thought of simply as types 1 to 6, though short grammatical explanations are given for those who want the more technical terms.

Type 1. "The man *who left* was John" *(subject clauses)*
In all languages it is possible to have clauses in which the *subject* of the relative clause is the link to the main clause, i.e "who" in this case.

Type 2. "The car *that he crashed* was John's" ***(object clauses)***
In most languages it is also possible to have sentences like this in which the grammatical ***object*** of the relative clause is the link to the main clause, here "that".

Type 3. "The person *that he gave the cheque* was Tom" ***(indirect object clauses)***
In some languages the link to the main clause is through the ***indirect object*** — often referring to the person who receives something. Here "that" acts as indirect object of "gave"

Type 4. "The person *to whom he gave the cheque* was John" ***(object of preposition clauses)***
Another possible link between the relative and the main clause is through prepositions like "to". In English this type of clause is effectively the same as type 3, with the addition of "to".

Type 5. "The man *whose book I borrowed* was furious" ***(possessive clauses)***
Next comes the relative clause linked through ***possessive*** words such as "whose".

Type 6. "The man *than whom I am taller* is John" ***(object of comparison clauses)***
Finally come relative clauses using "than" as a link, i.e. expressing some kind of comparison. It is difficult to find natural-sounding examples in English, though they are possible.

This is not just a list of six types of relative clause but is arranged in a particular order — hence the name Accessibility *Hierarchy*. Some languages such as English have clauses of all six types. Others such as Basque only have types 1 to 4 and do not allow 5 and 6. Others such as Welsh have types 1 and 2, but do not not allow 3–6. A few such as Malagasy only have type 1 and no others. The important factor is that ***all*** languages start at the top of the hierarchy with type 1, and go some way down it. No language starts at type 2 and leaves type 1 out, or has 1 and 4 but skips 2 and 3, and so on. In other words the difference between languages is how far down the hierarchy they go. The Accessibility Hierarchy is a general rule which all languages obey; if a language has type 1 then it may have type 2, but it can't have type 2 without also having type 1, and so on.

How is the Accessibility Hierarchy relevant to L2 learning? The first language of the learner, say French, will have a certain range of relative clauses starting from type 1. The L2 of the learner, say English, may have a different range of clauses also starting from type 1. L2 learners might start with type 1, go on to learn type 2, and so on down the list. The Accessibility Hierarchy in this case would correspond to a sequence of acquisition. But it is also relevant to the processing of language. Popular writers use only the first few types of relative clause; intellectual writers such as Virginia Woolf use the whole range. The psychological difficulty of relative clauses varies in accordance with the Hierarchy, type 1 being least difficult to understand, type 6 most difficult. It is also possible that L2 learning may be based on the L1 knowledge and the types used in the first language carried over to the second. L2 learners could start by assuming a new language has the same constructions as the first language. If the L1 has type 6 relative clauses, the learners presume the L2 has them too.

Susan Gass (1979) found that the difficulty for EFL learners indeed seemed to follow the Hierarchy with type 1 the easiest type and type 6 the most difficult, rather than that learners depended on the L1. There was one major exception: type 5 (possessive clauses) were much easier than expected, coming between types 1 and 2 in terms of difficulty, rather than after type 4. Other research has generally found that the L2 sequence of acquisition corresponds to the Accessibility Hierarchy. It should, however be pointed out that other explanations for the phenomenon have been put forward, such as the processes of comprehension.

The question is what this means for teaching. At one level it broadens the idea of grammar. Topics such as the Accessibility Hierarchy need to be looked at as well as more conventional ideas. It is as important to know where the L2 fits on the Hierarchy as it is to know about the passive voice or the more familiar parts of grammar. The obvious conclusion might seem to be that, everything else being equal, teaching should follow the order of the Accessibility Hierarchy, teaching type 1 (subject clauses) first, then type 2 (object clauses), etc. Often in some sense this has already been intuitively part of language teaching. In the elementary level textbook *English in Perspective* (Dalzell & Edgar, 1988) the first teaching page already has type 2, "Find the thing your partner describes"; page 22 has type 1 as in, "Choose the words which interest you"; the rarer types do not appear.

But the obvious conclusion may be wrong. Given that all languages adhere to the Hierarchy, learners would simply have to discover how far the language goes down it. If they know it has type 5 (possessive), they can work out it must have type 2, type 3 , and so on. Suppose that **all** learners expect the Accessibility Hierarchy to be true. Then, if they know how far down the hierarchy the language comes, they can extrapolate all

---

L2 learning of relative clauses

A. L2 learners broadly follow the Accessibility Hierarchy as a sequence of acquisition (Gass).
1. **subject** relatives: "The man who left was John."
2. **possessive** relatives:"The man whose book I borrowed."
3. **object** relatives: "The car that he crashed was John's."
4. **object of preposition** relatives: "The person he gave the cheque to was Tom"

B. If L2 learners are taught clauses way down the Accessibility Hierarchy, they can fill in the intervening gaps (Eckmann), e.g. learners taught only object of preposition clauses "The person he gave the cheque to was Tom" knew subject clauses "The man who left was John." and object clauses "The car that he crashed was John's." better than those students who had been taught them directly

the other possible clauses. Eckman and his colleagues (1988) divided some EFL students into 3 groups. One group were taught type 1 (subject), a second group type 2 (object), a third group type 4 (preposition clauses), all for one hour. Then they tested how well the students knew *all* three types, not just the one they had been taught. The third group, who had only been taught type 4 were, not surprisingly, the best group of the three at these; but they were also the best at type 1 and type 2 clauses! In other words they had worked out the other types better than those who had started from the top of the hierarchy and worked their way down. By virtue of the common features of all languages, L2 learners can 'extrapolate' from one structure to others. The straightforward logical teaching sequence, essentially from easy to difficult, may be less effective than the reverse order. Giving the students an example of the most difficult form is sometimes useful.

5. Principles and parameters grammar

Keywords

> *Universal Grammar:* the language faculty built-in to the human mind consisting of principles and parameters

> *principles of language:* aspects of human language present in all human minds, e.g. the principle of structure dependency — why you cannot say "Is John the man who happy?"

> *parameters:* aspects that vary from one language to another within tightly set limits, e.g. the pro-drop parameter has two settings that distinguish pro-drop languages which do not need subjects expressed (Spanish, Chinese) and non-pro-drop languages in which they must be expressed (English, German)

So far grammar has been seen in terms of morphemes, patterns or structures, and universals spread across many languages. All of these capture some aspect of L2 learning and contribute to our knowledge of the complete process. A radically different way of looking at grammar that has become popular in recent years however tries to see what human languages have in common because of the nature of the human mind. This is the Universal Grammar theory associated with Noam Chomsky, for example Chomsky (1988). Universal Grammar (UG) sees the knowledge of grammar in the mind as having two components — 'principles' that all languages have in common and 'parameters' on which they vary. All human minds are believed to possess the same language principles. They differ over the settings for the parameters for particular languages.

principles

A fairly simple example of a principle is *structure-dependency*. How might you explain to someone how to make questions in English such as "Is Sam the cat that is black?" One possible instruction is:

"Start from the sentence: 'Sam is the cat that is black' and move the second word 'is' to the beginning."

But while this works in this instance, it obviously will not work for "The old man is the one who's late" as it would produce "Old the man is the one who's late?".

To remedy this you might suggest:

"Move the copula 'is' to the beginning of the sentence."

But this also does not work as it will not prevent someone mistakenly saying "Is Sam the cat that black?". It is important *which* "is" is moved. The only instruction that works properly is to say:

"Move the copula 'is' in the main clause to the beginning of the sentence".

This instruction depends on the listener knowing enough of the structure of the sentence to be able to distinguish the main clause from the relative clause. In other words it presupposes that they know the structure of the sentence. This is what is meant by 'structure-dependent'. Anybody producing a question in English takes the structure of the sentence into account. Inversion questions in English, and indeed in all other languages, involve a knowledge of structure, not just of the order of the words. There is no particular reason why this should be so; computer languages do not behave like this for instance nor do mathematical equations. It is just a feature of human languages that they depend on structure. In short structure-dependency is one of the language principles that is built-in to the human mind.

This type of grammar affects the nature of interlanguage. As described earlier, there appeared to be few limits on how the learners' interlanguage grammars developed. Their source might be partly the learners' first languages, partly their learning strategies, partly other sources. However the human mind always uses its built-in language principles, so interlanguages too conform to these principles. It would be literally inconceivable for the L2 learner, say, to produce questions that were *not* structure-dependent. And indeed no-one has yet found sentences said by L2 learners that breach the known language principles such as structure-dependency. Interlanguages do not vary without limit but conform to the overall mould of human language since they are stored in the same human minds. Like any scientific theory this may be proved wrong. Tomorrow someone may find a learner who has no idea of structure-dependency. But so far no-one has found clear examples of learners breaking universal principles.

parameters

How do parameters capture the differences between languages? One variation is whether the grammatical subject of a declarative sentence has to be actually present in the sentence. In German it is possible to say "Er spricht" (he speaks) but impossible to say "Spricht" (speaks); declarative sentences must have subjects. The same is true for French, for English, and for a great many languages. But in Italian it is possible not only to say "Lui parla" (he talks) but also "Parla" (talks) without an expressed subject; declarative sentences are not required to have subjects. In Arabic and Chinese and many other languages the same is true. This variation is captured by the ***pro-drop parameter*** — so-called for technical reasons we will not go into here. In 'pro-drop' languages such as Italian or Chinese or Arabic the subject does not need to be actually present; in 'non-pro-drop' languages such as English or German it must always be present in declarative sentences. The pro-drop parameter variation has effects on the grammars of all languages; each of them is either pro-drop or non-pro-drop.

Children learning their first language at first start with sentences without subjects (Hyams, 1986). Then those who are learning a non-pro-drop language such as English go on to learn that subjects are compulsory. The obvious question for second language learning is whether it makes a difference if the L1 does not have subjects and the L2 does, and vice versa. Lydia White (1986) compared how English was learnt by speakers of French (a non-pro-drop language with compulsory subjects) and by speakers of Spanish (a pro-drop language with optional subjects). If the L1 setting for the pro-drop parameter has an effect, the Spanish-speaking learners should make different mistakes from the French-speaking learners. Spanish-speaking learners were much more tolerant of sentences like "In winter snows a lot in Canada" than were the French.

One attraction of this form of grammar is its close link to language acquisition. The parts of language that have to be learnt are the settings for the parameters on which languages vary. The parts which do not have to be learnt are the principles that all languages have in common. Learning the grammar of an L2 is not so much learning completely new structures, rules, etc as discovering how to set the parameters for the new language. The implications of this overall model for language teaching is described in greater detail in chapter Eight. For the moment we are simply concerned to point out that the study of grammar and of acquisition in recent years has been much more concerned with the development of abstract ways of looking at phenomena like pro-drop than with the conventional grammar of earlier sections. Language teaching will eventually miss out if it does not keep up with such new ideas of grammar (Cook, 1989a).

L2 learning of principles and parameters grammar

1. L2 learners do not need to learn principles such as structure-dependency as they will use them automatically
2. L2 learners need to acquire new parameter settings for parameters such as pro-drop, often starting from their L1

6. L2 learning of grammar and L2 teaching

Keywords

> *consciousness-raising*: helping the learner by drawing attention to features of the second language
>
> *language awareness*: helping the learner by raising awareness of language itself
>
> *sensitization*: helping the learners by alerting them to features of the first language
>
> *developmental sequence*: a consistent order in which learners acquire the L2, based, according to Pienemann and Johnston, on difficulty of language processing

Teachers are often surprised by what grammar means in L2 learning research and how much importance is given to it. While the grammar used here has some resemblance to the traditional and structural grammars with which teachers are familiar — 'structures', 'rules', and so on — the perspective has changed. Grammatical morphemes cut across the teaching categories of prepositions, articles, and forms of "be". The Accessibility Hierarchy puts together information about relative clauses rather differently from most grammarbooks. The theory of principles and parameters puts grammar on a different plane from anything in language teaching. Hence teachers will not find any quick help with carrying out conventional grammar-teaching from such forms of grammar. But they will nevertheless understand better what the students are learning and the processes through which they are going. To take two examples, sentences with missing subjects and deviant relative clauses are both common in students' work and can be simply explained by the pro-drop parameter and by the Accessibility Hierarchy. Both are insightful ways of looking at learning which teachers have not hitherto been conscious of.

Let us gather together some of the threads about grammar and teaching in this chapter. If the syllabus that the student is learning from includes grammar in some shape or form, this is not a matter of just structures and rules but of a range of highly complex phenomena, some of which have been discussed in this chapter. The L2 learning of grammar has turned out to be wider and deeper than anyone supposed. It ranges from morphemes such as "the" to negative elements such as "not" to universal hierarchies of relative clauses to parameters about the presence of subjects. Above all, grammar is competence in the mind rather than rules in a book; one crucial end-product of teaching is that students should be able to 'know' language in an unconscious sense, so that they can put it to good use. Teaching has to pay attention to the internal processes and knowledge the students are building up in their minds.

Grammar is also relevant to the sequence in which elements of language are taught. Of necessity language teaching has to present the various aspects of language in order rather than introducing them all simultaneously. The conventional solution used to be a sequence of increasing grammatical complexity, teaching the present simple first, and the past perfect continuous passive last, because the former is much 'simpler' than the latter. When language use became more important to teaching, the choice of a teaching sequence was no longer straightforward since it was aspects of communication that now had to be sequenced. For example the textbook *Opening Strategies* (Abbs & Freebairn, 1982) uses an order based on language functions: Lesson 1 "Ask for and say numbers", Lesson 2 "Ask about people's nationality", Lesson 4 "Say what you want", Lesson 11 "Give permission", Lesson 14 "Identify belongings", and so on. Any function-based order runs into problems in arriving at a logical sequence; is 'requesting' simpler or more complex than 'complaining'? Hence grammar began to creep back in to textbooks because it was easier to arrange in order. *Opening Strategies* in addition to its functional order has a grammatical order, starting with the present simple tense of "be", going on to the present tense of full verbs, then past simple of "be", followed by present continuous, and so on. Clearly such grammatical sequencing should be related in some way to more recent ideas of the L2 learning of grammar.

L2 learning research has often claimed that there are definite orders for learning language, such as the Accessibility Hierarchy for relative clauses, and orders of difficulty, such as the order for grammatical morphemes. What should teachers do about this? Four extreme points of view can found:

1. **Ignore the parts of grammar that have a particular L2 learning sequence**, as the learner will anyway follow these automatically. Nothing teachers can do will help or hinder the student who is progressing through the grammatical morpheme order from "-ing" to "the" and "a". Teachers should therefore get on with teaching the thousand and one *other* things that the student needs and let nature follow its course.

2. **Follow the L2 learning order as closely as possible in the teaching.** There's no point in teaching "not" with "any" to beginners because the students are not ready for it. Instead teachers should concentrate on sentence-external "no", which is learnable at the first stage, "not" which is learnable at the next, and so on. So the order of teaching should follow the order found in L2 learning as much as possible.

3. **Teach the last things in an L2 learning sequence** *first*. Relative clauses with possessive "whose" should be taught before relative clauses using the object because the student will extrapolate from one to the other, as Eckmann has shown. The students can best be helped by being given the extreme point of the sequence and having to fill in the intermediary positions for themselves.

4. **Ignore grammar altogether.** Some might argue that, if the students' goals are to communicate in a second language, grammar is an optional extra. Obviously this depends upon the definition of grammar: in the sense that any speaker of a language knows the grammatical system of the language then grammar is not disposable in this way but plays a part in every sentence anybody produces or comprehends for whatever communicative reason.

These positions are so simplified and extreme that no-one would hold to them completely. A more complex application to teaching is proposed by Pienemann and Johnston (1987) who suggest there are two types of acquisition sequence: developmental and variational. A *developmental sequence* is caused by the learner's problems with processing language, particularly with sorting out strings of words into sentences. The early sequence for English has six stages:

i)   The learner produces single words or formulas — "I don't know"
ii) The learner then produces strings of elements, that is to say 'simple sequences of words'
iii) The learner can distinguish the beginnings and endings of strings, shown by the ability to say "Yesterday I sick" as well as "I sick yesterday"
iv) The learner can next identify different types of element in the string, and produces questions in which the verb is moved to the beginning such as "Can you tell me?"
v)   The learner can identify and move elements in the string, as in questions with wh-words — "What are you studying at Tech?"
vi) The learner next acquires the ability to break a string into smaller strings and recombine them in different ways, shown by complex sentences such as "He asked me to go"

A *variational sequence* on the other hand incorporates factors which differ from one person or situation to another. One example is the omission of items from the sentence as in "I go station". The converse example is the oversupply of items such as the too frequent use of the present continuous, "I am living in London" when "I live in London" is intended. This separation between two types of sequence is then important for language teaching as the implications of the two types can be rather different. With developmental sequences the teacher has to fall in with the sequence in some way; Pienemann (1986) puts this as the Teachability Hypothesis: 'the course of second language development cannot be altered by factors external to the learner'. Variational sequences are much more under the learner's control and so can be changed by the teacher. The application of sequences to teaching depends upon what kind of sequence we are looking at, whether the developmental and variational sequences, orders of difficulty or of acquisition, or others.

Fuller discussion of the implications of L2 order of learning or difficulty depends on the rest of teaching. It must balance grammar against language functions, vocabulary, classroom interaction, and much else that goes on in the classroom. Teachers do not necessarily have to choose between these alternatives once and for all. A different decision may have to be made for each area of grammar or language and each stage of acquisition. But L2 learning research is starting to provide information about sequences which will eventually prove a gold-mine for teaching. In general, information on the L2 learning of grammar is often neutral between teaching techniques. It is not making claims about the experiences that learners have had so much as giving a factual description of their language development.

Making grammar conscious

The question of whether grammar should be explained to the students must be raised, not for the last time. The use of explicit explanation implies that L2 learning can be quite different from L1 learning. The fact that children learn their first language without resort to conscious understanding does not mean that adults cannot learn a second language in this way. Justifying conscious understanding in L2 learning involves separating L2 learning from L1 learning with respect to whether the learners get explanations. The belief that L2 learning can potentially make use of explanation underlies distinctions such as those made by Harold Palmer (1922) between 'spontaneous capacities' for acquiring speech and 'the studial capacity' through which people study language, and by Krashen (1981a) between 'acquisition' and 'learning' (the latter being conscious and available only to older learners), and by many others. An important issue is *what* is learnt. I can tell you facts about languages such as Japanese or Gboudi that their native speakers could not. This does not mean I can say a single word, let alone a sentence, of Japanese or Gboudi in a comprehensible way. Conscious explanation is a way of teaching facts about the language — that is to say a form of linguistics. If this is the aim of teaching, as has indeed often been the case, conscious understanding is acceptable as a form of L2 learning.

But mostly grammatical explanation has relied on the assumption that rules that are learnt consciously can be converted into processes that are known unconsciously. The French subjunctive was explained to me at school, not just to give me academic knowledge of the facts of French, but to help me to write French. After a period of absorption, this conscious rule would become part of my unconscious ability to use the language. Rutherford (1987) and others have been advocating '*consciousness raising*' in teaching — 'the drawing of the learner's attention to features of the target language'. This functions as an aid to help the students avoid some of the pitfalls rather than an end in itself. Unlike traditional grammar teaching, it tackles grammatical topics such as the Accessibility Hierarchy and the pro-drop parameter.

Stephen Krashen however has persistently denied that consciously acquired rules change into normal speech processes in the same way as grammar acquired unconsciously, for example in Krashen (1981a). If Krashen's view is accepted, people who are taught by conscious explanation can only produce language by laboriously checking each sentence against their conscious repertoire of rules, as many had to do with Latin at school. Or they can use it for certain 'tips' or rules of thumb such as '*i* before *e* except after *c* or before *g*'. While not taking sides here, perhaps one should remember that many graduates of European universities who learnt English primarily by going through traditional grammars have turned into fluent spontaneous speakers of English. This at least suggests that the conversion of conscious rules to non-conscious processes does indeed take place for some highly academic students. This 'conversion' model of L2 learning is discussed further in chapter Eight.

More indirect uses for grammar have also been put forward in recent years. One suggestion by Eric Hawkins (1984) is for *'language awareness'*: the learners' general awareness of language should be raised as a preliminary to L2 teaching, partly through grammar. If the students know the kind of thing to expect, they are more receptive to it. Hawkins suggests 'an exploratory approach' where the pupils investigate grammar by for example deciding where to insert "see-through" in the sentence "She put on her cosy, old, blue, nylon, blouse". They invent their own labels for grammar, rather than being taught a pre-established system. As Hawkins puts it, 'grammar approached as a voyage of discovery into the patterns of the language rather than the learning of prescriptive rules, is no longer a bogey word'. It is not the teaching of particular points of grammar that matters but the overall increase in the pupil's language sensitivity. The textbook *Learning to Learn English* (Ellis & Sinclair, 1989) provides some exercises to make EFL learners more conscious of their own predilections, for instance suggesting ways for the students to discover grammatical rules themselves. Philip Riley (1985) has suggested *'sensitization'* of the students by using features of the L1 to help them understand the L2, say by discussing puns to help them see how speech is split up into words. Increasing awareness of language may have many educational advantages and indeed help L2 learning in a broad sense. It has however no particular licence from the types of grammar considered in this chapter.

Further reading

A good overview of grammatical morphemes research is in Dulay, H., Burt, M., and Krashen, S. (1983). *Language Two*. Newbury House. An introduction to principles and parameters grammar can be found in Cook, V.J. (1988a). *Chomsky's Universal Grammar: an Introduction*, Blackwell. Otherwise the reader is referred to the books and articles cited in the text.

3
Learning other components of language

This chapter looks at some of the other components of language that are involved in L2 learning — pronunciation, vocabulary, and discourse — and presents the main trends in these areas that have potential for language teaching. While the L2 acquisition of grammar has been widely studied, these other components have been covered much more patchily and are hardly referred to in most standard introductions to L2 learning research. Nor, despite their relevance to teaching, has much yet been done to apply them to actual teaching.

1. Acquisition of pronunciation

Keywords

phonemes: the sounds of a language that are systematically distinguished from each other e.g. "s" from "t" in "sin" and "tin"

syllable structure: the way in which consonants (C) and vowels (V) may be combined into syllables in a particular language

epenthesis: adding extra vowels or consonants to the syllable, e.g. "Espain" for "Spain"

Voice Onset Time (VOT) — the moment when voicing starts during the production of a consonant

intonation: the rise and fall in the pitch of the voice during speech

Language conveys meanings from one person to another through spoken sounds or written letters. Native speakers know how to pronounce the words, sentences and utterances of their first language. At one level they can tell the difference in pronunciation between "drain" and "train", the sound patterns of the language, at another the difference between "Fine", "Fine?", and "Fine!", the intonation patterns in which the voice rises and falls. Languages make different use of the vast repertoire of sounds available to human beings and they structure them into syllables in different ways. Languages also differ in the ways they use intonation.

It is impossible to imagine a non-handicapped speaker of a language who couldn't pronounce sentences in it, at least comprehensibly to others.

The study of the pronunciation system of language is known as phonology', the study of the sounds themselves being called 'phonetics'. One side of phonology is the sounds of the language that are systematically distinguished from one another — its 'phonemes'. The sound "s" for instance is different from the sound "t" in English, so the word "sin" means something different from "tin". English combines a limited set of around 45 phonemes to get all the words of the language -"sin", "tin", "fin", etc. In this section the pronunciation of words has sometimes to be given in phonetic transcript, as the written language can often not convey the sound differences accurately. For example the written letter "i" is pronounced as /ai/ in "I", /i/ in "limit", /ə: / in "first", and probably in other ways as well.

Pronunciation textbooks like ***Ship or Sheep?*** (Baker, 1981) present the student with pairs of words — "car" /ka:/ versus "cow" /kau/, or "bra" /bra:/ versus "brow" /brau/. The student learns how to tell which is which and then hears and repeats sentences with a high concentration of particular phonemes such as "I've found a mouse in the house" or "This is the cleanest house in town" or the traditional tongue-twisters such as "He ran from the Indes to the Andes in his undies". The type of L2 learning implied by this technique resembles the ways of teaching structural grammar described in the last chapter in its emphasis on practice rather than communication. Pronunciation is considered a set of habits for producing sounds. The habit of producing the sound /i/ is acquired by repeating it many times and by being corrected when it is pronounced wrongly. Learning to pronounce a second language means building up new pronunciation habits and overcoming the bias of the first language. Only by saying "car" /ka:/ and "cow" /kau/ many times is the contrast between /a:/ and /au/ acquired.

These notions clash with most current ideas of phonology in linguistics and language learning. There is no evidence that children learn the phonemes of their first language by repeating them one at a time or in pairs, as the teaching technique suggests. Moreover phonology concentrates less on the phoneme and more on abstract relationships of sounds and structures. It is not just the view of language learning that has changed but also the idea of what is actually learnt.

The concept of interlanguage applies as much to pronunciation as to grammar. L2 learners have their own rules for pronunciation, which are not just pale shadows of the target language. A German learner of English who says "pup" /pʌb/ for "pub" /pʌb/ is using a rule of 'voicing' that means he will also say /gut/ for "good" /gud/, /pi:s/ for "peas" /pi:z/, and so on. While many of these pronunciation rules are related to the learner's first language, they nevertheless still make up a unique temporary system — an interlanguage. What counts is the complex system inside the learner's head, not the target rules or the first language habits'.

Learning syllable structure

Part of interlanguage phonology is the rules for forming syllables. Syllables

are formed out of combinations of consonants (C) such as /t/, /s/, /p/, etc,
and vowels (V) such as /i/, or /ai/. English syllables must have a vowel, apart
from some so-called syllabic consonants — /n/ as in /bʌtn/. One difficulty for
the L2 learner concerns the ways the consonants can be combined — the
permissible consonant clusters. English combines /p/ with /l/ as in "plan"
/plæn/ or with /r/ as in "pray" /prei/ but not with /f/ or /z/, so there are
no English words like "pfan" or "pzan" that start /pf.../ or /pz.. /. Aliens
in Larry Niven stories for instance are identified by the reader because
their names have non-English clusters — "tnuctipun" /tn/ and "ptavvs" /pt/.
Even when languages have the same consonants they vary in the ways they
combine them in syllables. L2 learners often try by one means or another to
make English syllables fit their L1s. Examples are Koreans saying /kə la:s/
for "class", Vietnamese saying /də wait/ for "Dwight", and Arabs saying
/bilæstik/ for "plastic". To make English conform to the syllable structures
of their first languages, they are inserting extra vowels, a process known as
'epenthesis'.

The compulsory vowel in the English syllable may be preceded or followed by one or more consonants. So "lie" /lai/ which has a consonant-
vowel (CV) structure and "sly" /slai/ which starts with a two consonant
cluster (CC) are both possible, as are "eel" /i:l/ with VC and "eels" /i:lz/
with VCC. Clusters of several consonants can also occur at the end of
"lengths" /lengkθs/ or the beginning of "splinter" /splintə/. While the English syllable can have several consonants before or after the central vowel,
the syllable structure of some languages allows only a *single* consonant
before or after the vowel. Japanese for instance has no consonant clusters
and most syllables end in a vowel. Some L2 learners leave consonants out
of words if they are not allowed in their L1. Cantonese speakers, whose L1
syllables have no final consonants, turn English "girl" /gə:l/ into "gir" /gə:/
and "Joan" /dʒəun/ into "Joa" /dʒəun/. Arabic syllables too can be CV but
not CCV, i.e. there are no two consonant clusters. "Straw" /strɔ:/ could not
be a possible syllable in Arabic because it starts with a three-consonant
cluster CCC.

So Egyptian-Arabic learners of English often add an epenthetic vowel
/i/ to avoid two- or three- consonant clusters. "Children" /tʃildrən/ becomes
"childiren" /tʃidirən/ in their speech because the CC combination /dr/ is
not allowed. "Translate" /trænzlait/ comes out as "tiransilate" /tirænzileit/
to avoid the two consonant CC sequences /tr/ and /sl/. A feature of their
first language phonology is being carried over into English. Ellen Broselow
(1988) found that the insertion of epenthetic vowels reveals quite small
differences between first languages. Iraqi speakers of Arabic add epenthetic
/i/ like Egyptians, but they say "chilidren" /tʃilidrən/ rather than "childiren"
/tʃildirən/, and "itranislate" /itrænizleit/ rather than "tiransilate" /tirænzileit/.
The ways in which they avoid the consonant combinations /ld/ and /ns/
show that their dialect of Arabic differs slightly in syllable structure from
the Egyptians. The phonological systems of these L2 learners are unique
interlanguages. Neither their first language nor their second have epenthetic
vowels. The clash between the syllable structures of the L1 and L2 is
resolved by the temporary expedient of adding vowels, a true interlanguage

solution. It is not just the sequence of phonemes in the sentence that matters but the abstract syllable structure that governs their combinations. Hence the phonology of the syllable in the interlanguage shows effects from the L1, although it is a system of its own, which is neither L1 nor L2.

Learning to voice consonants

Let us now jump from phonology to phonetics and examine how some of the actual sounds of speech are produced. James Flege (1986) has argued that L2 learners have more problems with sounds that are similar to those in their L1 than with new sounds that are completely different. One fruitful area that bears on this is '*Voice Onset Time*' (VOT). A speaker who is producing the stop consonant /g/ in the English word "got" /gɔt/ is doing two things:

(i) blocking the back of the mouth with the tongue and then releasing this blockage — the actual 'stop'. All stop consonants such as /g/, /p/, /b/, /t/, etc, are produced by completely stopping the air coming out of the mouth for a brief moment with the tongue or the lips and then letting the air out suddenly — the 'release'.

(ii) producing 'voice' by vibrating the vocal chords against each other. Voice can be felt by putting the hand against the front of the throat and feeling the vibration in /z/ and the lack of vibration in /s/. The chief but not the sole difference between so-called voiced sounds such as /d/ or /z/ and unvoiced sounds such as /t/ or /s/ is whether such voicing takes place.

An important aspect of stop consonants that varies from one language to another is the moment when voicing *starts* as the person produces the consonant. Voice Onset Time is the name for the actual moment this occurs. In English the Voice Onset Time for /g/ varies. It can come about 100 thousandths of a second (milliseconds or msec) before the stop is released or it can occur at the same moment as the release. So long as the speaker starts to voice within these time limits, the sound is heard as voiced. In the unvoiced English sound /k/ as in "cot" /kɔt/ voicing starts around 100 msec *after* the stop is released. Any stop with a delay in voicing of 100 msec will be heard as unvoiced. This is shown in the following rough diagram:

(100 msec before release) −100	(actual moment of release) 0 msec	(100 msec after release) +100

English /g/   ᄿᄿᄿᄿᄿᄿᄿᄿᄿᄿᄿᄿᄿᄿᄿᄿᄿᄿᄿᄿᄿᄿᄿᄿᄿᄿᄿᄿᄿᄿ

English /k/ {   ᄿᄿᄿᄿᄿᄿᄿᄿᄿᄿᄿᄿᄿᄿᄿᄿᄿᄿᄿᄿ

     ᄿᄿᄿᄿᄿᄿᄿᄿ

Voice Onset Time in English stop consonants

An English stop is heard as a voiced /g/ *either* if the Voice Onset Time happens before the release (−100 msec) *or* is simultaneous with the release (0 msec). On the other hand the sound is heard as an unvoiced /k/ if the

Voice Onset Time occurs after the release (+100 msec). This is another way of saying that English unvoiced stops are 'aspirated' — followed by a silent puff of air.

In Spanish however the distinction between the voiced and unvoiced sounds is made differently. A voiced sound such as /g/ has an early Voice Onset Time of −100 msec, as in English. But an unvoiced sound such as /k/ has a Voice Onset Time simultaneous with the release (0 msec) rather than after it. In other words the English late Voice Onset Time does not occur, as we see in the diagram.

(100 msec before release) −100	(actual moment of release) 0 msec	(100 msec after release) +100

Spanish /g/ 〰〰〰〰〰〰〰〰〰〰〰〰〰〰〰〰〰〰〰〰〰〰

Spanish /k/   〰〰〰〰〰〰〰〰〰〰〰〰〰〰

Voice Onset Time in Spanish stop consonants

Although both languages have voiced and unvoiced stops, their systems of voicing differ. Both Spanish and English speakers agree that stop consonants with early Voice Onset Time are voiced and that stops with a later Voice Onset Time are unvoiced. But a Spanish speaker interprets a stop where the voicing is simultaneous with the release as a /k/, an English speaker hears it as a /g/.

Nathan (1987) found that Spanish learners of English gradually acquire the English 0 msec Vowel Onset Time for the stop /g/, something which does not actually matter for English speakers at all as −100 msec will do just as well. As Nathan puts it, 'once they have marked English voiceless stops as distinctive from voiced ones, . . . it is no longer necessary to keep the voiced ones quite as distinct'. L2 learners are not just learning the major differences between phonemes; they are learning subtle differences that do not even matter to native speakers. Arabic learners similarly carry over the shorter VOTs of Arabic to English. An interesting side-effect is the carryover to the first language; French learners of English pronounce the /t/ sound in French with a longer Vowel Onset Time than monolinguals (Flege, 1987) Spanish/English bilinguals also behave similarly so far as Voice Onset Time is concerned in both English and Spanish (Williams, 1977). It makes no difference to their perception of stops which language is used. Research has also looked at the question of age and the L2 learning of VOT. English-speaking adults were unable to distinguish the Hindi voiced/voiceless distinction between /tʰ/ and /dʰ/ while seven-month-old English babies could (Werker *et al*, 1981).

So far the discussion has mostly been illustrating differences between L2 learners due to the transfer of some aspect of their L1. One should emphasise however that there are universal processes shared by all L2 learners. For example the simplification of consonant clusters happens almost regardless of L1. The earlier example of Germans having trouble with voicing in English may be due to a universal preference for 'devoicing' of final consonants rather than transfer of the German equivalent. Similarly the use of CV syllables by many L2 learners could reflect a universal tendency rather than transfer from specific L1s. Major (1986) claims that the early stages of L2 learning are characterized by interference from the L1 but the later stages start to reveal universal processes of acquisition common to both L1 and L2 learning. While epenthesis may often depend upon the structure of the L1, it is nevertheless a process that appears to be available to all L2 learners.

The teaching of pronunciation

What does this research show for teaching? Most language teachers use 'integrated pronunciation teaching', as Joanne Kenworthy (1987) calls it, in which pronunciation is taught as an incidental to other aspects of language. The teacher corrects wrong pronunciations when they arise on an *ad hoc* basis. It is doubtful whether such incidental correction does much direct good as it most often consists of isolated phonemes and relies on the efficiency of correction as a teaching technique. It may indirectly serve to raise the students's awareness of pronunciation.

More crucially the learning of sounds is not just a matter of mastering the phonemes of the second language along with their predictable variants. At one level it is learning the rules of pronunciation for the language, such as those for forming syllables; at another level it is learning precise control over Voice Onset Time. While the phonemes of the language are indeed important, pronunciation difficulties are often not to do with specific phonemes so much as with more general principles — in the case of English as L2, voicing for German students, syllable structure for Arabic students, Voice Onset Time for Spanish students, and so on. Language teaching should then pay more attention to such general features of pronunciation rather than the phoneme.

Learners have their own interlanguage phonologies — temporary rules of their own. The sounds of the language are not just separate items on a list but are related in a complex system. Correcting a single phoneme may not have any effect on their pronunciation or may have the wrong effect. It is like taking a brick out of a wall and replacing it with another. Unless the replacement fits exactly in the structure of the whole wall all the other bricks will move to accommodate it, or at worst the wall will fall down. Understanding how to help students' pronunciation means relating the faults first to their current interlanguage and only secondly to the target. It will not suffice to compare their speech with what native speakers say and then correct them without taking into account the two systems of the interlanguage and the target. All in all the conventional techniques of discrimination of sounds, correction of 'mistakes', and imitation of phonemes are only scratching the surface. They are not directly linked either to much of what the student has to learn or to the processes of learning. Pronunciation teaching has stood still for a generation; it is time exercises and techniques started to be used that grasped the fact that pronunciation is more than the phoneme and learning is more than repetition.

L2 Learning of Pronunciation

Syllable structure:
L2 learners simplify consonant clusters, often to fit the L1
  — L2 learners add extra 'epenthetic' vowels, often to fit the L1
Voice Onset Time
  — L2 learners gradually acquire the L2 way of voicing
  — their L1 is affected by their knowledge of the L2
Intonation
  — L2 learners are still capable of discriminating 'tones'
  — L2 learners have strategies for dealing with 'new' intonation
Teaching uses
  — teachers should be less aware of the phoneme, more of the
    other aspects of pronunciation
  — correction of individual phonemes may be useless
  — the teaching of awareness of pronunciation is as beneficial
    the teaching of specific points

The learning and teaching of intonation

Intonation is the way that the pitch of the voice goes up and down during speech. Chinese is a 'tone' language that separates different words purely by intonation: "¯ma" with level tone means "mother", "vma" with fall-rise tone means "house". Adult L2 learners have no problems in distinguishing Chinese tones, though with less confidence than native speakers of Chinese (Leather, 1987). Adults learning Thai, another tone language, were much worse at learning tones than children (Ioup *at al*, 1987). On the other hand research has looked at L2 learning of Portuguese and English, which are 'intonation' rather than 'tone' languages (Cruz-Ferreira, 1987?). Rather than differences between words in these languages intonation shows a variety of grammatical points (e.g. question versus statement), discourse connections (e.g. when a topic starts and finishes), and speakers' attitudes (e.g. politeness versus rudeness). In this case learners have no problems with similar intonation patterns in L1 and L2 but use strategies for unfamiliar patterns based on their idea of the range of the intonation and the extent to which they can deduce meanings from the actual words in the sentence.

Specialized intonation textbooks like my own *Active Intonation* (Cook, 1968) often present the learner with a graded set of intonation patterns for understanding and for repetition, starting, say, with the difference between rising "Well?" and falling "Well", and building up to more complex patterns through comprehension activities and imitation exercises. But the teaching techniques again mostly depend on ideas of practice and repetition; students learn one bit at a time, rather than having systems of their own; they repeat, they imitate, they practice, all in a very controlled way.

Some teaching methods aim simply at making the student aware of the nature of intonation rather than at improving specific aspects of it. Several examples can be found in *Teaching English Pronunciation* (Kenworthy, 1987). For instance Kenworthy suggests getting two students to talk about holiday photographs without using any words other than "mmm", "ah", or "ooo". This makes them aware of the crucial role of intonation without necessarily teaching them any specific English intonation patterns, the objective underlying many of the communicative intonation exercises in my own textbook *Using Intonation* (Cook, 1979). It resembles the consciousness-raising approach to grammar teaching. Dickerson (1987) made detailed studies of the usefulness of giving pronunciation rules to L2 learners, concluding that they are indeed helpful. Chapter Eight looks at such 'conversion' models in more detail.

2. Acquisition of vocabulary

Keywords

> *components of meaning*: the meaning of some words can be broken up into separate components, e.g. the word "boy" has components "human", "male" and "young"

> *prototype theory*: words have whole meanings divided into basic level ("table"), superordinate ("furniture") and subordinate ("coffee table")

> *frequency*: either how many times a word occurs in speech or how often it is practiced by a student

Grammar provides the overall patterns, vocabulary the material to put in the patterns. To understand "Peter sat on the floor" properly the listener needs to know not only that "sat" refers to a physical state, but also that it is usually preceded by a grammatical subject that refers to something that is alive; in other words you can't say "The rock sat the man". "Sat" is related to other words such as "lie" and "stand", and it is associated in the mind with "cat" and "bat" and "chair". All of these are part of the speaker's knowledge of English vocabulary. Using "sat" properly means not just knowing how it is defined in the dictionary, but how it relates to all the other words in the language, and how and when it may be used in sentences. Dictionaries can give a false idea that vocabulary is a list of words, each with one or more meanings attached to them. Instead words are related to each other in many ways, and this is how they are remembered and stored.

Some students still learn vocabulary lists in which each L1 word has a one-word L2 translation; English "man" is "homme" in French and so on. Some teachers try to get the students to associate each word with an image or an object; they hold up a picture of a man and say "This is a man". Both these teaching techniques imply that learning vocabulary means learning individual words one at a time. But the relationships between words are as important as the meaning of the word in isolation — how "man" contrasts with "woman" and with "boy" is as important as the meaning of the word itself.

Words are not coins you exchange from one language to another according to a fixed exchange rate. Changing five pounds into 35 French francs is not the same as changing "beer" into "bière" because the word "beer" depends on the complex system of words for drinks in English and on the place of beer in the culture. Even the actual substance referred to can change when the word changes; "bière" does not refer to the same substance as "beer", being a light cool lager rather than a dark warm bitter due to the different yeasts involved requiring different brewing and storage temperatures. Linguists sometimes claim that no word can be exactly translated into another language. Jespersen (1904) illustrated this through translations of the word "bat" into other languages; the French "chauvesouris" emphasises its baldness and its resemblance to a mouse, the Latin "vespertilio" suggests the evening when the bat is out, and the Danish "flagermus" suggests its flapping. The word "pub" corresponds to nothing in any country other than England, as seen by the variety of tourist bars mistakenly called pubs all over the world. An American "deli" again is unrecognizable in other countries. Learning the vocabulary of a second language is not just memorizing equivalent words between languages ("red" means "rouge"), or learning the definition of the word ("red" is "a colour typically seen in blood") or putting it in context ("Rudolph the red-nosed reindeer") — but learning the meaning relationships between "red" and all the other words in English within the full context of cultural life.

Meaning components

One way of analyzing vocabulary is to break the meaning of a word up into smaller components. Thus the meaning of "girl" is made up of "female", "human", and "non-adult". The meaning of "apple" is made up of "fruit", "edible", "round", and so on. Much of the dispute about gender discrimination in English comes down to whether the meaning of "man" necessarily has the component "male" as well as "human" and "adult", and whether "girl" is made up of "young" as well as "female"! Breaking meaning up into components has been used in first language acquisition to study the development of words such as "before" and "big" in English children. At one stage they know one component of the meaning but not the other. They know "big" and "small" share a meaning component to do with size but think they both mean "big"; or they know that "before" and "after" are to do with "time" but do not know which one means "prior" (Clark, 1971). L2 beginners in English indeed found it much easier to understand "Mary talks before Susan shouts" than "Caroline sings after Sally dances" (Cook, 1977).

A version of this components approach can be found in textbooks such as *The Words You Need* (Rudzka *et al*, 1981). Students look at a series of 'Word Study' displays displaying the different components of meaning of words. For example a chart gives words that share the meaning 'look at/over' such as "check", "examine", "inspect", "scan", and "scrutinize". It shows which of them have the component of meaning 'detect errors', which 'determine that rules are observed', and so on. Students are encouraged to build up the idea of the vocabulary as consisting of such components while reading texts.

Learning a second language can literally mean seeing the world in a different way; English "brown" does not refer to exactly the same colour as French "brun". This has an effect on the first language. A monolingual speaker of Korean uses the word "paran sekj" (blue) to mean something greener and less purple than a Korean who also knows English (Caskey-Sirmons and Hickson, 1977). Languages vary slightly in how they divide up the colours in which their speakers see the world. The same is true of the sense of taste. Speakers of Bahasa Malaysia are particularly good at distinguishing saltiness, reflected in the many expressions for salt in their language — "masin kitchup" (salty like soy sauce), "masin ayer laut" (salty like sea water), "masin garam" (salty like salt), and "masin maung" (horribly salty) (O'Mahoney *et al*, 1977). Nor is this effect confined to vocabulary. People whose first language has the word order colour + object ("black cat") tend to sort objects such as blue squares and yellow triangles out by colour while those whose language has the order object + colour ("gatto nero") tend to sort them out by shape (Hooton and Hooton, 1977).

The prototype theory of vocabulary

Nevertheless many aspects of meaning cannot be split up into components but are appreciated as wholes. An influential approach of this type is Eleanor Rosch's *'prototype'* theory (Rosch, 1977). An English person who is asked to give an example of a typical bird is more likely to say "sparrow" than "penguin" or "ostrich"; sparrows are closer to the prototype for "birds" than penguins and ostriches. Rosch's theory suggests that, rather than components of meaning, there is an ideal of meaning in our minds — "birdiness" in this case — from which other things depart. Speakers have a central form of a concept in their minds and the things they see and talk about correspond better or worse with this prototype.

Prototype theory also claims that children first learn words that are 'basic' because they reflect aspects of the world, prototypes, that stand out automatically from the rest of what they see. "Sparrow" is a 'basic level' term compared to a 'superordinate level' term like "bird", or a 'subordinate level' term like "house sparrow". The basic level of vocabulary is easier to use and to learn. On this foundation children build higher and lower levels of vocabulary. Some examples of the three levels of vocabulary in different areas are seen in the diagram on the next page.

L1 children learn the basic level terms like "apple" before they learn the superordinate term "fruit", or the subordinate term "Golden Delicious". They start with the most basic level as it is easiest for the mind to perceive. Only after this has been learnt do they go on to words that are more general or more specific. Cook (1982) showed that L2 learners first acquired basic terms such as "table", second more general terms like "furniture", and finally more specific terms like "coffee table". Rosch's levels are therefore important to L2 learning as well as to first language acquisition.

This this sequence, however, is different from the usual order of presentation in language teaching in which the teacher or textbook introduces or practices a whole group of words simultaneously. "You have just moved house. Decide which pieces of furniture are to go in which room; armchair, television, bed . . ." Here all three levels of vocabulary are being taught at once — superordinate "furniture", basic "bed", and subordinate "armchair". According to prototype theory, this method is misguided. The most important early words are basic level terms. The human mind automatically starts from this concrete level rather than from a more abstract level or a more specific one. Starting by teaching vocabulary items that can be easily shown in pictures fits in with the Rosch theory. A drawing can be readily recognized as a chair but is less easy to see as an armchair or as furniture. Hence prototype theory ties in with the audiovisual method of language teaching that introduces new vocabulary with a picture of what it represents, in an appropriate cultural setting. This theory has particular implications for teaching of vocabulary at the beginning stages.

superordinate terms	furniture		bird	fruit	
basic level terms	table	chair	sparrow	apple	strawberry
subordinate terms	coffee table	armchair	field sparrow	Golden Delicious	wild strawberry

Learning and remembering vocabulary

The problem lies not just in learning L2 words, but also in remembering them. Harry Bahrick (1984) investigated how well English learners remembered Spanish words eight years after they had learnt them. He found that a word that is learnt after only one or two presentations is remembered better than one that takes several presentations to learn. How well people remember something depends on how deeply they process it. Repeating words as strings of sounds is low-level processing and badly remembered; working out how words fit in the grammatical structure of the sentence is deeper and leads to better memory; using the meanings of words together within the whole meaning of the sentence is the deepest level of processing and ensures the best memory. Bahrick's research also suggested that a word is remembered best if it is practised every 30 days rather than at more frequent intervals (Bahrick *et al*, 1987). This contradicts the belief common among teachers that every word should be practised as often as possible within a short timespan. It is *how* the word is practised that is important rather than how often.

A familiar precept of vocabulary teaching is that the most frequently used words in the target language are usually taught first. Almost all beginners books restrict the vocabulary they introduce in the first year to about a thousand of the most frequent items. The textbook **Break Into English** (Carrier *et al*, 1985) for instance covers 'approximately 900 lexical items'; the American course *I love English* (Capelle *et al*, 1985) lists about 750 words. Traditional syllabuses for language teaching usually include lists of the most frequent words. An up-to-date version of this is seen in the **COBUILD English Course I** (Willis & Willis, 1987) which was based on a vocabulary count several million words long. The first lesson teaches 91 words including "person" and "secretary", unlikely to be in opening lessons of other coursebooks.

Though frequency may indeed form a logical basics for teaching, L2 learning research has little to say about it one way or another. Carter (1988) has proposed that a language has a 'core' vocabulary found in all its uses, plus 'subject' cores specific to specialist subject matters, and a non-core vocabulary. Advanced Danish university students of English tested by Dollerup *et al*, (1989) knew the high frequency 'core' words, but many also knew many low frequency words. The difference between good Danish readers and bad readers was not a straightforward matter of the better the students the rarer the words they knew. Hence a simple grading for language teaching from core frequent words to non-core infrequent words step-by-step does not seem justified.

Frequency also means how often something is repeated by the student, the implication being that to learn a word you have to use it several times. Again Bahrick's research suggests something rather different. First of all words are remembered best if they are learnt quickly with few presentations. Hence teachers should make the first occurrence of the word memorable rather than practising it several times. An example of this might be that students appear to have no problems in remembering swear-words they have heard only once! Bahrick's approach also suggests that, if teachers want students to remember something for periods longer than a year or two, they need to space the presentations over quite long intervals of days.

First language influences on vocabulary

A further question is the extent to which the first language vocabulary influences the learning of the second. This is not so obvious as with grammar. Learners may fill in gaps in their knowledge of the new language with items from the first. When the languages are closely related, this may be effective. If you don't know the French word for "beer", it is likely that "Je veux un beer" will get some results. But also the ways in which the mind organizes the vocabulary of your first language have an influence on how it perceives the second. Eric Kellerman (1986) looked at how students learn words with several meanings, such as the English word "eye", which ranges from "potato eye", "peacock's eye", "electronic eye", "human eye", "eye of a dice", to "eye of a needle". The reason he chose to investigate "eye" was that the Dutch word "oog" happens to have the same range of meanings. So you would expect Dutch students of English to have no problems with transferring the meanings of "oog" to English, but this wasn't the case. Dutch students tended to assume that the English word "eye" could *not* have the same meanings as Dutch "oog". This tendency actually increased the more advanced they were. Kellerman found two causes for this. One was that the closer the meaning was to the base meaning of the word, that is to say "human eye", the more likely it was to be transferred. A meaning such as "eye of a dice" is remote from the base and so is thought by the students to be very unlikely in English. The other cause was how often the particular meaning of a word occurs. The more frequent a meaning the more likely the students are to transfer it. The meaning "eye of a peacock" is infrequent and so students assume it cannot be shared by two languages even if it is not far from the base meanings. A similar example to Kellerman's is the word /lidxot/ in Hebrew (Levenston, 1979). English-speaking learners have no problems in learning the meaning 'postpone', but have the greatest difficulty in seeing that the same word can also mean 'reject'.

A question that has often been asked by psychologists is whether the L2 user has two mental dictionaries or one. Research into the processing of semantic meaning showed that people take about the same time to say whether a "table" is "furniture" in their L1 as in their L2 (Caramazza *et al*, 1980). Hence they would seem to have one mental store of words. Other research has shown however that speed of mental access to a word is helped by hearing another word in the same language rather than a word in the speaker's other language (Kirsner *et al.*, 1980). This suggests that the two dictionaries are separate in the mind. So the simple question about one dictionary or two at the moment is unanswerable. One suggestion is that there are indeed two separate underlying stores of knowledge but that they interact during speech processing in ways that are not under the speaker's control.

Vocabulary and teaching

i. *Teaching the complexity of word meaning*

One consequence of L2 vocabulary research for teaching is that L2 learning of vocabulary is not just learning a word once and for all but learning the range of meanings that go with it. The problems associated with going from the first language to the second are not just the transfer of the actual words but also the relationships and overtones they carry in the L1. As an English speaker I cannot conceive how "postpone" and "reject" could be the same word in another language. Most uses of vocabulary in textbooks imply that words have single meanings: books that have vocabulary lists usually give single word translations. The German course *English for You* (Graf, 1983) for instance lists one translation for "bar" (Bar) and one for "write" (schreiben), where many might be necessary.

A traditional teaching technique was the memorizing of wordlists. A recent variant is the psychology-inspired 'mnemnotechnics' technique in which students acquire L2 words by associating them with incongruous images or sounds in the L1 — the French "hérisson" (hedgehog) is remembered through an image of the English sound-alike "hairy son" (Gruneberg, 1987). However many words one learns in this way it is doubtful if they will form part of one's active vocabulary. I have been waiting since school days for the opportunity to use the French word "la jubé" (roodloft), memorized for a vocabulary test, but I have never yet seen a roodloft let alone had anything to say about one. Teaching has unfortunately often counted items rather than meanings. The textbook *Break into English* (Carrier *et al.*, 1985) indeed has 900 lexical items — but how many meanings per word? Going against this tradition, the *COBUILD English Course I* (Willis & Willis, 1987) makes a point of listing a range of meanings for a word, five for "heavy", and six for "so", to take two words from Book 1.

ii. *Putting words in structures*

An aspect of vocabulary that has become important in recent years is the position of the word in the structure of the sentence. For example the verb "faint" can only occur with a grammatical subject such as "Martin" in "Martin fainted", never with an object "Martin fainted John". The verb "meet" on the other hand has to have an object "He met John", not "He met". Some verbs are followed by subordinate clauses — "I hoped Mary would go" rather than grammatical objects "I hoped Mary". A speaker of English knows not just what a word means and how it is pronounced but also how it fits into sentences. The Universal Grammar model of language acquisition, to be described in chapter Eight, claims that learning how each word behaves in sentences is crucial. Maurice Gross (1990) found 12,000 'simple' verbs in French of which no two could be used in exactly the same way in sentences. While there is no L2 research on the links between

---

L2 learning of Vocabulary

Components theory: the meanings of words break up into components, which are learnt separately

Prototype theory:
basic terms ("potato") are learnt before subordinate ("Idaho potato") and superordinate terms ("vegetable")

Depth of processing: type of practice counts more than frequency
Transfer of meaning from the L1 is caused by two factors:
— closeness to base meaning
— frequency of occurrence

Mental dictionaries; unclear whether L2 learners have one or two

Teaching uses:
— basic level words should be taught first
— some words may be taught through components of meaning
— it is how the word is practised not how often, that is important
— remember students transfer L1 meanings as well as the words themselves
— teaching should not separate words from their structural context

vocabulary and syntax of this type as yet, nevertheless teaching cannot ignore that the student has to learn not just the meaning and pronunciation of each word, but how to use it.

3. Acquisition of conversational discourse

Keywords

interactive discourse: spontaneous language with give-and-take

listener-related talk : language for 'chat' and maintenance of social life

information-related talk: language for transfer of information

discourse move: here used for the speaker's choice of what to do in the conversation, e.g. opening moves such as 'greeting'

adjacency pair: a pair of discourse moves that often go together, e.g. question and answer

language function: the reason why someone says something, e.g. apologising, arguing etc

Interaction in discourse

Normally sentences are not said in isolation but spoken in a particular situation. They do not mean much without knowing how the successive sentences are linked together, and how they relate to the situation. In one sense 'discourse' concerns how the participants influence each other while talking. They interrupt, they ask for more information, they adapt what they are saying, but they cannot take back what they have said, even if they can try and say it again. Henri Holec (1985b) calls this *'interactive discourse'* as there is a give-and-take between the participants. Hence interactive discourse usually occurs in speech rather than writing. But language can also consist of connected speech or writing that has been prepared and gone over, so that the sequence in which it was first devised is not the same as the sequence in which it is encountered. Usually this is written language, for instance a set of instructions on how to work a video-recorder, but sometimes it may be prepared speech such as talks or lectures. This is 'non-interactive' discourse in Holec's terms in that the reader or listener cannot affect what happens.

A related distinction made by Gillian Brown and her colleagues (1984) is between *listener-related* talk and *information-related* talk. Listener-related talk — 'chat' — forms the basis of social life. People talk to each other to maintain social relationships. Information-related talk however has the purpose of transferring information from speaker to listener. It might be a doctor directing a nurse how to treat a patient, or a passenger telling a cab-driver where to go, or a teacher imparting information in a classroom. While both listener-related and information-related talk are usually interactive in Holec's terms, perhaps only information-related talk can be non-interactive.

Brown and her colleagues also draw attention to an important difference between short and long turns at speaking. Speaking at length poses quite different problems from saying one or two sentences. As they put it, 'students who are only capable of producing short turns are going to experience a lot of frustration when they try to speak the foreign language'. Native speakers too need training in various aspects of discourse. The ability to follow non-interactive discourse or to produce long turns may be vital aspects of mother-tongue teaching. The L2 teaching problems differ according to whether the students are capable of doing these in their first language or not.

This chapter deals chiefly with discourse in the interactive listener-related sense; information aspects of discourse are discussed in the next chapter, and classroom discourse in chapter Six.

Discourse moves in conversation

If two people are talking, each of them has a choice of what to say and how to say it. There are certain opening moves for the conversation that can be chosen, then a choice of follow-up moves, a further choice of conversational moves linked to these, and so on until the final exchange that ends the conversation. So a conversation might start with ritualistic greetings:

> *Hello, John.*
> *Hello, Mary.*

Then one speaker broaches a topic of conversation, which continues for a while:

> *Have you heard about Brian?*
> *No? What's happened?*
> *Oh he's gone off to Australia.*
> *How amazing!*

The conversation continues till the speakers signal a close:

> *Well I'd better be off now. Goodbye.*
> *Cheerio.*

Some of these exchanges are as predictable as the steps in a waltz. If one person says a greeting — "Hello" - the other has to say a greeting in return — "Hello". Other exchanges come in '*adjacency pairs*' with straightforward linguistic connections between the moves. A question "What's happened?" has to be followed by an answer such as "He's gone off to Australia". Other connections are less obvious; a move that gives information — "He's gone off to Australia" - calls for a polite reaction "How amazing!". Much of conversation is made up of such pairs of moves — greeting and reply, question and answer, statement and reaction. Some psychologists such as Bruner (1983) have suggested that a child learns the first language through such routines. One example is the peekaboo game that parents play with small babies — hiding something, then bringing it out with a cry of "boo". Mothers gradually develop this routine so that the child takes part in increasingly complex sequences of moves. The child is learning how to build up structures of interaction in which language becomes steadily more important. Conversational interaction is vital for children, not just for the moves themselves that they are learning, but for the grammatical rules and lexical items they are using in the moves — for the way they learn all the components of language through interaction. The components of language are learnt through the moves of conversation.

Much of this knowledge of interaction is transferred from the first language. Knowing how to construct a conversation in one language means it can be done in another, to some extent. Languages do not differ over the moves themselves so much as over what makes up the moves. We all greet each other; we all ask questions and provide answers; but we do so differently in different languages. The main difficulty in going from one language to another is conventions over politeness. Germans prefer more direct ways of making a request than such indirect English forms as "Could you tell me the way to the station please?". Japanese consider it polite not to disagree with the speaker.

Evelyn Hatch (1978) has advocated an approach to L2 learning based on *Conversation Analysis* — the analysis of conversations between native and non-native speakers. One of her examples is a telephone conversation between a native speaker and a foreign student called Pauline who is trying to get her thesis typed:

> Native: *Which university is it for?*
> Pauline: *Yes I have a more 100.*
> Native: *Pardon me?*
> Pauline: *I have more 100 pages.*
> Native: *Yes but is it for UCLA? Or USC?*
> Pauline: *UCLA.*
> Native: *I see. Well is it typed?* . . .

Conversation Analysis sees the moves of conversation as closely linked to the topic of discussion. The prime need is for the participants to make clear what they are talking about. One opening move is *topic-nomination*, when the speaker tries to establish the topic of conversation — "Which university is it for?". The other participant has to acknowledge the topic, perhaps incorrectly — "Yes I have a more 100". When things go wrong, as they obviously do here, the speaker resorts to *topic clarification* to make the topic clear — "Pardon me?" Other conversational moves are *priming* where the non-native tries to get help from the native — "The how you say year" - and *repairs* where the non-native corrects herself — "He's got a bar, a car".

Teaching conversational discourse

The art of conversation is keeping this channel of communication open so that everyone knows what they are talking about. In native to non-native conversations the native uses more topic clarification moves than usual because of the increased unintelligibility of L2 speech. The non-native needs particular moves for stating topics unambiguously and for making certain they are continuing to be understood. While all these indeed occur from time to time in native-to-native speech, the proportions of each move inevitably change in conversations involving non-native speakers. Cook (1985) found for instance that non-native speakers are more formal and polite than native speakers when making requests from strangers and when thanking them. They tend to say "Thank you very much" rather than "Thanks" for example, regardless of who they are speaking to. Porter (1986) compared natives and non-natives on the same discussion tasks. The non-natives had a smaller repertoire of ways of expressing themselves, for example, not using the past tense for giving their opinions, and expressing disagreement directly rather than through face-saving 'hedges'.

The fact that conversation consists of moves and the idea that learning takes place through conversational moves can come together in teaching. My own beginners book *People and Places* (Cook, 1980) used a teaching exercise called a 'conversational exchange'. The students, for example, are shown pictures of various clothes; they hear model conversations showing two conversational moves, stating opinion and reacting:

> Jenny: *Joe's suit is very nice.*
> Edna: *Is it?*
> Jenny: *Peter's jeans are horrible.*
> Edna: *Are they?*

Then they have to supply Edna's side of the conversation for a few exchanges, working out the appropriate answer according to their opinion of the clothes. Finally the students supply both sides of the conversation. The basic concept was indeed that learning takes place through interaction in limited exchanges: conversation is taught as linked conversational moves. As soon as possible in each exercise, the students have to choose which expression to use and have to fit it into the situation meaningfully. They are going through a learning sequence through practising a series of moves.

Conversational Analysis comes close to some communicative teaching through its belief that second languages are learnt under the pressure of conversation. Interacting with other people through a series of conversational moves is not just what the learners are aiming at: it is the actual means of learning. But the concept of a 'move' outlined here is not quite the same as the idea of 'function' in most communicative teaching, which is usually concerned with functions such as 'arguing' or 'apologizing' that might occur in several different conversational moves. Topic nomination on the other hand is a move that may be expressed through several different functions — asking, requesting, stating, and so on. It is part of the structure of discourse rather than an isolated item to be learnt. Functions have mostly been put into lists — arguing, complaining, thanking — rather than seen as inter-linked discourse moves. The teacher using a communicative method should perhaps remember that functions never occur by themselves but always in a sequence of conversational moves. However, as with the rest of this chapter, the L2 research base for interactive discourse is fairly narrow. While there are many lists of communicative functions for teaching and many accounts of the gaps that L1 children and L2 learners have in their knowledge, hardly any research has dealt with the crucial relationship between such discriptions and the actual process of L2 learning, vital as this is to its teaching application.

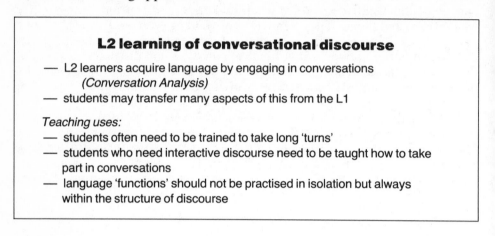

L2 learning of conversational discourse

— L2 learners acquire language by engaging in conversations
   (Conversation Analysis)
— students may transfer many aspects of this from the L1

Teaching uses:
— students often need to be trained to take long 'turns'
— students who need interactive discourse need to be taught how to take part in conversations
— language 'functions' should not be practised in isolation but always within the structure of discourse

Reading

Few readily accessible treatments of the areas covered in this chapter exist. Of the technical books and articles referred to, a good collection on phonology is James, A. and Leather, J. (eds.) (1986). *Sound Patterns In Second Language Acquisition*, Foris, Dordrecht, and a good introduction to transfer is Odlin, T. (1989). *Language Transfer*, CUP.

4

Processes in using second languages

So far this book has dealt chiefly with a learner's knowledge of language of various kinds, that is to say 'competence'. This is not of much avail without the ability to understand or produce speech or writing. People may know they want to say something, and have the grammar, the vocabulary, and the sounds to say it with, but this knowledge is useless if they cannot actually say or comprehend anything. This aspect of language is called 'performance'. This chapter examines five areas of performance related to L2 learning and using. Some aspects of memory and language and cognitive processing are involved in both L1 and L2 processing, other aspects such as codeswitching between languages are unique to L2 use, some aspects such as communication strategies are the subject of dispute as to whether they are unique to L2 learning or shared.

1. short term memory processes

Keywords

Short Term Memory (STM): the memory used for keeping information for periods of time up to a few seconds

working memory: the memory system used for holding and manipulating information while various mental tasks are carried out (Baddeley)

articulatory loop: the means by which information is kept in working memory by being audibly or silently articulated

cognitive deficit: the limitations on processing information in a second language

Memory to most people probably means a store that is used for remembering information for long periods. You have a good memory if you are able to recall people's names, or dates in history. However memory plays a much wider role in language use. Anything that is stored in the mind for any length of time involves some form of memory. In this sense memory is involved in all aspects of the processing of the sentence. Listeners remember the beginning of the sentence while processing the end, they retrieve the patterns and meanings of words from their memory and they work out the relationship of the sentence to its context from information in their memory; they store the meaning of the sentence in their memory so that they can recall it seconds or years later. The different types of information in the sentence have to be processed in different ways and at different levels of memory.

A starting point is Short Term Memory (STM). This refers to the processing of information for periods of time up to a few seconds — the memory process used for remembering a phone number while dialling it. Information is stored in STM quite briefly, and is then usually forgotten. A typical test of STM is the number of digits that can be remembered. Adult native speakers have STMs that store around 7 digits at a time, i.e. have a span of 7190236, varying slightly according to the exact way in which their span is tested and according to other factors. Perhaps not entirely by coincidence a local phone number in England is around six digits, e.g. 872212, that is to say safely within the normal STM span.

In a second language memory of span is reduced. Glicksberg (1963) found that L2 learners' span in English improved from 6.4 digits at the beginning of an eight-week course up to 6.7 at the end. Both spans were below that for native speakers, who scored 7.1 digits on his test. My own STM tests found that at an early stage of English L2 learners could remember 5.9 digits on average (Cook, 1977). At an advanced level they could remember 6.7. So there was an initial shortfall from the 8 digits that natives scored on this test seen in the following diagram.

Short Term Memory Spans in Adult EFL Learners (Cook, 1977)

Beginners
Advanced
Natives

1 2 3 4 5 6 7 8

L2 learners' spans increased as their English improved, yet they were still slightly below the native speaker normal span even at advanced stages. Later research tested the STM of English school-children learning French in both the L1 and the L2 (Cook, 1979). At about the age of 12 their span was 7.5 digits in English, 4.7 in French. By 14 their spans were 8.2 in English, and 5.4 in French. While the students' span is improving in French, it is also improving in English. At each stage there is a gap between their spans for English and French.

Short Term Memory Spans in Schoolboy French Learners (Cook, 1979)

12-year-old French
12-year-old English
14-year-old French
14-year-old English

1 2 3 4 5 6 7 8

Working memory and the articulatory loop

The question is: what stops us remembering more than seven or eight digits in our L1 and fewer than that in the L2? Alan Baddeley (1986) has put forward a theory which accounts for aspects of STM called 'working memory'. In this, working memory is used for processing information while the mind works on various tasks. Its capacity is restricted by the 'articulatory loop'. Information tends to fade rapidly from working memory within a second or two. When people try to remember something, they repeat it over and over to themselves, as with phone numbers, sometimes audibly, sometimes not. They are articulating the sounds, even if they do not say them. To keep the information in working memory from fading it must be repeated over and over. This constant repetition makes up the articulatory loop. Whatever you're trying to remember circulates round this loop. The speed that information goes round the loop governs how much can be remembered. That is to say, the faster a person can repeat things the more they can remember. Memory span is restricted by speed of articulation.

Articulatory loop theory of working memory (simplified)

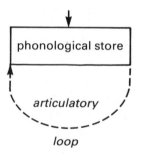

phonological store

articulatory

loop

Not only is the number of words restricted but also their length. More monosyllabic words can be remembered than those with many syllables, because they take longer to articulate. It is easier to remember "Chad, Burma, Greece, Cuba, Malta" than "Czechoslovakia, Somaliland, Nicaragua, Afghanistan, Yugoslavia". The articulatory loop restricts how much can be recycled. Speed of speech is related to the capacity of working memory. Fast speakers have better spans than slow speakers, everything else being equal. And finally there is the comparison across languages. Welsh digits have longer vowels than English ones and hence take longer to say. Sure enough, Welsh people have smaller spans for digits than English speakers. Chinese speakers, however, can say Chinese digits more rapidly and so have greater spans.

Working memory is not therefore an independent part of the mind but is related to pronunciation and to language use. Baddeley regards working memory as a historical by-product of the use of language. Human beings would not have an articulatory loop if they did not have language. Using an L2 means learning how to process information for a second time to the extent that working memory depends upon the first language. In unpublished research Gordon Brown and I found that speed of speaking in English schoolboys learning French was related to working memory span in the two languages. Service (1989) looked at Finnish children learning English in a working memory model and found some development with language experience but not the straightforward link between speed of articulation and progress that might have been expected. She concluded that the children had problems with the phonological store itself rather than the loop.

Teaching and working memory

i. *STM involvement in classroom activities*

Working memory is involved in everyday performance in second language use and in the classroom. The restrictions on the learner's ability to speak the language are caused just as much by memory limits as by the difficulty of the syntax, vocabulary, and so on. A Cambridge university lecturer once told me that the acid test of whether a candidate deserved a scholarship in modern languages was how long a sentence he or she could repeat in the L2. If the mind can't handle enough words, it is impossible to actually process speech. The articulatory loop theory suggests this is linked to fluency of pronunciation. Audiolingual teaching sets great store on the students' pronunciation. Communicative teaching by and large has concentrated on fluency without paying any special attention to pronunciation. Those who emphasise listening as the core skill postpone pronunciation and production in general till the student is ready for it. But training students to speak swiftly and accurately may have helpful side effects on their working memory and hence on their general ability to process language.

ii. *ubiquitousness of working memory*

The second consequence for teaching is the realization that everything the student does or says in the L2 is related in some way to STM. Even asking the students to repeat an L2 sentence is a test of their L2 memory, let alone asking them to comprehend it. So far this chapter has discussed the span for unconnected digits. Memory for sentences is restricted by factors other than the sheer number of words. Different syntactic structures affect the memory processes. Baddeley (1986) showed that passive sentences take longer to understand than active sentences and that they use up more space in working memory. Part of the difficulty in comprehending L2 syntax is the load it puts on the student's memory.

In some sense teachers have always been aware of these restrictions. Two colleagues and I had a rule of thumb for writing structure drills, which was that the student's answer should never be more than fifteen syllables long. We were putting an intuitive limit to the demands on the student's memory. Teachers giving dictation similarly split the text up into the phrases or chunks they think the students' memories can handle. Teaching that takes account of memory limitations will certainly be more effective.

Cognitive deficit in L2 use

Such restrictions are examples of the more general fact that cognitive processes work less efficiently through the second language. Magiste (1979) measured how fast German-speaking children learning Swedish in Sweden carried out production tasks such as naming pictures, and comprehension tasks such as "Mark the third letter from the left". After a year in Sweden the comprehension tasks took about twice as long in the L2 as in the L1 and the production tasks about three times as long. Only after 4–6 years for production and 4–5 years for comprehension did the students become as quick in Swedish as in German. It thus took several years to attain the same ease in the L2 as in the L1, even though they had been living in the country where it was spoken.

The same restrictions on cognitive processes in an L2 are found in other tasks. If L2 learners are asked to count the number of flashes of light from a bulb in two seconds, they underestimate them more in the L2 than in the L1 (Dornic, 1969). People are much worse at mental arithmetic in their second language than in their first (Marsh and Maki, 1978). In general the mind is less efficient in an L2 whatever it is doing; there is an L2 'cognitive deficit', as it is sometimes called. Indeed this deficit has often been used to tell which of a bilingual's languages is dominant.

Memory is also related to the learner's age. Memory processes develop as the child matures rather than being fully present from the beginning. So the way that a child handles information in an L2 is different from that of an adult. For example STM capacity in the L1 was said earlier to be related to pronunciation and to the articulatory loop. This should have been qualified by pointing out that children under 5 do *not* use sounds in STM tasks and they do *not* repeat things to themselves in the same way as adults (Ornstein and Naus, 1978). Adult Venezuelan students of English use adult-like memory processes in English rather than child-like processes (Cook, 1981a). They carry over their adult ways of processing to a second language rather than reverting to childlike ways. Age affects the memory processes that the L2 learner can apply because the learner is at a particular stage in the development of memory. And the age of L2 learners varies in ways that the age of L1 children does not.

L2 learning, Short-Term Memory, and Working Memory

— the span of L2 learners is more restricted than in their L1
— STM span increases as L2 learners develop
— working memory span in the L2 is related to how fast people can speak
— L2 users have a 'cognitive deficit' which makes many of their cognitive processes work slightly less well in the L2

Teaching uses:
— remember that all teaching activities involve an STM load as well as a language load
— pronunciation teaching may benefit students' STM span
— do not expect students to cope with the same ease with L2 tasks that they would find easy in the L1, even when these do not appear to involve language

Although they are still not well-understood in L2 learning, these short-term memory processes have overall implications for the classroom, even if they have been intuitively taken into account by teachers already. The things teachers ask students to do must not be beyond their cognitive capacity in the L2, which is substantially below that in their L1. I remember as a teacher asking near-beginners in English to do mental arithmetic and being shocked how bad they were at it. Cognitive deficit provides a simple explanation. Any classroom activity involves memory processes to some degree and these are restricted in the L2.

2. Reading and longer-term memory processes

Keywords:

> *schema* (pl. schemas or schemata): the background knowledge on which the interpretation of a text depends

> *script*: 'a predetermined stereotyped sequence of actions that defines a well-known situation' (Schank and Abelson)

Reading is also a cognitive process that is restricted in the L2. Reading, like speaking, occurs in a context rather than in isolation. The meaning of a text is not found just in the sentences themselves, but is derived from the previous knowledge stored in the reader's mind and the processes through which the reader tackles it. I look out of my window and see an empty road, as anybody else would do sitting in the same position. However to me the emptiness means my wife has gone out, since the family car is not there, to my son it means the bus for school has not yet arrived, to my daughter it means the postman is late. The same scene is interpreted in different ways according to our background information and predilections.

Schema theory

A famous experiment by Bransford and Johnson (1982) asked people to read texts such as the following:

> The procedure is actually quite simple. First you arrange things into different groups depending on their makeup. Of course, one pile may be sufficient depending on how much there is to do. If you have to go somewhere else due to lack of facilities that is the next step, otherwise you are pretty well set. It is important not to overdo any particular endeavour. That is, it is better to do too few things at once than too many. . . .

To make sense of this text a particular piece of information is required: the passage is about washing clothes. A person who doesn't have this information does not get much out of the text. If the topic is known, the passage is straightforward and the comprehension level is much higher. The sentences themselves do not change when we know the topic, but the interpretation they have in our minds does. The background knowledge into which a text fits, sometimes called the schema, plays a large role in how it is read.

L2 readers too need to know what the passage is about. Adams (1983) gave American students of French the same texts as Bransford and Johnson and tested whether they were better or worse at learning new vocabulary when they were told what the passage was about. Her results showed first that they were better at learning vocabulary in the first language, secondly that knowing what the passage was about helped them equally in both languages. Hence this kind of background knowledge is relevant to both L1 and L2 processing. Patricia Carrell (1984) tested L2 learners of English with the same Bransford and Johnson texts to see not only whether the presence or absence of context made a difference to how much they could understand, but also the importance of whether the text had precise words like "clothes" and "washing machine", or vague words like "things" and "facilities". Both advanced learners and natives once again found lack of context affected their comprehension. However intermediate L2 learners also found the use of vague words was a hindrance. The provision of context varied in importance according to the stage of L2 learning. At the early stages of L2 learning, linguistic aspects of the words are as important to understanding as context. One interesting side effect of Carrell's research was that, while native speakers had a fair idea of how difficult the passages were for them to understand, non-natives did not!

'Scripts' and discourse

A crucial element in the understanding of discourse was given the name of '*script*' by Roger Schank in the 1970s (Schank and Abelson, 1977). The concept of the script came out of attempts to build computer programs that would understand human languages. The problem was that the computer did not know obvious things that human beings take for granted. Suppose a text reads, "Bill had some hamburgers in a restaurant". Straightforward as this sentence seems, our understanding of it relies on several unconscious assumptions about restaurants. What did Bill do with the hamburgers? He ate them, because that's what you go to restaurants to do. Did he cook the hamburgers? Of course he didn't. Did he fetch them himself? Probably not. Did Bill pay for them? Of course he did. In our minds there is a script for restaurants that specifies that they are places where they supply you with food that you pay for. None of this information needs to be given in the text as our minds supply it automatically. Only if the actual event does **not** conform with our background knowledge for restaurants will it be mentioned — if it's self-service, if they've run out of food, or if Bill sneaks out without paying his bill. The mind supplies such information automatically from the background script in its memory. A script is then according to Schank and Abelson (1977) 'a predetermined, stereotyped sequence of actions that defines a well-known situation'. While in recent years Schank has developed his ideas beyond this, nevertheless the script has been a very influential view of how memory is organised.

Some scripts are virtually the same for speakers of different languages;

others differ from one country to another. The script for eating-out may require all restaurants to have waitress-service, or to be takeaway, or to have cash desks by the exit or other variations. I remember once arguing that American hotels are not proper hotels because they have large entrance lobbies rather than cosy lounge areas; my British script for hotels implies lounges. Wherever there are such differences between two scripts, the L2 learners will be at a loss. They unwittingly have different expectations and they have an unpleasant shock when something turns out different. A self-service restaurant that calls for payment in advance by naming the dishes you want can be an unpleasant trial for visitors to Italy! Or indeed the script may be totally absent; I have no script for a Finnish sauna. Many of the stereotyped problems of foreign travel that people recount show conflicts between scripts — eating sheeps' eyes, loos for mixed sexes, tipping taxidrivers, asking if food tastes good, all are absent from the scripts in particular cultures.

An important aspect of discourse is how the background information contributed by the script relates to the purposes of conversation. Say someone is attempting to book a plane ticket in a travel agent's. The participants have their own ideas of what they expect to get out of the conversation; the travel agent needs to know what information he needs to find out and then how to ask the customer to supply it. There is an expected framework of information necessary for the task of booking a ticket to be accomplished. The customer has to supply bits of information to fit this framework. Both participants are combining background knowledge of what goes on in travel agent's with the specific goal of booking a ticket — almost a definition of communicative teaching!

Scripts and schema theory in teaching

Carrell (1983) has produced a set of recommendations for language teachers, based on her own research and that of others. On the one hand she points to the importance of vocabulary, revealed in her experiments with tests outlined earlier. The L2 learner needs to be supplied with the vocabulary that the native takes for granted. On the other hand Carrell sees teaching as building up the learner's background knowledge. Thus she stresses pre-reading activities that build up background knowledge, partly through providing them with appropriate vocabulary through activities such as word association practice. The techniques she suggests develop processing strategies for the text such as flow-charting or diagramming activities. Materials should not only be interesting, but also be conceptually complete; a longer passage or an in-depth set of passages on a single topic is better than short unconnected passages.

Perhaps none of these ideas will be completely new to the practising teacher. Reading materials have after all been stressing content and background for some time. Pre-reading exercises are now standard. Communicatively oriented reading tasks meet many of her requirements. In the textbook *Reasons for Reading* (Davies and Whitney, 1979), for example, a unit on "Persuasion" starts by setting the context firmly in a restaurant with a specimen menu and conversation and by practising vocabulary for good and bad, for food, and so on. It goes on to develop the students' interpretation of advertisements for Oxford marmalade and for Sealink ferries. All the desirable ingredients seem there even if the balance and overall sequence are slightly different.

The benefit for the teacher is an increased awareness of the difficulties that L2 learners face with texts. These are not just a product of the processing of the text itself but of the background information that natives automatically read into it. L2 learners have 'cognitive deficits' with reading that are not caused by lack of language ability but by difficulties with processing information in an L2. Even at advanced levels, L2 learners still cannot get as much out of a text as in their first language, even if on paper they know all the grammar and vocabulary. Cambridge university students tested by Long and Harding-Esch (1977) for example not only remembered less information from political speeches in French than in English but also added more false information! Furthermore advanced L2 learners still read their second language much more slowly than they read their first (Favreau *et al.*, 1982). The problem with reading is not just the language but the whole process of getting meaning from texts.

The importance of background information through scripts and similar mental structures is much wider than the area of reading. The processing of written texts is distinctive in that the reader has to depend only on his or her own script. In speaking, someone else is usually there to help or hinder by interacting with the speaker in one way or another. As with pronunciation, reading involves important low-level processes as well as high-level comprehension. The discussion here has not been about the teaching of reading itself, i.e. literacy, but about teaching L2 students to read in a new language, which is a rather different issue. The actual literacy skills become important either when the L2 learners cannot read in their own language or when the writing system of their L1 is very different. Chinese learners of English have one type of problem in that Chinese uses characters which have no relationship to the spoken form. Greek or Russian learners of English have another set of problems in that the letters are different, rather than the system. Many other L2 learners have problems in that English writing is further from the spoken form than that in their first languages, say Italian.

L2 learning, reading and memory processes

— knowledge of conventional situations (scripts) is important to L2 use
— background knowledge (schemata) is important to L2 learners
— use of 'vague words' hinders lower level learners
Teaching uses:
— build up students' background knowledge
— vocabulary should be emphasized in the teaching of texts
— allow for students' inherent loss of efficiency in processing the L2

3. Processes in listening

Keywords

> *parsing*: the process through which the mind works out the grammatical structure and meaning of the sentence
>
> *top-down* and *bottom-up*: starting from the sentence as a whole and working down to the smallest parts of it, versus starting from the smallest parts and working up
>
> *decoding* versus *codebreaking*: processing language to get the 'message' versus processing language to get the 'rules'

Guides to the teaching of listening appear almost every year; some textbooks are aimed specifically at listening, others include listening components. Yet there is little L2 research concerned with the process of listening as part of the speaker's use of language. Listening does not even figure as a topic in most introductions to L2 learning. This section first looks briefly at the process of listening itself and then develops the use of listening as a vehicle for learning, the most discussed aspect in recent years. It will not discuss the actual processing of speech sounds, already mentioned in chapter Three.

Elements of listening

Most introductions to the comprehension of speech stress three elements: access to vocabulary, parsing, and memory processes.

i. *Access to words*

At one level, in order to comprehend a sentence you have to work out what the words mean. The mind has to relate the words that are heard to the information that is stored about them in the mind — their meanings, etc. For example, a native speaker can answer the question "Is the word 'blish' English?" almost instantaneously, somehow working through many thousands of words in a few moments. Such feats show the human mind is extraordinarily efficient at organizing the storage of words and their interconnections. The context automatically makes particular meanings of words available to us. To a person reading a research article, the word "table" means a layout of figures. To someone reading about antiques it means a piece of furniture. To someone reading a surveyor's report on a house it means the depth at which water appears in the ground, and so on. Somehow the context limits the amount of mental space that has to be searched to get the right meaning. Take the sentence "The dog was run over by a bus". As people listen to it, they are retrieving information about the words. They know that "the" is an article used with certain meanings, here probably something to do with a dog that is already relevant to the conversation. Next "dog" summons up the meanings of "dog" important to this context, its relationships to other words such as "bark" etc, and the probable other words that contrast with it or come in the same context such as "cat". "Run" connects in our mental dictionary with the verb "run", with its range of meanings and its irregular past form, and to expectations that it is going to be followed by a noun phrase object, as we saw in chapter Three. In addition there are the links between the L1 vocabulary and the L2 vocabulary; using a second language means accessing a more complicated mental dictionary.

ii) *parsing*

Parsing refers to how the mind works out the grammatical structure and meaning of the sentences it hears. Take a sentence such as "The man ate breakfast". To understand the sentence fully means being able to tell who is carrying out the action and what is affected by the action, and to realise that "ate breakfast" goes together as a phrase while "man ate" does not. Even if our minds are not consciously aware of the grammatical technicalities, nevertheless they are working out the structure of the sentence automatically. Grammar is not just in the back of our minds but is active while we are listening.

The process of parsing can be either 'bottom-up' or 'top-down'. 'Bottom-up' means building the sentence up in our minds bit by bit, putting the sounds into words, the words into phrases, the phrases into a whole sentence. So "the" is put with "man" to get a noun phrase "the man"; "ate" goes with "breakfast" to get a verb phrase "ate breakfast"; and the noun phrase "the man" and the verb phrase "ate breakfast" go together to yield the structure of the whole sentence. 'Top-down' parsing on the other hand means starting from the whole sentence and breaking it down into smaller and smaller bits. Given a sentence like "The man ate breakfast" the top-down process tries to find a noun phrase, which in turn means trying to find first an article "the" and then a noun "man". If it succeeds, it next tries to find a verb phrase, which means trying to find a verb "ate" and a noun phrase "breakfast". If the quest to find a noun phrase and a verb phrase succeeds, it has found a sentence, complete with its structure.

In principle the mind could parse the sentence in either the bottom-up or the top-down direction. In practice listeners get the best of both worlds by using both types of process. Features such as the intonation pattern allow them to fit words and phrases within an overall structure, a top-down process. Particular words indicate the start of a phrase and allow them to build it up word by word, a bottom-up process. J. Michael O'Malley and his colleagues (1989) found that effective L2 learners used both top-down approaches of listening for intonation or phrases and bottom-up approaches of listening for words, while ineffective listeners concentrated on a bottom-up process. When parsing failed, they fell back on a range of other strategies, the least effective being translation.

iii.*memory processes and cognition*

The memory processes in listening are closely connected to those discussed earlier. All comprehension depends on the storing and processing of information by the mind. Call (1985) for instance found that sheer memory for digits was less important to comprehension than memory for sentences.

The extent of the memory restriction in an L2 depends upon how close the task is to language. Hence getting the students to do tasks that are not concerned with language may have less influence on their learning than language-related tasks, for example comprehension activities using maps and diagrams may improve the learners' problem-solving abilities with map and diagrams but may be less successful at improving those aspects of the learners' mental processes that depend on language.

A further point that applies to listening as much as to reading is that vital aspects of the process are contributed by the listener. At the lowest level, the actual "p" sounds of speech have to be worked out by the mind. While the actual sounds in "pit", "spit", and "top" differ in terms of Voice Onset Time, the English person nevertheless hears a /p/ in each of them; the listener's ear somehow imposes the idea of a /p/ on the soundwaves it hears. The meaning of words such as "bus" and "breakfast" is not present in the sentence itself but is retrieved from the listener's mental dictionary to match the sequence of sounds that is heard. The sentence also has to be actively parsed by the listener to discover the phrases and constructions involved. As with reading, the listener's knowledge of the context of situation and background knowledge of the culture and society are crucial to listening comprehension. I recently invited some overseas students to a party at eight o'clock; some of them asked me if I meant eight in the morning or eight in the evening. Though it was not mentioned in my invitation, my cultural expectation was that parties take place in the evening. The scripts and schemas talked about in relation to reading are equally involved in listening. Our mental pictures of restaurants and stations come into play as soon as the appropriate situation is invoked. Any sentence listeners hear is matched against their mental models of the world as reflected in scripts and schemas. If the models of speaker and listener differ too much, they have problems in comprehending each other. O'Malley *et al.*, (1989) found that effective listeners helped themselves by drawing on their knowledge of the world, or on their personal experiences, or by asking questions of themselves.

The teaching of listening

How does this view of listening compare with that in teaching guides such as Mary Underwood's *Teaching Listening* (Underwood, 1989) She recognizes three stages of teaching — *pre-listening* where the students activate their vocabulary and their background knowledge, *while-listening* where 'they develop the skill of eliciting messages', and *post-listening* which consists of extensions and developments of the listening task. Some of the elements are similar. It is rightly considered important to get the students' background scripts working and the appropriate vocabulary active in their minds. What seems overlooked is parsing. Listeners do need to know the structure of the sentence in some way. Teaching has mostly ignored the process of syntactic parsing, perhaps because of its unwelcome overtones of grammar. But, as with reading, some attempt could be made to train both top-down and bottom-up parsing skills.

A development in the past ten years has been task-based teaching of listening. The students carry out a task in which they have to listen for information in a short piece of discourse and then have to fill in a diagram, check a route on a map or correct mistakes in a text. The *COBUILD English Course I* (Willis & Willis, 1987) for example asks the students to listen to tapes of people speaking spontaneously and to work out information from them. Lesson 9 has a recording of Chris telling Philip how to get to his house in Birmingham. The students listen for factual information, such as which buses could be taken; they make a rough map of the route, and they check its accuracy against the A–Z map of Birmingham. One teaching motivation for this approach is the practical necessity for the teacher of checking that comprehension is taking place. Unfortunately in normal language use there is no visible feedback when someone has comprehended something. A visible sign of comprehension is useful to the teacher to see if the student has understood. This check can range from a straightforward question to an action based on what has happened. If you shout "The room's on fire" and nobody moves, you assume they have not understood. Much teaching of listening comprehension has consisted of the student having to show some sign of having comprehended, whether through answering questions, carrying out tasks, or whatever.

The other motivation for task-based listening activities is that information is being transferred for a communicative purpose. Task-based listening stresses the transfer of information rather than the social dimension of language teaching. In the COBUILD example the student is practising something that resembles real world communication. It is sad, however, that the information that is transferred in such activities is usually about trivial topics or irrelevant to the students' lives. The factual information the students learn in the COBUILD exercise is how to get around in Birmingham, somewhere only a few of them are ever likely to go! Often such exercises deal with imaginary towns, or even treasure islands. On the one hand task-based exercises often neglect the educational value of the content that can be used in language teaching. On the other much psychological research shows that, the more important the information is to the listener, the more likely it is to be retained.

Such techniques do not so much teach listening as decorate the listening process with a few frills. They suggest that conscious attention to information will improve all the other aspects of listening, which is hardly justified by the research described here. If word access, parsing, and memory processes are improved by these activities, this is an accidental by-product. Perhaps listening cannot be trained directly and the best the teacher can do is devise amusing activities during which the natural listening processes can be automatically activated.

Listening-based methods of teaching

So far listening has been taken as a process of *decoding* speech — working out the 'message' from the sentence you hear just as a spy decodes a secret message by using a code he or she already knows. However the main focus in recent discussions of teaching methodology has been on listening as a way of **learning** language rather than as a way of **processing** language. Logically L2 learners can't learn a language if they never hear it; the sounds, the words, the structures, have to come from somewhere. This process can be called *codebreaking* — listening means working out the language code from the 'message' just as a cryptographer works out an unknown code from an intercepted message. Decoding speech has the aim of discovering the message using processes that are already known. Codebreaking speech has the aim of discovering the processes themselves from a message.

One of the first to interpret listening as codebreaking was James Asher's *Total Physical Response Method* (TPR) (Asher, 1986), which claimed that listening to commands and carrying them out was an effective way of learning a second language. A specimen TPR lesson reported by Asher (1986) consists of the teacher getting the students to respond to the commands:

> Walk to the window.
> Touch the window.
> Walk to the table.
> Touch the table.
> Juan, stand up and walk to the door.
> Jaime, walk to the table and sit on the table.

and so on. The students follow the directions the teacher gives. TPR came from psychological theories of language learning and extensive research has been carried out into it. Its unique feature is the emphasis on learning through physical actions. As Asher puts it, 'In a sense, language is orchestrated to a choreography of the human body'.

Other listening-based methods have also been successful. Postovsky (1974) described how students who were taught Russian by methods that emphazise listening were better than students taught in a conventional way. According to Gary and Gary (1981a; 1981b) the benefits of concentrating on listening are that students do not feel so embarrassed if they don't have to speak, the memory load is less if they listen without speaking, classroom equipment such as taperecorders can be used more effectively for listening than for speaking, and so on. Classroom research has confirmed that there are distinct advantages to listening-based methods, as we see in the collection by Winitz (1981). One of the major schisms in contemporary teaching methodology is between those who require students to practise communication by both listening and speaking and those who prefer students to listen for information without speaking. This will be discussed in chapter Nine.

Krashen brings these listening-based methods together through the notion of 'comprehensible input'. He claims that 'acquisition can take place only when people understand messages in the target language' (Krashen and Terrell, 1983). Listening is motivated by the need to get messages out of what is heard. L2 learners acquire a new language by hearing it in contexts where the meaning is made plain to them. Ideally the speech they hear has enough 'old' language that the student already knows and makes enough sense in the context for the 'new' language to be understood and absorbed. How the teacher gets the message across is not particularly important. Pointing to one's nose and saying "This is my nose", working out "nose" from the context in "There's a spot on your nose", looking at a photo of a face and labelling it with "nose", "eyes", etc., all of these are satisfactory provided that the student discovers the message in the sentence.

Krashen claims that *all* teaching methods that work utilize the same 'fundamental pedagogical principle' of providing comprehensible input: 'if *x* is shown to be "good" for acquiring a second language, *x* helps to provide CI [comprehensible input], either directly or indirectly' (Krashen, 1981b). Krashen's codebreaking approach to listening became a strong influence on language teachers in the 1980s. It is saying essentially that L2 acquisition depends on listening — decoding *is* codebreaking.

But this theory does not say what the processes of decoding *are* and how they relate to codebreaking. The statement that teaching should be meaningful does not get us very far by itself. Most teachers have already been trying to make their lessons convey messages. Comprehensible input is too simplistic and too all-embracing a notion to produce anything but the most general guidelines on what a teacher should do. It pays little heed to the actual processes of listening or learning but promises that everything will be all right if the teacher maximises comprehensible input. As advice this is too vague; the teacher can do anything, provided the students have to make sense of the language that is addressed to them.

L2 learning and Listening processes

— L2 listening is an active process involving background schemas etc
— both 'top-down' and 'bottom-up' parsing is involved
— ineffective L2 students rely too much on bottom-up parsing
Teaching uses:
— teaching involves both decoding messages from language and codebreaking the language system from what is heard
— task-based listening may be dangerous if it is too task-specific

---

4. Codeswitching by second language users

Keywords

> *codeswitching*: going from one language to the other in midspeech when both speakers know the same two languages

The processes discussed so far are employed by all language users in one way or another. People use similar memory processes, reading processes, and listening processes in both the L1 and the L2, even if they are less efficient at using them in the L2. This section however looks at a process peculiar to the use of the L2, namely *codeswitching* from one language to another. To illustrate codeswitching in action, here are some sentences recorded by Zubaidah Hakim in a staffroom where Malaysian teachers of English were talking to each other. "*Suami saya dulu* slim and *trim tapi sekarang* plump like drum" (Before my husband was slim and trim but now he is plump like a drum), "*Jadi* I *tanya*, how can you say that when . . . *geram betul* I" (So I asked how can you say that when . . . I was so mad), and "Hero you *tak datang hari ni*" (Your hero did not come today). What is happening here is a constant switching between English and Bahasa Malaysia. One moment there is a phrase or a word in English, the next a phrase or word in Bahasa Malaysia. Sometimes the switch between languages occurs between sentences rather than within them. It is often hard to say which is the main language of the conversation or indeed of the sentence.

Codeswitching is found all over the world where bilingual speakers talk to each other. According to François Grosjean (1989), bilinguals have two modes of using language. One is when they speak either one language or the other, the other mode is when they codeswitch from one to the other during the course of speech. Bilingual codeswitching is neither unusual or abnormal; it is an ordinary fact of life in many multilingual societies. The box on the next page gives some example of codeswitching drawn from various sources, as well as some of the previous examples.

The interesting questions about codeswitching are why and when it happens. A common reason for switching is to report what someone has said, as in the following example where a girl who is telling a story switches from Tok Pisin (spoken in Papua New Guinea) to English to report what the man said: "*Lapun man ia cam na tok*, 'oh yu poor pussiket'" (The old man came and said 'you poor pussycat'). In one sense whenever a book cites sentences in other languages, it is a codeswitch! A second reason for switching is to use markers from one language to highlight something in another. The Japanese/English "She *wa* took her a month to come home *yo*" uses "wa" to indicate what is being talked about, its function in Japanese.

Another reason is that some topics are more appropriate to one language than another. Mexican Americans for example prefer to talk about money in English rather than in Spanish — "La consulta era (the visit cost) *eight dollars*". One of my Malaysian students told me that she could express romantic feelings in English but not in Malay. Sometimes the reason for codeswitching is that the choice of language shows the speaker's role. A Kenyan man who was serving his own sister in a shop started in their own Luiyia dialect and then switched to Swahili for the rest of the conversation to signal that he was treating her as an ordinary customer. And often bilinguals use fillers and tags from one language in another, as in the Spanish/English exchange "Well I'm glad to meet you", "*Andale pues* and do come again." (OK swell . . .). The common factor underlying these examples is that the speaker assumes the listener is fluent in the two languages. Otherwise such sentences would not be a bilingual codeswitching mode of language use but would be either interlanguage communication

---

Some examples of codeswitching between languages

Bahasa Malaysian/English: "*Suami saya dulu* slim and trim *tapi   sekarang* plump like drum" (Before my husband was slim and trim but now he is plump like a drum)

Spanish/English "*Todos los Mexicanos* were riled up" (All the Mexicans were riled up)

Dutch/English "*Ik heb een kop* of tea, tea or something" (I had a cup of tea or something)

Russian/French "*Chustvovali, chto* le vin est tiré et qu'il faut le boire" (They felt that the wine is uncorked and it should be drunk).

Tok Pisin/English: "*Lapun man ia cam na tok*, 'oh yu poor pussiket'" (The old man came and said 'you poor pussycat')

Japanese/English "She *wa* took her a month to come home *yo*"

---

strategies or attempts at one-up-manship, similar to the use by some English speakers of Latin expressions such as "*ab initio* learners of Spanish" (Spanish beginners).

How does codeswitching relate to language structure? According to one set of calculations about 84% of switches within the sentence are isolated words, say the English/Malaysian "Ana *free* hari ini" (Ana is free today) where English is switched to only for the item "free". About 10% are phrases as in the Russian/French "Imela une femme de chambre" (She had a chambermaid). The remaining 6% are switches for whole clauses as in the German/English "*Papa, wenn du das Licht ausmachst*, then I'll be so lonely" (Daddy, if you put out the light, I'll be so lonely). But this still doesn't show when a switch from one language to another can take place.

The theory of codeswitching developed by Poplack (1980) claims that there are two main restrictions on where switching can happen:

i. **The 'free morpheme constraint'**. This means that the speaker may not switch language between a word and its endings unless the word is pronounced as if it were in the language of the ending. Thus an English/Spanish switch "run*eando*" is impossible because "run" is distinctively English in sound. But "flip*eando*" is possible because "flip" could be a Spanish word.

ii) **The 'equivalence constraint'**. This means that the switch can come at a point in the sentence where it does not violate the grammar of either language. So there are unlikely to be any should be no French/English switches such as "a car *americaine*" or "une *American* voiture" as they would be wrong in both languages. It is possible however to have the French/English switch "*J'ai acheté* an American car" (I bought an American car) because both English and French share the construction in which the object follows the verb.

Codeswitching and language teaching

What does codeswitching have to do with language teaching? The profile of the proficient L2 user includes the codeswitching mode of language. It is not something that is peculiar or unusual. If the bilingual knows that the listener shares the same languages, codeswitching is likely to take place for all the reasons given above. For many students the ability to go from one language to another is highly desirable.

The Institute of Linguists' examinations in Languages for International Communication test whether candidates can mediate between two languages. At beginners level this may be reading an L2 travel brochure or listening to L2 answerphone messages to get information that can be used in the L1. At advanced stages it might be researching a topic through reading and conducting interviews in order to write an L1 report. In this international use of a second language the L2 learner is not becoming an imitation native speaker but is a person who can stand between the two languages, using both when appropriate. While this is not in itself codeswitching, it involves the same element of having two languages readily available rather than functioning exclusively in one or the other. One possibility is to utilize '*reciprocal*' language teaching in which students switch language at predetermined points (Cook, 1989b). This method pairs students who want to learn each other's languages and makes them alternate between the two languages, thus exchanging the roles of teacher and student. My own experience of this was on a summer course that paired French teachers of English with English teachers of French. For one day all the activities would take place in French, for the next day everything would be in English, and so on throughout the course.

But codeswitching proper can also be exploited as part of actual teaching methodology. When the teacher knows the language of the students, the

---

L2 learning and Codeswitching

Codeswitching is the use of two languages within the same conversation, often when the speaker is:
— reporting what someone has said
— highlighting something
— discussing particular topics
— emphasising a particular social role
Codeswitching consists of 84% single word switches, 10% phrases, 6% clauses
Teachers should remember:
— the classroom is often a natural codeswitching situation
— there is nothing wrong or peculiar about codeswitching
— principles exist for codeswitching in the classroom

classroom itself is often a codeswitching situation. The lesson starts in the L1, or the control of the class takes place through the L1, or the L1 slips in in other ways. Use of the L1 is an important indication of the extent to which the class is 'communicative', as we see in chapter Six. Perhaps codeswitching is inevitable in the classroom if the teacher and students share the same languages and should be regarded as natural.

Rodolpho Jacobson has developed a teaching method known as the 'New Concurrent Approach' (Faltis, 1989) which gets teachers to balance the use of the two languages within a single lesson. The teacher is allowed to switch languages at certain key points. In a class of English taught to Spanish children, the teacher can switch to Spanish when concepts are important, when the students are getting distracted, or when the student should be praised or told off. The teacher may switch to English when revising a lesson that has been already given in Spanish.

5. Communication strategies

Keywords

Communication strategies

— mutual attempts to solve L2 communication problems by participants (Tarone)
— individual solutions to psychological problems of L2 processing
(Faerch & Kasper)
— ways of filling vocabulary gaps in L1 or L2 (Kellerman)

L2 learners are attempting to communicate through a language that is not their own. It is different from children learning a first language where mental and social development go hand in hand with language development. Hence, unlike L1 children, L2 learners are always wanting to express things for which they do not have the means in the second language. In the eighties there was considerable debate about the communication strategies L2 learners employ to cope with this problem. Here we shall look at three different approaches to communication strategies. The detailed lists of strategies used by these approaches are summarized in the box on page 70 which can be referred to during this section.

Communication strategies as social interaction

Elaine Tarone (1980) emphasizes social aspects of communication. Both participants are trying to overcome their lack of shared meaning. She sees three overall types of strategy — communication, production, and learning, the first of which we will consider here. When things go wrong, both participants try to devise a communication strategy to get out of the difficulty. One type of strategy is to paraphrase what you want to say. Typical strategies are:
— *approximation*. Someone who is groping for a word falls back on a

strategy of using a word that means approximately the same, say "animal" for "horse", because the listener will be able to deduce from the context what is intended.

— *word coinage*. Another form of paraphrase is to make up a word to substitute for the unknown word — "airball" for "balloon".
— *circumlocution*. L2 learners talk their way round the word — "when you make a container" for "pottery".

All these strategies rely on the speaker trying to solve the difficulty through the L2.

A second overall type of communication strategy is to fall back on the first language. Examples are:

— *translation* from the L1. A German-speaking student says "Make the door shut" rather than "Shut the door".
— *language switch*. "That's a nice tirtil" (caterpillar), distinct from the codeswitching discussed above because the listener does not know the L1.
— *appeal for assistance*. "What is this?"
— *mime* what you need. My daughter succeeded in getting some candles in a shop in France by singing "Happy Birthday" in English and miming blowing out candles.

A third overall type of strategy is to *avoid* talking about things you know are difficult in the L2, whether whole topics or individual words.

Bialystok (1990) compared some of these strategies in terms of effectiveness and found that listeners understand word coinage much better than approximation, circumlocution, or language switch.

Communication strategies as psychological problem-solving

The approach of Faerch and Kasper (1984) concentrates on the psychological dimension of what is going on in the L2 speaker's mind. L2 learners want to express something through the second language but encounter a problem. To get round this psychological difficulty, they resort to communication strategies. Faerch and Kasper divide these into two main groups — *achievement* (trying to solve the problem) and *avoidance* (trying to avoid it).

i. achievement strategies

These subdivide into *cooperative strategies*, such as appealing to the other person for help, which are mostly similar to Tarone's list, and *noncooperative* strategies where the learner tries to solve the problems without recourse to others. One form of non-cooperation is to fall back on the first language when in trouble by:

— *codeswitching*. The speaker skips language — "Do you want to have some ah Zinsen?" (the German word for "interest")
— *foreignerisation*. A Dane literally translating the Danish word for vegetables into English as "green things".
In the light of the discussion on codeswitching above these strategies seem likely to occur when the listener knows both languages, as in many research and teaching situations.

Another overall grouping is *interlanguage strategies* that are based on the learner's evolving L2 system rather than on the L1. Among these Faerch and Kasper include:

— *substitution* Speakers substitute one word for another, say "if" for "whether" if they cannot remember whether "whether" has an "h".
— *generalisation*. L2 speakers use a more general word rather than a more particular such as "animal" for "rabbit".
— *description*. Speakers can't remember the word for "kettle" and so describe it as "the thing to cook water in".
— *exemplification*. Speakers give an example rather than the general term "cars " for "transport".
— *word-coining*. That is, making up a word when you don't know it such as inventing an imaginary French word "heurot" for "watch".
— *restructuring*. The speaker has another attempt at the same sentence, as in a learner struggling to find the rare English word "sibling" "I have two — er — one sister and one brother".

ii. *avoidance strategies*
   These Faerch and Kasper divide into:

— *formal avoidance* The speaker avoids a particular linguistic form, whether in pronunciation, in morphemes, or in syntax.
— *functional avoidance*. The speaker avoids different types of function.

Archistrategies

To some extent Tarone's social communicative strategies and Faerch and Kasper's psychological strategies are complementary ways of coping with the problems of communicating in a second language. But, as we have seen, they end up as rather long and confusing lists of strategies. Eric Kellerman and his colleagues (1987) feel that these approaches can be considerably simplified. The common factor to all communication strategies is that the L2 learner has to deal with not knowing a word in a second language; it is vocabulary lack that is crucial. The strategies exist to plug gaps in the learners' vocabulary by allowing them to refer to things for which they do not know the L2 words. The apparent variety of strategies can be reduced to three more general 'archistrategies':

i. The *approximative* archistrategy. The learner substitutes a word whose meaning is as close as possible. Using "bird" for "robin" or "chest" for "breast" is substituting a word that is reasonably close in meaning to the one intended.
ii. The *analytic* archistrategy. The learner builds up a picture of what the missing word means by describing it. So the word "knife" might be replaced by "large sharp thing" and "breast" by "the part between throat and legs".
iii. The *linguistic* archistrategy. The learner fills the gap with a word from the first language. Thus "breast" might be substituted by the Dutch word "borst" or "alimony" by "alimentation" derived from the Dutch equivalent "alimentatie". According to their devisers, these three archistrategies cover

---

Different approaches to L2 Communication Strategies

Socially-motivated strategies for solving mutual lack of understanding (Tarone)
— paraphrase (approximation, word coinage, circumlocution)
— falling back on L1 translation, language switch, appeal for assistance, mime
— avoidance

Psychologically motivated strategies for solving the individual's L2 problems of expression (Faerch & Kasper)
1 Achievement strategies:
— cooperative strategies (similar to list above)
— noncooperative strategies
— codeswitching
— foreignerisation
— interlanguage strategies (substitution, generalisation, description, exemplification, word-coining, restructuring)
2 Avoidance strategies:
— formal (phonological, morphological, grammatical)
— functional (actional, propositional, modal)

Archistrategies to compensate for lack of vocabulary (Kellerman)
— approximative (substitutes one word for another)
— analytic (describes the properties of the object in question
— linguistic (uses something from the L1 instead)

---

much the same ground as those discussed earlier and are much easier to look for in learners' speech.

They lead, however, to an interesting conclusion. The linguistic archi-strategy requires knowledge of another language and hence is unique to L2 learning. However the approximative and analytic strategies are the same as those used in native speech when speakers cannot remember the word they want to use. Describing which parts of my car needed repairing to a mechanic, I said "That cross bar that holds the bonnet down", an approximative strategy, and "There's oil dripping from that sort of junction in the pipe behind the engine", an analytic strategy. These strategies not only allowed me to communicate without knowing the correct words; they mean I never need to learn them — I still don't know what these parts of the car are called. Such strategies occur more frequently in L2 learners' speech only because they know fewer words than native speakers. The strategies are used by native speakers in the same way as L2 learners when they too do not know the words, as any conversation overheard in a shop selling do-it-yourself tools will confirm. Kellerman and his colleagues believe that these compensatory strategies are a part of the speaker's communicative competence that can be used in either language when needed rather than something peculiar to L2 learning. (Kellerman *et al.*, 1990).

So it is not clear whether strategies need to be taught. L2 learners resort to these strategies in the real-world situation when they do not know words. This does not mean that it may not be beneficial for students to have their attention drawn to them so that they are reminded that these strategies can indeed be used in an L2. They form part of the normal repertoire of their communicative competence. In any teaching activity that encourages the learners to speak outside their normal vocabulary range they are bound to occur. An exercise in the textbook *Keep Talking* (Klippel, 1984) suggests that the students describe their everyday problems such as losing their keys and not being able to remember names, and other students suggest ways of solving them. If the students do not know the word for "key" say, they might ask the teacher (a cooperative strategy), or look it up in a dictionary (a non-cooperative strategy). Or they might attempt an analytical archistrategy — "the thing you open doors with". With the exception of dictionary use, these strategies can be safely ignored by the teacher. They are there if the students need them but they need not form the teaching point of an exercise. One danger with teaching activities that make the students communicate spontaneously is that sheer lack of vocabulary forces the students back onto these strategies. Hence the teacher should keep the likely vocabulary load of non-teacher-controlled activities within certain limits, ensuring that students already know enough of the vocabulary not to be forced back onto compensatory strategies for too much of the time. Or the teachers can treat them as ways of discovering and teaching the vocabulary the students lack. Further discussion of the teaching of strategies occurs in the section on learning strategies in the next chapter.

Reading

For the areas of *short-term memory processes, reading,* and *listening,* readers are recommended to the original sources referred to in the chapter, as no book-length L2 learning treatments exist that cover the areas adequately. *Codeswitching* is described in many books on bilingualism, particulary Romaine, S. (1989). *Bilingualism* (OUP). One perspective on *communication strategies* can be found in Bialystok, E. (1990). *Communication Strategies*, Blackwell, Oxford.

5

Learners as individuals

So far this book has concentrated on the things that L2 learners have in common. Teachers usually have to deal with students in groups rather than as individuals; it is what all the class do that is important. However, ultimately language is not learnt by groups, but by individuals. At the end of the class, the group turns into 25 individuals who go off to use language as they will. Features of the learner's personality or mind encourage or inhibit L2 learning. The concern of the present chapter is then with how L2 learners vary as individuals.

1. Motivation: what sort of motivation is good for L2 learning?

Keywords

> *integrative motivation*: learning the language to take part in the culture of its people

> *instrumental motivation*: learning the language for a career reason or other practical reason

> *additive bilingualism*: L2 learning that adds to the learner's capabilities

> *subtractive bilingualism*: L2 learning that takes away from the learner's capabilities

Some L2 learners do better than others because they are better motivated. The child learning a first language cannot really be spoken about in terms of good or bad motivation. Language is one means through which all children fulfil their everyday needs, however diverse these may be. One might as well ask what the motivation is for walking or for being a human being. In these terms the second language is superfluous for many classroom learners, who can already communicate with people and use language for thinking. Their mental and social life has been formed through their first language.

Motivation has chiefly been talked about in L2 learning in terms of two types of favourable motivation — *integrative* and *instrumental* motivation, introduced by Lambert and Gardner in a series of books and papers

(Gardner and Lambert, 1972; Gardner, 1985). The integrative motivation reflects whether the student identifies with the target culture and people in some sense, or rejects them. The more that a student admires the target culture — reads its literature, visits it on holiday, looks for opportunities of practising the language, and so on — the more successful the student will be in the L2 classroom.

The instrumental motivation on the other hand reflects whether the student is learning the language for an ulterior motive unrelated to its use by native speakers — to pass an examination, to get a certain kind of job, and so on. For example I learnt Latin at school because a classical language was an entry requirement for university. A survey of young people in Europe found that 29% wanted to learn more languages to increase their career possibilities, while 14% wanted them in order to live, work, or study in the country (Commission of the EC, 1987). The largest category, 51%, however were motivated by 'personal interest'. The last figure is a reminder that integrative and instrumental motivations are only two of the possible kinds of motivation. Gardner and Lambert (1972) for example also recognised the possibility of 'manipulative' or 'intellectual' motivations.

L2 motivation should not therefore be considered as a forced choice between these two. Both types are important. A student might learn an L2 well with an integrative motivation or with an instrumental one, or indeed with both, for one does not rule out the other, or with other motivations. The relative importance of these has been shown to vary from one part of the world to another. In Montreal learners of French tend to be integratively motivated, in the Philippines learners of English tend to be instrumentally motivated (Gardner, 1985). Some of the different contexts of L2 learning are discussed in chapter Seven.

The distinction between integrative and instrumental motivation has been used by many researchers as a point of reference. Clement and Kruidenier (1983) for example compared L2 learners who were learning English or French in different Canadian contexts and found four main factors shared by all groups. One was indeed *pragmatic goals*, similar to instrumental motivation. But instead of the integrative motivation they found two factors, *travel*, and *seeking new friendships*. In addition there was a factor of *acquiring knowledge*. The two-way division into instrumental and integrative obscures important motivations common to learners and conceals important differences.

Motivation and teaching

Nevertheless students will find it difficult to learn a second language in the classroom if they have **neither** instrumental **nor** integrative motivation, as is probably often the case in school language teaching. School-children have no particular contact with the foreign culture and no particular interest in it, nor do their job prospects depend on it. Only 36% of pupils in England thought learning French would be useful to them, according to the Assessment of Performance Unit (1986). Teachers of French in England try to compensate for this lack by cultivating both types of motivation in their students, say by stressing the career benefits that knowledge of a second language may bring, or by building up interest in the foreign culture through exchanges with French schools or samples of French food.

Otherwise teachers may have to go along with the students' motivation, or at least be sufficiently aware of the students' motivation so that any problems can be smoothed over. Course books then reflect the writer's assessment of the students' motivation. The Hungarian English course **Angol Nyelv Alapfokon** (Edina and Ivanne, 1987) uses English primarily in Hungarian scenes such as entertaining English guests, tours of Budapest for English visitors, shopping ("The oranges are 25 forints"), and letters home from sons in the army. It concentrates on jobs for which English is necessary, such as travel representatives, airline stewards, tourist guides, and journalists. It assumes that an important part of the motivation of Hungarian students is instrumental and that integration into an English-speaking culture is less important.

Whether this fits with the motivation of actual Hungarian students, only their teachers can say. On the other hand, the British coursebook **Blueprint One** (Abbs & Freebairn, 1990) stresses the life-style of middle-class young adults in England or visiting England — booking holidays, tourist trips, living in 'typical English houses . . . with three bedrooms and a bathroom', interested in ballet, caravanning, clothes, shopping and eating out. Again this will be valuable with students interested in this life-style, and alienating for those who prefer something else.

A problem teachers face is that motivations for L2 learning are deep-rooted in the students' minds and in their cultural backgrounds. This is incorporated in Gardner's Socio-educational model of L2 learning to be discussed in chapter Eight. Whatever the teacher does may be powerless against the many other influences on the students. The general issue is how the student's cultural background fits the background projected by the L2 culture. Lambert (1981; 1990) makes an important distinction between **additive** and **subtractive** bilingualism. In additive bilingualism the learners feel they are adding something new to their skills and experience by learning a new language, without taking anything away from what they already know. In subtractive bilingualism they feel that the learning of a new language threatens what they have already gained for themselves. Successful L2 learning takes place in additive situations; learners who see the L2 as diminishing themselves will not succeed.

This relates directly to many immigrant or multi-ethnic situations; a group that feels in danger of losing its identity by learning a second language does not learn the L2 well. Some Chilean refugees I taught in the 1970s often lamented their lack of progress in English. However much they consciously wanted to learn English, subconsciously they saw it as committing themselves to permanent exile and thus to subtracting from themselves as Chileans. It is not motivation for learning as such which is important to teaching but motivation for learning a **particular** second language. Monolingual UK children in a survey conducted by the Linguistic Minorities Project (1983) showed a preference in order of popularity for learning German, Italian, Spanish and French. Young people in the EC as a whole however had the order of preference English, Spanish, German, French and Italian (Commission of the EC, 1987).

In an ideal teacher's world students would enter the classrooms admiring the target culture and language, wanting to get something out of the L2 learning for themselves, and thirsting for knowledge. In practice teachers have to be aware of the reservations and preconceptions of their students. What they think of the teacher, and what they think of the course heavily affect their success. This is what teachers can influence rather than the learners' more deep-seated motivations, as we see in later chapters. Motivation also goes in both directions. High motivation is one factor that causes successful learning; successful learning, however, may cause high motivation. The latter process of creating successful learning which can spur high motivation, may be under the teacher's control, if not the former. The choice of teaching materials and the information content of the lesson for example should correspond to the motivations of the students. As Lambert (1990) puts it while talking about minority group children, 'The best way I can see to release the potential [of bilingualism] is to transform their subtractive experiences with bilingualism and biculturalism into additive ones.'

Motivation and L2 learning

— both integrative and instrumental motivations may lead to success, but lack of either causes problems
— successful learning can be based on: pragmatic goals, travel, seeking new friendships, acquiring knowledge
— motivation in this sense has great inertia

Teaching implications:
— recognize variety and nature of motivations
— work with student motivation in materials and content

---

2. Aptitude: are some people better at learning a second language than others?

Keywords

aptitude: usually the ability to learn the L2 in an academic classroom

Modern Language Aptitude Test (MLAT): testing phonemic coding, grammatical sensitivity, inductive language learning ability, rote learning

memory-based learners these rely on their memory rather than grammatical sensitivity

analytic learners these rely on grammatical sensitivity rather than memory

even learners these rely on both grammatical sensitivity and memory

It is popularly believed that some people have a knack for learning second languages, and others are rather poor at it. Some immigrants who have been in a country for twenty years are very fluent. Others from the same background and living in the same circumstances for the same amount of time speak the language rather poorly. Given that their ages, motivations, and so on are the same, why are there such differences? As always the popular view has to be qualified to some extent. Descriptions of societies where each individual uses several languages daily, such as Central Africa or Pakistan, seldom mention people who cannot cope with the demands of a multilingual existence, other than those with academic study problems. Differences in L2 learning ability are apparently only felt in societies where L2 learning is treated as a problem rather than an everyday fact of life.

Tests of aptitude

So far the broad term 'knack' for learning languages has been used. The more usual term however is 'aptitude'; some people have more aptitude for learning second languages than others. But aptitude has almost invariably been used in connection with students in classrooms. It does not refer to the knack that some people have for learning in real-life situations but to the ability to learn from teaching. In the 1950s and 1960s considerable effort went into establishing what successful students had in common. The *Modern Languages Aptitude Test* (MLAT) broadly speaking requires the student to carry out L2 learning on a small scale. It incorporates four main factors that predict a student's success in the classroom (Carroll, 1981). These are:

i. *'phonemic coding ability'*: how well the student can use phonetic script to distinguish phonemes in the language.

ii. *'grammatical sensitivity'*:whether the student can pick out grammatical functions in the sentence.

iii. *'inductive language learning ability'*: whether the student can generalise patterns from one sentence to another.

iv. *'rote learning'*:whether the student can remember vocabulary lists of foreign words paired with translations.

Such tests are not neutral about what happens in a classroom nor about the goals of language teaching. They assume that learning words by heart is an important part of L2 learning ability, that the spoken language is crucial, and that grammar consists of structural patterns. In short MLAT mostly predicts how well a student will do in a course that is predominantly audiolingual in methodology rather than in a course taught by other methods. Wesche (1981) divided Canadian students according to MLAT and other tests into those who were best suited to an 'analytical' approach and those who were best suited to an 'audiovisual' approach. Half she put in the *right* type of class, half in the *wrong* (whether this is acceptable behaviour by a teacher is another question). The students in the right class 'achieved superior scores'. It is not just aptitude in general that counts but the right kind of aptitude for the particular learning situation. Predictions about success need to take into account the kind of classroom that is involved rather than being biased towards one kind or assuming there is a single factor of aptitude which applies regardless of situation.

Krashen (1981a) suggests aptitude is important for 'formal' situations such as classrooms, and attitude is important for 'informal' real-world situations. While aptitude tests are indeed more or less purpose-designed for classroom learners, this still leaves open the existence of a general knack for learning languages in real-life settings, which is different from the notion of aptitude as defined here. Horwitz (1987) anticipated that a test of cognitive level would go with communicative competence and a test of aptitude with linguistic competence. She found however a strong link between the two tests.

Peter Skehan (1986) argues for a slightly different set of factors. He looked at soldiers learning foreign languages and found three groups of successful learners:

i. *'memory-based'* learners were usually younger and were not particularly sensitive to grammar but had good memories.

ii. *'analytic'* learners were slightly older, group and were poorer at memory but had good grammatical sensitivity.

iii. *'even'* learners were good overall.

So there seemed to be two sides of aptitude — a memory-based side and a language-based side. Lack of memory capability in older students can be compensated for by greater grammatical sensitivity. Lack of grammatical sensitivity in younger students can be compensated for by better memory. Students do well if they have both attributes but they also do well if they have either of them.

Aptitude and teaching

The problem for language teachers is what to do once the students have been tested for academic learning aptitude. There are at least three possibilties:

i. *select students who are likely to succeed* in the classroom and bar those who are likely to fail. This would however be unthinkable in most settings with open access to education.

ii. *stream students into different classes* for levels of aptitude, say highfliers, average, and below average. The Graded Objectives Movement in England for instance set the same overall goals for all students at each stage but allowed them different periods of time for getting there (Harding *et al.*, 1981). In the UK all pupils take the same GCSE (General Certificate of Secondary Education) examination in French but can choose how many aspects of language they wish to be examined on, varying from three tests to achieve at best a Grade E up to seven tests to achieve at best a Grade A (Eastern Examining Board, 1986). Aptitude is then related to the speed with which students reach the final stage and to the number of aspects they are examined on at the final stage.

iii. *provide different teaching for different types of aptitude* with different teaching methods and final examinations. This might lead to varied exercises within the class, to parallel classes, or to self-directed learning. In most educational establishments this would be a luxury in terms of staffing and accommodation, however desirable.

The overall lesson is to see students in particular contexts. The student whose performance is dismal in one class may be gifted in another. Any class teaching is a compromise to suit the greatest number of students. Only in individualised or self-directed learning perhaps can this be overcome.

Aptitude for L2 learning

— most aptitude tests predict success in L2 academic classrooms
— aptitude breaks down into different factors such as memory and grammatical sensitivity

Teaching implications
— eliminating students without aptitude (if allowable on other grounds)
— streaming students according to aptitude into fast and slow streams
— arranging different teaching for learners with differnt types of aptitude

---

3. Learning strategies: how do learners vary in their approaches to L2 learning?

Keywords

learning strategy: a choice that the learner makes while learning or using the second language that affects learning

Good Language Learner strategies: the strategies employed by people known to be good at L2 learning

metacognitive strategies: these involve planning and directing learning at a general level

cognitive strategies: these involve specific conscious ways of tackling learning

social strategies: these involve interacting with other people

This section looks at the learning strategies used by L2 learners. A learning strategy here refers to a choice that the learner makes while learning or using the second language that affects learning, as distinct therefore from discourse moves (chapter Three) or communication strategies (chapter Four), both of which aim at language use. A summary box of the main strategy types is given on page 80.

Good Language Learner strategies

People who are good at languages might tackle L2 learning in different ways from those who are less good or they might behave in the same way but more efficiently. One interesting theme is the *Good Language Learner* (GLL) *strategies*. Naiman, Frohlich, Stern and Todesco (1978) tried to see what people who were known to be good at learning languages had in common. They found six broad strategies shared by GLLs:

GLL strategy 1: *find a learning style that suits you*
Good language learners become aware of the type of L2 learning that suits them best. While they conform to the teaching situation to start with, they soon find ways of adapting or modifying it to suit themselves. Thus some GLLs supplement audiolingual or communicative language teaching by reading grammar books at home, if that is their bent. Others seek out communicative encounters to help them compensate for a classroom with an academic emphasis.

GLL strategy 2: *involve yourself in the language learning process*
GLLs do not passively accept what is presented to them but go out to meet it. They participate more in the classroom, whether visibly or not. They take the initiative and devise situations and language learning techniques for themselves. Some listen to the news in the L2 on the radio; others go to see films in the L2.

GLL strategy 3: *develop an awareness of language both as system and as communication*
GLLs are conscious not only that language is a complex system of rules but also that it is used for a purpose; they combine grammatical and pragmatic competence. In other words GLLs do not treat language solely as communication or as academic knowledge but as both. While many learn lists of vocabulary consciously, many also seek out opportunities to take part in conversations in the L2, one even driving a truck for the L2 opportunities it yielded.

GLL strategy 4: *pay constant attention to expanding your language knowledge*
GLLs are not content with their knowledge of a second language but are always trying to improve it. They make guesses about things they do not know; they check whether they are right or wrong by comparing their speech with the new language they hear; and they ask native speakers to correct them. Some are continually on the lookout for clues to the L2.

GLL strategy 5: *develop the L2 as a separate system*
GLLs try to develop their knowledge of the L2 in its own right and eventually to think in it. They do not relate everything to their first language but make the L2 a separate system. One common strategy is to engage in silent monologues to practice the L2. I have sometimes told my students to give commentaries in the L2 to themselves about the passing scene.

Language learning strategies

The Good Language Learner (GLL) Strategies (Naiman, Frohlich, Stern & Todesco)
1 find a learning style that suits you
2 involve yourself in the language learning process
3 develop an awareness of language both as system and as communication
4 pay constant attention to expanding your language
5 develop the L2 as a separate system
6 take into account the demands that L2 learning imposes

Learning strategies (O'Malley & Chamot):
— *Metacognitive strategies*: (planning learning, monitoring your own speech, self-evaluation, etc)
— *Cognitive strategies*: (note-taking, resourcing, elaboration, etc)
— *Social strategies*: (working with fellow students or asking the teacher's help)

GLL strategy 6: *take into account the demands that L2 learning imposes*
GLLs realise that L2 learning can be very demanding. It seems as if you are taking on a new personality in the L2, and one which you do not particularly care for. It is painful to expose yourself in the L2 classroom by making foolish mistakes. The GLL perseveres in spite of these emotional handicaps. "You've got to be able to laugh at your mistakes", said one.

Some qualifications need to be made to this line of research. First of all it only describes what GLLs are aware of; this is what they *say* they do rather than what they actually do. The magic ingredient in their L2 learning may be something they are quite unaware of, and hence does not emerge from interviews. Secondly the strategies are similar to what teachers probably supposed to be the case. This is partly a limitation of the original research. Most of the GLLs studied were highly educated people themselves working in education, probably rather similar to the readers of this book. The strategies are familiar because we are looking at ourselves in a mirror. As with aptitude, there may be an alternative set of strategies employed by people who are non-academic GLLs in natural settings.

Types of learning strategies

Extensive research that goes much deeper into learning strategies has been carried out by O'Malley and Chamot (1990) within an overall model of L2 learning based on cognitive psychology. They have defined three main types of strategy used by L2 students.

i. *'metacognitive'* strategies involve planning and thinking about learning, such as planning one's learning, monitoring one's own speech or writing, and evaluating how well one has done.

Language teaching and learning strategies

— exploit the GLL strategies that are useful to the students
— develop the student's independence from the teacher with 'learner training' or self-directed learning
— make students aware of the range of strategies they can adopt
— provide specific training in metacognitive strategies
— remember the similarities and differences between learning a second language and learning other school subjects

---

ii. *'cognitive'* strategies involve conscious ways of tackling learning, such as note-taking, resourcing (using dictionaries and other resources), and elaboration (relating new information to old).

iii. *'social'* strategies mean learning by interacting with others, such as working with fellow-students or asking the teacher's help.

They found that cognitive strategies accounted for 53% of those reported by ESL students, the most important being advanced preparation — as one student put it "You review before you go into class" - and self management, "I sit in the front of the class so I can see the teacher's face clearly" (O'Malley *et al.*, 1985a). Metacognitive strategies accounted for 30%, the most important being self-management and advance preparation. Social strategies made up the remaining 17%, consisting about equally of cooperative efforts to work with other students and of questions to check understanding. The type of strategy varies according to the task the students are engaged in (O'Malley *et al.*, 1990). A vocabulary task calls forth the metacognitive strategies of self-monitoring and self-evaluation and the cognitive strategies of resourcing and elaboration. A listening task leads to the metacognitive strategies of selective attention and problem identification as well as self-monitoring, and to the cognitive strategies of note taking, inferencing and summarizing as well as elaboration.

Learning strategies and language teaching

How can teachers make use of learning strategies? The chief moral is that the students often know best. It is the learners' involvement, the learners' strategies, and the learners' ability to go their own ways that count, regardless of what the teacher is trying to do. Poor students are those who depend most on the teacher and are least able to fend for themselves. The students must be encouraged to develop independence inside and outside the classroom. Partly this can be achieved through 'learner training' — equipping the student with the means to guide themselves by explaining strategies to them. The idea of learner-training shades over into self-directed learning, in which the students take on responsibility for their learning. They choose their goals; they control the teaching methods and materials; they assess how well they are doing themselves. This is dealt with further in Chapter Nine.

It may not have occurred to students that they have a choice of strategies which affect their learning. Teaching can open up their options. My intermediate EFL course *Meeting People* (Cook, 1982) asked students to discuss four GLL strategies. The intention was to make them aware of different possibilities rather than specifically to train them in any strategy. A more thorough approach is seen in the textbook *Learning to Learn English* (Ellis & Sinclair, 1989), which aims 'to enable learners of English to discover the learning strategies that suit them best'. One set of activities practises metacognitive strategies. The opening questionnaire for instance asks the students 'Do you hate making mistakes?', 'Do you like to learn new grammar rules, words, etc by heart?', and so on. The results divide the students into 'analytic', 'relaxed', and 'a mixture'. A second set of activities practise cognitive as well as metacognitive strategies. Teaching speaking for instance starts with reflection ('How do you feel about speaking English?'), knowledge about language ('What do you know about speaking English?'), and self-evaluation ('How well are you doing?'). Another guide for teachers, *Language Learning Strategies* (Oxford, 1990), provides a wealth of activities to heighten the learners' awareness of strategies and their ability to use them, for example 'The old lady ahead of you in the bus is chastising a young man in your new language, listen to their conversation to find out exactly what she's saying to him'.

Strategy-training assumes that conscious attention to learning strategies is beneficial. This is a different proposition from claiming that the strategies themselves are beneficial. Strategy-training in a sense assumes that the strategies are teachable. While the idea that GLLs need to 'think' in the L2 may strike the students as a revelation, this does not mean they can put it into practice. They may indeed find it impossible or disturbing to try to think in the second language and so feel guilty they are not living up to the image of the GLL. For example the GLLs studied in Canada clearly had above average intelligence; less intelligent learners may not be able to use the usual GLL strategies. Many strategies cannot be changed by the teacher or the learner, however good their intentions. Bialystok (1990) argues in favour of training that helps the students to be aware of strategies in general rather than teaches specific strategies.

Nevertheless research by O'Malley and Chamot (1990) provides some encouragement for strategy-training. They taught EFL students to listen to lectures using their three types of strategy. One group were trained in cognitive strategies, such as notetaking, and social strategies, such as giving practice reports to fellow students. A second group were in addition trained in metacognitive strategies, for example paying conscious attention to discourse markers such as "first", "second", and so on. A third group were not taught any strategies. The metacognitive group improved most for speaking, and did better on some, but not all, listening tasks. The cognitive group were better than the control group. Given that this experiment only lasted eight 50-minute lessons spread over eight days, this seems as dramatic an improvement as could reasonably be expected. Training students to use particular learning strategies improves their language performance. But, as O'Malley and Chamot (1990) found, teachers may need to be convinced that strategy training is important, and may themselves need to be trained in how to teach strategies.

The learning strategies mentioned suit any academic subject. It is indeed a good idea to prepare yourself for the class, to sit near the teacher, and to take notes whether you are studying physics, cookery, or French. Those who believe in the uniqueness of language feel language learning is handled by the mind in ways that are different from other areas. Some consciously accessible learning strategies that treat language as a thing of its own may be highly useful for L2 learning, say the social strategies. But metacognitive or cognitive strategies treat language like any other part of the human mind. Hence they may benefit students with academic leanings who want to treat language as a subject but may not help those who want to use it for its normal functions in society, that is unless of course such knowledge translates into practical ability to use the language, one of the controversies discussed in chapter Eight.

4. Age: are young L2 learners better than old learners?

Keywords:

> *Critical Period Hypothesis*: the claim that human beings are only capable of learning language between the age of two years and the early teens

> *immersion teaching*: teaching the whole curriculum through the second language, best known from experiments in Canada

Undoubtedly children are popularly believed to be better at learning second languages than adults. People always know one friend or acquaintance who started learning English as an adult and never managed to learn it properly and another who learnt it as a child and is indistinguishable from a native. Linguists as well as the general public often share this point of view. Chomsky (1959) has talked of the immigrant child learning a language quickly while 'the subtleties that become second nature to the child may elude his parents despite high motivation and continued practice'. My new postgraduate overseas students prove this annually. They start the year by worrying whether their children will cope with English and they end it by complaining how much better the children speak than themselves.

This belief in the superiority of young L2 learners was enshrined in the Critical Period Hypothesis — the claim that human beings are only capable of learning language between the age of two years and the early teens — which was held to apply to both L1 and L2 learning (Lenneberg, 1967). A variety of explanations were put forward for the apparent decline in adults, physical factors such as the loss of 'plasticity' in the brain, and 'lateralisation' of the brain, social factors such as the different situations and relationships that children encounter compared to adults, and cognitive explanations such as the interference with natural language learning by the adult's more abstract mode of thinking (Cook, 1986). It has often been concluded that teachers should take advantage of this ease of learning by teaching the child a second language at as early an age as possible.

Evidence for the effects of age on L2 learning

But research evidence in favour of the superiority of young children has proved surprisingly hard to find. Much research, on the contrary, shows that age is a positive advantage. English-speaking adults and children who had gone to live in Holland were compared using a variety of tests (Snow & Hoefnagel-Hohle, 1978). At the end of three months, the older learners were better at all aspects of Dutch except pronunciation. After a year this advantage had faded and the older learners were better only at vocabulary. Studies in Scandinavia showed that Swedish children improved at learning English throughout the school years, and that Finnish-speaking children under 11 learning Swedish in Sweden were worse than those over 11 (Eckstrand, 1978). Although the Total Physical Response method of teaching with its emphasis on physical action appears more suitable to children, when it was used for teaching Russian to adults and children the older students were consistently better (Asher and Price, 1967).

Even with the immersion techniques used in Canada in which English speaking children are taught the curriculum substantially through French, late immersion pupils were better than early immersion students at marking number agreement on verbs, and at using 'clitic' pronouns ("le", "me" etc) in Object Verb constructions (Harley, 1986). To sum up, if children and adults are compared who are learning a second language in *exactly the same way*, whether as immigrants to Holland, or by the same method in the classroom, adults are better. The apparent superiority of adults in such controlled research may mean that the typical situations in which children find themselves are better suited to L2 learning than those adults encounter. Age itself is not so important as the different interactions that learners of different ages have with the situation and with other people.

Usually children are thought to be better at pronunciation in particular. The claim is that an authentic accent cannot be acquired if the second language is learnt after a particular age, say the early teens. For instance, the best age for Cuban immigrants to come to the United States so far as pronunciation is concerned is under 6, the worst over 13 (Asher and Garcia, 1969). Ramsay and Wright (1974) found younger immigrants to Canada had less foreign accent than older ones. But the evidence mostly is not clearcut. Indeed Ramsay and Wright's evidence has been challenged by by Cummins (1981). Other research shows that, when the teaching situation is the same, older children are better than younger children even at pronunciation. An experiment with the learning of Dutch by English children and adults found imitation was more successful with older learners (Snow and Hoefnagel-Hohle, 1977). Neufeld (1978) trained adults with a pronunciation technique that moved them gradually from listening to speaking. After 18 hours of teaching, 9 out of 20 students convinced listeners they were native speakers of Japanese, 8 out of 20 that they were native Chinese speakers.

It has become common to distinguish short term benefits of youth from long term disadvantages of age. David Singleton (1989) sums up his authoritative review of age with the statement 'The one interpretation of the evidence which does not appear to run into contradictory data is that in naturalistic situations those whose exposure to a second language begins in childhood in general eventually surpass those whose exposure begins in adulthood, even though the latter usually show some initial advantage over the former'. Adults start more quickly and then slow down. Though children start more slowly, they finish up at a higher level. My own view is that much of the research is still open to other interpretations (Cook, 1986). The studies that show long-term disadvantages mostly use different methodologies and different types of learners from those conducted into short-term learning. In particular the long-term research has by coincidence mostly used immigrants, particularly to the United States, but the short-term research has used learners in educational systems elsewhere. Hence factors such as immigration cannot at present be disentangled from age.

Age and Language Teaching

How should a language teacher take the student's age into account? One question is when L2 teaching should start. This also involves how long the learners are going to be studying. If they are intending to spend many years learning the L2, they might as well start as children rather than as adults since they will probably end up better speakers. If they are going to learn the L2 for a few years and then drop it, like the majority of learners perhaps, there is an advantage for adults who would reach a higher standard during the same period. But as Bernard Spolsky (1989a) points out, 'Educational systems usually arrive first at a decision of optimal learning age on political or economic grounds and then seek justification for their decision.' When to teach children a second language is usually not decided by language teachers or L2 learning experts.

The other question is whether the use of teaching methods should vary according to the age of the students. At particular ages students prefer particular methods. Teenagers may dislike any technique that exposes them in public; role-play and simulation are in conflict with their adolescent anxieties. Adults can feel they are not learning properly in play-like situations and prefer a conventional formal style of teaching. These are not factors that affect L2 learning directly. Adults learn better than children from the 'childish' activities of Total Physical Response — if you can get them to join in! Age is by no means crucial to L2 learning itself. Spolsky (1989a) describes three conditions for L2 learning related to age.

i. 'formal' classroom learning requires 'skills of abstraction and analysis'. That is to say if the teaching method entails sophisticated understanding and reasoning by the student, as for instance a traditional grammar-translation method, then it is better to be older.

ii. the child is more open to L2 learning in informal situations. Hence children are easier to teach through an informal approach.

iii. the natural L2 situation may favour children. The teaching of adults requires the creation of language situations in the classroom that in some ways compensate for this lack. An important characteristic of language spoken to small children is that it is concerned with the 'here and now' rather than with the absent objects or the abstract topics that are talked about in adult conversation — adults do not even talk about the weather much to a two-year-old! That is to say ordinary speech spoken by adults to adults is too sophisticated for L2 learning. Restricting the language spoken to the beginning L2 learner to make it reflect the here-and-now could be of benefit. This is reminiscent of the audiovisual and situational teaching methods, which stress the provision of concrete visual information through physical objects or pictures in the early stages of L2 learning. But it may go against the idea that the content of teaching should be relevant and should not be trivial, to be discussed in the next chapter.

Age in L2 learning

— to be older leads to better learning in the short term, other things being equal
— some research still favours child superiority at pronunciation but not reliably
— children get to a higher level of proficiency in the long term than those who start L2 learning while older, perhaps because adults slow down

Teaching uses:
— deciding when to teach the L2
— varying methods according to the student's age

---

5. Are other personality traits important to L2 learning?

Keywords:

>   *cognitive style*: a person's typical ways of thinking, seen as a continuum between *field-dependent* (FD) cognitive style in which thinking relates to context and *field-independent* (FI) style in which it is independent of context

>   *extrovert* and *introvert*: people's personalities vary between those who relate to objects outside themselves (extroverts) and those who relate to the contents of their own minds (introverts).

Though there has been research into how other variations between L2 learners contribute to their final success, it has produced a mass of conflicting answers. Mostly, isolated areas have been looked at rather than the learner as a whole. Much of the research is based on the non-uniqueness view of language and so assumes that L2 learning varies in the same way as other types of learning, say learning to drive or to type. One piece of research shows that something is beneficial; a second piece of research following up the same issue shows it is harmful. Presumably this conflict demonstrates the complexity of the learning process and the varieties of situation in which L2 learning occurs. But this is slender consolation to teachers, who want a straight answer.

'Cognitive style'

This term refers to a technical psychological distinction between typical ways of thinking. People are made to wait in a room. Without them knowing, the whole room is tilted while they are standing in it. Some people attempt to stand upright, others lean so that they are parallel to the walls. Those who lean have a *field-dependent* (FD) cognitive style; that is to say, their thinking relates to their surroundings. Those who stand upright have a *field-independent* (FI) style; they think independently of their surroundings. The usual test for cognitive style is less dramatic, relying on distinguishing shapes in pictures. Those who can pick out shapes despite confusing backgrounds are field-independent, those who cannot are field-dependent. Obviously these are tendencies rather than absolutes; any individual is somewhere on the continuum between the poles of FI and FD.

A difference in cognitive style might well make a difference to success in L2 learning most researchers have found that a tendency towards FI (field independence) helps the student with conventional classroom learning (Alptekin *et al.*, 1990). Hansen & Stansfield (1981) used three tests with L2 learners; those that measured the ability to communicate, those that measured linguistic knowledge, and those that measured both together. FI learners had slight advantages for communicative tasks, greater advantages for academic tasks, and greatest for the combined tasks. However since then Bacon (1987) found no differences between FD and FI students in terms of how much they spoke and how well they spoke. This illustrates again the interaction between student and teaching method; not all methods suit all students.

Cognitive style varies to some extent from one culture to another. There are variations between learners on different islands in the Pacific and between different sexes, though Field-Independence tends to go with good scores on a cloze test (Hansen, 1984). Of course there is no general reason why FI people in general are better or worse at cognitive functioning than those who are FD. FI and FD are simply two styles of thinking.

Personality

Perhaps an outgoing, sociable person learns an L2 better than a reserved, shy, person. Again, the connection is not usually so straightforward. Some researchers have investigated the familiar division between extrovert and introvert personalities. In Jungian psychology the distinction applies to two tendencies in the way that people interact with the world. Some people relate to objects outside them, some to the interior world. Rossier (1976) found a link between extroversion and oral fluency. There would seem a fairly obvious connection to language teaching methods. The introverts might be expected to prefer academic teaching that emphasizes individual learning and language knowledge; the extroverts audiolingual or communicative teaching that emphasizes group participation and social know-how.

Other individual variation

What else? Many other variations in the individual's mental makeup have been checked against L2 success.

Intelligence for example has some connection with school performance. There are links between intelligence and aptitude in classrooms as might be expected (Genesee, 1976).

Sex differences have also been investigated. The UK Assessment of Performance Unit (1986) found English girls were better at French than English boys in all skills except speaking. In my experience of talking with teachers it is true in every country that second languages are more popular school subjects among girls. Only one in four undergraduates studying in the Languages and Linguistics department at Essex are men.

Level of first language Level of knowledge of the L1 is also relevant. Some studies support the common teacher's view that children who are more advanced in their L1 are better at their L2. (Skehan, 1988)

Empathy Those students who are able to empathise with the feelings of others are better at learning L2 pronunciation, though this depends to some extent on the language the students are acquiring (Guiora *et al.*, 1972).

Many of the factors in this chapter cannot be affected by the teacher. Age is unchangeable, as are aptitude, intelligence, and most areas of personality. As teachers cannot change them, they have to live with them. In other words teaching has to recognise the differences between learners. At a gross level this is catering for the factors that a class have in common, say age and type of motivation. At a finer level the teacher has to cater for the differences between individuals in the class by providing opportunities for each of them to benefit in their own way. To some teachers this is not sufficient; nothing will do but complete individualization so that each student has his or her own unique course. For class teaching the aspects in which students are different have to be balanced against those that they share. Much L2 learning is common ground whatever the individual differences between learners may be.

Reading

Main sources for this chapter are: Skehan, P. (1989). *Individual Differences in Second-Language Learning*, Edward Arnold, London; O'Malley, J.M., & Chamot, A.U. (1990). *Learning Strategies in Second Language Acquisition*, CUP; Singleton, D. (1989). *Language Acquisition: The Age Factor*, Multilingual Matters, Clevedon.

6

Language and input in the L2 classroom

One question that has sometimes been asked is "Can second languages be taught?" Or, as Michael Long (1983) puts it less contentiously, 'Does second language instruction make a difference?'. Though a fair amount of discussion of this question has taken place, it is like asking a doctor if medical treatment benefits the patient. When the students are studying for educational benefit or for personal profit in places where the L2 has no function in the society, the question is beside the point since teaching is the chief or only source of the second language. Whatever they know, whatever they can say or understand, is an effect of teaching. Perhaps Greeks learning English in Athens might learn it better if they lived in London, or English people learn Chinese better if they lived in Beijing, but, as they don't have the chance, the comparison is hypothetical so far as practical implications for language teaching are concerned.

In societies where the second language is in actual use, L2 learning in the world outside can be compared with L2 learning inside the classroom. The issue of whether one is better than the other hardly arises since few L2 learners have the option of deciding between learning in a classroom or a street. It is a different question to ask whether the doctor's treatment was successful — to consider whether the students would have done better if they had been taught differently — but this involves the comparison of different teaching methods, not a dismissal of teaching. Perhaps one should point out, to the relief of teachers, that Long's survey of research concluded that instruction *does* in fact make a difference.

1. L2 learning inside the classroom

Keywords

> *leader* & *follower:* in some types of conversation one person has the right to lead the conversation while the others follow his or her lead

> *teacher-talk:* the amount of speech supplied by the teacher rather than the students

initiation: the opening move by the teacher

response: the student's response to the teacher's opening move

feedback: teacher evaluation of the student response

authentic speech: 'an authentic text is a text that was created to fulfil some social purpose in the language community in which it was produced' (Little *et al.*, 1988)

L2 learning inside and outside classrooms

It is however perfectly natural and proper to ask whether L2 learning is the same inside the classroom as outside. One extreme point of view sees the L2 classroom as a world of its own. Whatever it is that the students are doing, it is quite different from the 'natural' ways of learning language. Thus some teaching methods exploit deliberately 'unnatural' L2 learning. Grammar/translation teaching for instance is exploiting the other faculties the mind has available for L2 learning rather than making use of the 'natural' processes of the language faculty. At the opposite extreme is the view that all L2 learning, or indeed all language learning of L1 or L2, is the same. The classroom at best exploits this natural learning, at worst puts barriers in its way, as argued in the Krashen model (Krashen 1981a) developed in chapter Eight.

What evidence is there one way or the other? Some areas of grammar have been investigated in classrooms as well as in the world outside. Learners appear to go through the same sequence of acquisition in both situations. The order of acquisition for grammatical forms such as negation and questions was substantially the same for German children learning English at school as for those learning naturally (Felix, 1981). Three children learning English as a second language in London over a period of time started by producing "no" by itself or 'anaphoric' "no" with a separate sentence "Red, no" (Ellis, 1986). Sentences with external negation "No play baseball" were said before those with internal negation "I'm no drawing chair". This happened slowly over the period of a year, only one child producing a single sentence with an auxiliary within the sentence "This man can't read". The children were going through the usual stages in the acquisition of negation despite the fact that they were actually being taught negation during the course of the year. So it appears that much of the time students in classrooms learn second languages in the same way as learners who never go near them.

The language of classrooms in general

Let us start with the language interaction that occurs in all classrooms. Most face-to-face conversation is interactive and listener-related. Some situations however give one participant a more directive role than the others; one person can be called the 'leader' who takes the initiative, the other are 'followers' who respond to it. For example an interviewer has the right to guide the conversation and to ask questions that would be out of place in other situations. "How old are you?" addressed to an adult is unthinkable except in an interview. In the classroom this overall 'leader' role falls to the teacher. The exchange of turns between listeners and speakers is under the teacher's overall guidance, overtly or covertly. So, not surprisingly, about 70% of the utterances in most classrooms come from the teacher.

So far this resembles the child learning the first language in that adults often assume the same basic right to direct the conversation when talking to children. "How old are you?" is a frequent question from adults to children. The difference between the classroom and other leader-directed conversations lies in the way that the turns are structured. Let us take a short classroom exchange from Sinclair & Coulthard (1975):

Teacher: Can you tell me why you eat all that food? Yes.
Pupil: To keep you strong.
Teacher: To keep you strong. Yes. To keep you strong. Why do you want to be strong? . . . .

This exchange has three main moves:

i. *Initiation*. The teacher takes the initiative by requiring something of the student, say through a question such as "Can you tell me why you eat all that food?". The move starts off the exchange; the teacher acts as leader.

ii. *Response*. Then the student does whatever is required, here answering the question by saying "To keep you strong". So the move responds to the teacher's initiation; the student acts as follower.

iii. *Feedback*. The teacher does not go straight on to the next initiation but announces whether the student is right or wrong, "To keep you strong. Yes." The teacher evaluates the student's behaviour and comments on it in a way that would be impossible outside the classroom and unlikely even from many parents speaking to children.

This three-move structure of initiation, response, and feedback — or IRF as it is known — is very frequent in teaching. Even in lectures teachers sometimes attempt feedback moves with comments such as "That was a good question". Language teaching methods such as the academic or audiolingual rely heavily on this classroom structure. IRF was after all the format of the classic language laboratory structure drill. Other methods such as the communicative may discourage it because it is restricted to classroom language rather than being generally applicable. Nor is IRF the only characteristic of such exchanges. One common feature, illustrated by the "Yes" in "Can you tell me why you eat all that food? Yes.", is that the teacher selects and approves who is to speak next, a feature common to all leader/follower situations ranging from chairpeople at committee meetings to Congressional committees of investigation.

Language in the language teaching classroom

Are language teaching classrooms any different from other classrooms? Craig Chaudron (1988) cites figures from various sources about teacher talk; teacher talk takes up 77% of the time in bilingual classrooms in Canada, 69% in immersion classes, and 61% in foreign language classrooms. Werner Hullen (1989) found 75% of the utterances in German classrooms came from the teacher. A massive amount of the language the student hears is provided by the teacher.

The uniqueness of the L2 teaching classroom is that language is involved in two different ways. First of all, the organization and control of the classroom take place through language; secondly language is the actual subject matter that is being taught. A school subject like physics does not turn the academic subject back on itself. Physics is not taught through physics in the same way that language is taught through language. This twofold involvement of language creates a unique problem for L2 teaching. The students and teachers are interacting through language in the classroom, using the strategies and moves that form part of their normal classroom behaviour. But at the same time the L2 strategies and moves are the behaviour the learner is aiming at, the objectives of the teaching. The teacher has to be able to manage the class through one type of language at the same time as getting the student to acquire another type. There is a falseness about much language teaching that does not exist in other school subjects because language has to fulfil its normal classroom role as well as be the content of the class. N.S. Prabhu (1987) suggests dealing with this problem by treating the classroom solely as a classroom: 'learners' responses arose from their role as learners, not from assumed roles in simulated situations or from their individual lives outside the classroom'; the real language of the classroom is classroom language.

The teacher's language is particularly important to language teaching. Teachers of physics adapt their speech to suit the level of comprehension of their pupils, but this is only indirectly connected to their subject matter. The students are not literally learning the teacher's language. Teachers of languages who adapt their speech directly affect the subject matter — language itself. Like most teachers I have felt while teaching that I was adapting the grammatical structures and the vocabulary to what the students could take.

But is this subjective feeling right? Do teachers really change their speech for the level of learner or do they simply believe they do so? What is more, do such changes actually benefit the students? Observation of teachers confirms there is indeed adaptation of several kinds. Steven Gaies (1979) recorded student-teachers teaching EFL in the classroom. At each of four levels from beginners to advanced their speech increased in syntactic complexity. Even at the advanced level it was still less complicated than their speech to their fellow students. Chaudron (1983) compared a teacher lecturing on the same topic to native and non-native speakers. He found considerable simplification and rephrasing in vocabulary — "clinging" became "holding in tightly", and "ironic" became "funny". He felt that the teacher's compulsion to express complex content simply often led to 'ambiguous over-simplification on the one hand and confusingly redundant over-elaboration on the other'. Hullen (1989) found the Feedback move was prominent with about 30% of teacher's remarks consisting of "right", "ah", "okay", and so on.

What does this high proportion of teacher-talk mean for L2 teaching?

Several teaching methods have tried to maximize the amount of speaking by the student. The audiolingual method approved of the language laboratory precisely because it increased each student's share of speaking time. Communicative methods support pair-work and group-work partly because they give each student the chance to talk as much as possible. Other methods do not share this opinion that teacher talk should be minimised. Conventional academic teaching emphasizes factual information coming from the teacher. Listening-based teaching sees most value in the students extracting information from what they hear rather than in speaking themselves. One argument for less speech by the students is that at least the sentences that the students hear will be correct examples of the target language, not samples of the interlanguages of their fellow students.

Authentic and non-authentic language

A further distinction is between authentic and non-authentic language. Here is a typical textbook dialogue taken from *Flying Colours I* (Garton-Sprenger & Greenall, 1990):

> Nicola: Do you like this music?
> Roger: Not very much. I don't like jazz.
> Nicola: What kind of music do you like?
> Roger: I like classical music . . .

This is ***nonauthentic*** language specially constructed for its teaching potential. People in real-life conversations do not answer questions so explicitly, do not speak in full grammatical sentences, and do not keep to a clear sequence of turns. Instead they speak like these two people who were recorded while talking about ghosts for the coursebook *English Topics* (Cook, 1975):

> Mrs Bagg: Oh, how extraordinary.
> Jenny Drew: So . . . 'cos quite a quite a lot of things like that.
> Mrs Bagg: I mean were they frightened? 'Cos I think if I actually . . .
> Jenny Drew: No.
> Mrs Bagg: . . . saw a ghost because I don't believe in them really, I would be frightened, you know to think that I was completely wrong.

This is then an example of ***authentic*** language, defined by Little et al (1988) as 'created to fulfil some social purpose in the language community in which it was produced'. Until recently teaching provided the students with specially adapted language, not only simplified in terms of syntax and confined in vocabulary but also tidied up in terms of discourse structure. The belief was that such non-authentic language was vital to L2 learning.

With the advent of methods that looked at the communicative situation the students were going to encounter, it began to seem that the students were being handicapped by never hearing authentic speech in all its richness and diversity. Hence exercises and courses have proliferated that turn away from specially constructed classroom language to any pieces of language that have been really used by native speakers, whether tapes of conversations, advertisements from magazines, train timetables, or a thousand and one other sources.

Two justifications for the use of authentic text in communicative teaching are put forward by Little et al (1988):

i. *Motivation and interest*. Students will be better motivated by texts that have served a real communicative purpose

ii. *Acquisition-promoting content*. Authentic texts provide a rich source of natural language for the learner to acquire language from.

An additional reason put forward by Cook (1981b) is:

iii. *Filling-in gaps*. Designers of coursebooks and syllabuses may miss some of the aspects of language used in real-life situations. This lack can be filled most easily by giving students the appropriate real-life language.

It is a decision for the teacher whether authentic language should be used in the classroom or whether non-authentic language reflects a legitimate way-in to the language. In other words once again the choice is between decoding and codebreaking — are the processes of learning similar to those of use, so that authentic language is needed, or are they distinct, so that appropriate non-authentic language is helpful? Other factors involved in this decision will be the goals of the students and the other constraints of the teaching situation.

Language in classroom L2 learning

— teacher-talk makes up around 70% of classroom language
— language teaching classrooms are different from other subjects because language is not just the medium but also the content
— authentic speech may motivate and help communicative goals, if decoding equates with codebreaking
— non-authentic speech may be specially tailored to students' learning needs if codebreaking is seen as different from decoding

---

2. Language in the communicative classroom

Keywords

> *Communicative Orientation of Language Teaching*: the COLT scheme devised at OISE describes the activities that occur in communicative classrooms

Let us now look more closely at the nature of the language classroom. A scheme for describing what goes on in language teaching has been developed at OISE (Ontario Institute for Studies in Education) in Toronto, known as *COLT — Communicative Orientation of Language Teaching* (Frohlich *et al.*, 1985; Allen *et al.*, 1990). COLT measures the extent to which the activities of a classroom represent communicative teaching. An outline of the whole scheme is given on page 97. COLT has two parts: Part A, '*Classroom events*' categorizes the activities that take place in the classroom; Part B, '*Communicative features*' looks at what the actual activities consist of. The researchers sat in on four types of classes in Ontario: 'core French' classes which were ordinary foreign language classes, 'extended French' classes which, in addition, used French for teaching one or more other school subjects, 'French immersion' classes which used French for most school activities, and English as a Second Language (ESL) classes where non-English speaking students spent most of their day.

COLT Part A Classroom events

The types of classroom events considered in COLT are:

a) *What type of activity occurs?* These are not categorized in any particular way.

b) *How do the teachers and students participate in the activity?* Is teaching to the whole class, in small groups, or to individuals? The ESL classes had the most individual work, the extended French classes had the most teacher-talk.

c) *What content is talked about in the activity?* This is divided roughly into classroom management, discussion of language, discussion of other topics, and who controls the choice of topic. Classroom management took up less then 10% of the time; language as a topic ranged from 66% in an ESL class to 14% in a French immersion class.

d) *Which skills or combination of skills are being used?* The combinations of Listening-Speaking, and Listening-Speaking-Reading were the most common rather than single skill activities.

e) *What materials are being used?* This is seen in terms of the type (text, audio, or visual), the source (specially-constructed teaching materials or natural language), and the extent to which the materials control the teaching. Texts are divided into 'minimal' and 'extended', i.e. individual or connected sentences. Text materials predominated in the classroom. The French immersion made the highest use of extended text, the core French the lowest; the source was usually specially constructed materials.

Part A of COLT draws out the salient features of the classroom and distinguishes one class from another. This brings some surprises, such as the concentration on form in the ESL class. The devisers of COLT decided that a communicative class would probably have more group work, would focus on meaning, and the participants would choose the topics; the texts would be extended, and the language would be authentic rather than specially constructed. On this scale of 'communicativeness' the core French classes were least communicative, the French immersion most communicative.

COLT Part B Communicative features

Part B of COLT looks at how the participants in the classroom interact with each other, in particular:

a) *Which language is used, L1, or L2?*
b) *Is there is an information gap?* I.e. do the students have to exchange real pieces of information? Two overall categories are: requesting information and giving information.
c) *How long are the utterances?* I.e. does an utterance last for more than a sentence or two?
d) *Reaction to code or message.* This reflects whether the teachers draw attention to language mistakes.
e) *Does what one person says take account of what the others say?*
f) *Who initiates an exchange*? teacher or student?
g) *How restricted are the linguistic forms*? This ranges from the use of only single linguistic forms to the free use of any form.

While the teachers concerned mostly used the L1, the amount of sustained speech by teachers varied from 28% in the core French classes to 61% in the ESL. As with the communication strategies outlined in Chapter Four, whether to use the L1 or the L2 for solving communicative tasks is perhaps the crucial decision. In the Canadian classrooms while teachers often commented "Good" etc as an evaluation, they rarely followed up the content of the student's response. Students had the minimal amount of sustained speech in the core French class, the most in French immersion and ESL.

COLT does then bring out some interesting side-lights on the communicative classroom. The supposedly communicative class is often less different from the conventional class than might be supposed. When Allen *et al.*, (1990) looked only at the core French classes, they found that the students in more communicative classes appeared to achieve much the same proficiency as those in less communicative ones.

COLT confirms the impression that many teachers still think of an L2 class above all else as language practice. If the student's answer leads away from the language point that is being pursued, it is ignored, however promising the discussion might seem. Seldom does genuine communication take place in which the students and teacher develop a communicative exchange leading away from the language teaching point. Yet one of the early claims of the Direct Method pioneers was that genuine interchange of ideas was possible. Lambert Sauveur boasted that he could give a beginners class on any topic, and, when challenged to give a class on God, succeeded brilliantly (Howatt, 1984). The IRF exchange, and the evaluation move by the teacher in particular, is a constant reminder to the students that they are engaged in language practice, not in 'real' communication.

The approach exemplified by COLT looks at the language used in actual classrooms through the filter imposed by a particular scheme of analysis. Many such schemes for analysing classrooms have been devised, usually known by a set of initials such as FLint, FOCUS, or ECS, to take three of the better-known, described for example in Allwright (1988). COLT has the advantage that it is deliberately oriented towards a teaching approach that is current and that it looks at relevant aspects of the teaching process. Often information yielded by these schemes ends up as a mass of figures that either show the obvious — teachers talk more than students — or

---

Communicative Orientation of Language Teaching (COLT)

Part A: Classroom events

a *What type of activity occurs?*
b *How do the teachers and students participate in the activity?*
c *What content is talked about in the activity?*
d *Which skills or combination of skills are being used?*
e *What materials are being used?*

Part B 'Communicative features'
1 *Which language is used, L1, or L2?*
2 *Is there is an information gap?*
3 *How long are the utterances?*
4 *Reaction to code or message*
5 *Does what one person says take account of what the others say?*
6 *Who initiates an exchange?*
7 *How restricted are the linguistic forms?*

---

the obscure. Such research tends to intimidate teachers through the sheer complexity it reveals about the classroom. However *any* situation analysed in this fashion would seem as complex. The title of a book on discourse was *The First Five Minutes* (Pittenger *et al.*, 1960), and this accurately described the entire content — analysis of the first five minutes of a single interview. Most results from these schemes at present seem remote from most teachers' practical concerns.

3. Language input and language learning

Keywords

> *babytalk, motherese, foreigner-talk*: forms of language specially designed for listeners without full competence

> *postfigurative*: a culture in which people learn from older wiser guardians of knowledge

> *cofigurative*: a culture in which people learn from their equals

> *prefigurative*: a culture in which people learn from their juniors

The language of the language teaching classroom is distinctive because it is designed for language learning to take place. All languages have special varieties for talking to speakers who are believed not to speak very well — called 'babytalk' or 'motherese' to babies. These have similar characteristics in many language — exaggerated changes of pitch, louder volume, 'simpler' grammar, special words such as "bow-wow", or "walkies!", and so on.

Barbara Freed (1980) found that 'foreigner talk' addressed to non-native speakers also had simple grammar and a high proportion of questions with 'unmoved' question words, e.g. "You will return to your country when?" rather than "When will you return to your country?". But the functions of language in foreigner-talk were more directed at the exchange of information than at controlling the person's behaviour as in baby-talk. Most teachers rarely fall totally into this style of speech. Nevertheless experienced teachers have a distinct type of speech and gesture when speaking to foreigners.

But the fact that babytalk exists does not prove that it has any effect on learning. After all people have been talking to animals for years without any of them learning to speak. In other words babytalk and foreigner-talk varieties of language reflect what people believe less proficient speakers need — but their beliefs may be wrong. Many child language researchers feel that acquiring the first language does not depend upon some special aspect of the language that the child hears. The effects of babytalk on children's first language development have so far been impossible to prove. It may well be that its characteristics are beneficial but this is chiefly a matter of belief, given the many children who acquire the first language in far from optimal conditions. Some further aspects of input in language learning are discussed in relation to the UG model in chapter Eight.

Teaching and input

L2 learning differs from L1 learning in that the majority of students fall by the wayside before they get to a level equivalent to an L1 learner. An important element in L2 success appears to be how learners are treated — the teaching method used with them, the language they hear, and the environment in which they are learning. The purpose of language teaching in a sense is to provide optimal samples of language for the learner to profit from — the best 'input' to the process of language learning. Everything the teacher does provides the learner with opportunities for encountering the language.

At this point the mostly British-based communicative method of teaching parts company with the mostly American listening-based methods. The communicative methods have emphasised the learners' double role as listener and as speaker. A typical exercise requires students to take both roles in a conversation and not only to understand the information they are listening to but also to try to express it themselves. They are receiving input not only from the teacher but also from their peers in the class. The listening-based methods however confine the student to the role of listener. In a technique such as Total Physical Response the students listen and carry out commands but they do not have to speak. Hence the input they receive is totally controlled by the teacher. An example from Krashen and Terrell *The Natural Approach* (1983) consists of showing the students pictures and getting them to choose between them according to the teacher's description — "There are two men in this picture. They are young. They are boxing." This approach was encapsulated in the slogan "Maximise comprehensible input" discussed in Chapter Four.

Communicative teaching methods have often felt that it is beneficial to students to listen to authentic language consisting of judiciously chosen samples of unexpurgated native speech, as we have seen. Authentic speech evidently needs to be made comprehensible by one method or another if it is to be useful to the learner. Its deliberate avoidance of any concession to the learner needs to be compensated for in some way.

Implications for teaching

One overall lesson is that there is no such thing as *the* classroom. Classrooms vary in many ways. Some students have been hypnotised, some have studied in their sleep, some have seen LEGO blocks built into sentences, some have had the world of meaning reduced to a set of coloured sticks, some have sat in groups and bared their souls, others have sat in language laboratories repeating after the tape. The classroom is a variable, not a constant. Teachers can adapt it in whatever way suits their students. Nor should we forget that instruction does not only take place in classrooms. The self-motivated autonomous student can learn as efficiently as any taught in a class.

What advice can be given about input in the classroom?

1. *Be aware of the two levels at which language enters into the classroom.* Using the L1 for classroom management and instructions deprives the students of genuine examples of language use and sets a tone for the class that influences much that happens in the L2 activities. Overusing the 'leader' pattern of IRF teacher-talk undermines a communicative classroom by destroying the usual give-and-take of interaction outside the classroom.

2. *Be aware of the different sources of input.* Language may come first from the teacher, second from the textbook or teaching materials, and third from the other students, not to mention sources outside the classroom. All of these provide different types of language — the teacher the genuine language of the classroom, the textbook purpose-designed non-authentic language or authentic language taken out of its usual context, the other students 'interlanguage' full of non-native-like forms but at the same time genuine communicative interaction.

3. *The input that the students are getting is far more than just the sentences they encounter.* The whole context provides language; this includes the patterns of interaction between teacher and class and between students in the class, down to the actual gestures used. Many teachers ostensibly encourage spontaneous natural interaction from the students but they proclaim they are teachers controlling a class in every physical gesture they make.

4. *Students learn what they're taught.* This truism has often been applied to language classrooms; in general, students taught by listening methods turn out to be better at listening; students taught through reading are better at reading. The major source of language available to learners is what they encounter in the classroom. This biases their knowledge in particular ways. A teacher I observed was insisting that the students used the present continuous; hardly surprisingly his students were later saying things like "I'm catching the bus every morning". The teacher's responsibility is to make certain that the language input that is provided is sufficient for the

student to gain the appropriate type of language knowledge and does not distort it in crucial ways. While in many respects L2 learners go their own way in developmental sequences, etc., their classroom input affects their language in broad terms.

Culture and the classroom

Two links with other areas must be made. One concerns the individual in the classroom, the other the classroom as part of the society. The individual's attitudes to the classroom form an important component in L2 learning. The student's attitudes towards the learning situation as measured by feelings about the classroom teacher and level of anxiety about the classroom contribute towards the student's motivation. This is discussed further in chapter Eight.

So far as the society is concerned the expectations of the students and teachers about the classroom depend upon their culture. Margaret Mead (1970) makes a useful division between *postfigurative* societies in which people learn from wise elders, *cofigurative* societies in which they learn from their equals, and *prefigurative* societies in which they learn from their juniors. Many cultures view education as postfigurative. The classroom to them is a place in which the wise teacher imparts knowledge to the students. Hence they naturally favour teaching methods that transfer knowledge explicitly from the teacher to the student, such as academic teaching methods. Other cultures see education cofiguratively. The teacher designs opportunities for the students to learn from each other. Hence they prefer teaching methods that encourage group and pair work. Mead feels that modern technological societies are often prefigurative, as witness the ease with which teenagers master computers, compared to their parents. There is not to my knowledge a language teaching parallel to this last type, unless in certain 'alternative' methods.

So certain teaching methods will be dangerous to handle in particular societies. Whatever the merits of the communicative method, its attempts to promote non-teacher-controlled activities in China were at first perceived as insults to the Confucian ethos of the classroom which emphasized the benefits of learning texts by heart (Sampson, 1984). In Mead's terms

---

Classroom input and language teaching

Everything the teacher does provides the learner with opportunities for encountering the language.
— Be aware of the two levels at which language enters into the classroom.
— Be aware of the different sources of input.
— The input that the students are getting is far more than just the sentences they encounter.
— Students learn what they're taught.
— What works in the classroom in one cultural milieu will not work in another

a cofigurative method was being used in a postfigurative classroom. A teaching method has to suit the beliefs of the society about what activities are proper for classrooms. It usually goes beyond the language teacher's brief to decide the overall concept of the classroom in a society. The different links between L2 learning and societies are followed up in the next chapter.

Reading

Two books that give a wealth of information on the language teaching classroom are: Chaudron, C. (1988). *Second Language Classrooms: Research on Teaching and Learning*, CUP; Ellis, R. (1990). *Instructed Second Language Acquisition*, Blackwell. The use of authentic texts in teaching is fully described in Little, D., Devitt, S., and Singleton, D. (1988). *Authentic Texts in Foreign Language Teaching: Theory and Practice*. Authentik, Dublin

7

Multilingual societies and the goals of language teaching

To most people in England it seems remarkable that someone can use more than one language in their everyday life; to most people in the Cameroon there is nothing surprising in using four or five languages in the course of a day. To some acquiring a second language is a difficult feat; to others it is ordinary and unexceptional. Probably more people in the world are like the typical Cameroonian than the typical Englishman. Harding and Riley (1986) point out 'there are 3000–5000 languages in the world but only about 150 countries to fit them all into'. The European Commission survey (1987) into young people found that 83% of 20–24 year olds in Europe had studied a second language. Knowing a second language is a normal part of human existence; it may well be unusual to know only one language. This chapter looks at some of the roles that second languages play in people's lives and sees how they can be interpreted as goals of language teaching.

1. The different roles of second languages in societies

Keywords

> *elite bilingualism: either* the choice by parents of bringing up children through two languages, *or* societies in which members of a ruling group speak a second language

> *official language:* language(s) recognized by a country for official purposes

> *multilingualism;* countries where more than one language is used for everyday purposes

Bilingualism by choice

Some people speak two languages because their parents decided to bring them up bilingually in the home. This so-called 'elite' bilingualism is not forced on the parents by society or by the educational system but is their free choice. Often one of the languages is the majority language of the country, the other a minority language spoken as a native by one parent. Sometimes both parents speak a minority language themselves but feel the majority language should also be used in the home. However Saunders (1982) describes how he and his wife decided to bring up their children in German in Australia through neither of them were native speakers of German. Others have three languages in the family; Philip Riley's children speak English and Swedish at home and French at school.

This choice by the parents also extends in some countries to educating their children through a second language, for example in the International School movement across Europe, or in the English language boarding schools that exist in countries from Kenya to India to Chile. Attending such schools usually depends upon having money or upon being an expatriate; it is mostly a preserve of the middle-classes. While L2 learning is often considered a 'problem' in the education of lower-status people, it is seen as a mark of distinction in higher-status people. Bilingualism by choice mostly takes place outside the main educational contexts of L2 teaching, according to a variety of approaches depending on the parents' wishes; accounts of these will be found in the self-help manuals written for parents by Arnberg (1987), by de Jong (1986), and by Harding and Riley (1986).

Second languages for religious use

Some people speak a second language because of their religious beliefs. For centuries after its decline as an international language, Latin functioned as a religious language of the Catholic Church. Muslims read the Koran in Arabic, regardless of whether they live in an Arabic-speaking country like Saudi Arabia, or in a country like Malaysia where Arabic has only a religious function. Jews outside Israel continue to learn Hebrew so that they can pray in it and study the Bible and other sacred texts. In parts of India, Christianity is identified with English, in Ethiopia with Aramaic. Though the language of religious observances is specialized, it is nevertheless a form of second language use. Again this type of L2 learning is distinct from most classroom situations and will not be discussed further here.

Official languages and L2 learning

According to Laponce (1987) there are 32 countries that recognize more than one language for official purposes. Switzerland has three official languages (German, French, and Italian), and one national language (Romansh), and uses Latin on its stamps ("Helvetia"). The Singapore government uses English, Mandarin, Malay, and Tamil. Canada is officially bilingual in English and French. But the fact that a country has several official languages does not mean that any individual person speaks more than one; the communities may be entirely separate. Mackey (1967) claims that 'there are fewer bilingual people in the bilingual countries than there are in the so-called unilingual countries'. Few Canadians for instance use both English and French in daily life. Instead the French and English speakers live predominantly in different parts of the country from each other — as do the German, French and Italian speakers in Switzerland, and the French and Dutch speakers in Belgium. It is necessary in many of these countries to teach speakers of one official language to use another official language; Afrikaans-speaking civil servants in South Africa need English, their English-speaking counterparts in Canada need French. This does not necessarily mean that each official language is equally favoured; few Swiss would bother to learn Romansh as a second language.

Sometimes a language can become an official language with at first few, if any, native speakers. Hebrew was revived by a popular movement in Israel long before being adopted by the new state. The teaching of Hebrew in Israel did not just educate one group in the language of another but created a group of people who spoke a second language that would become the first language of their children. In some countries an official language is selected that has, at least to start with, a small proportion of native speakers, for example Swahili in Tanzania, where only 10% of the population are native speakers. Another pattern is found in Zaire where French is the official language but there are four 'national languages', Kiswahili, Ciluba, Lingala, and Kikongo, which are used as lingua francas among speakers of different mother tongues.

Multilingualism and L2 learning

Regardless of whether they have more than one official language, most countries contain large numbers of people who use other languages. England uses one language for official purposes; nevertheless the Linguistic Minorities Project (1983) found 30.7% of children in the London Borough of Haringey spoke languages other than English at home. Some countries however consist almost entirely of speakers of a single language; 99.3% of the inhabitants of Japan speak Japanese (Grosjean, 1982). Others conceal a variety of languages under one official language. France has an estimated nine million people who are bilingual in other indigenous languages, not taking into account two million migrant workers from Portugal and North Africa (Valdman, 1976; Harding and Riley, 1986). The population of the United States in 1976 included nearly 28 million, or one in six of those over 14, who had a non-English mother tongue, most of whom were born in the USA (Wardhaugh, 1987).

Mobility also plays a part in multilingualism. Some countries for one historical reason or other have included static populations of speakers of different languages, sometimes called 'internal colonies'. Great Britain has had speakers of Welsh, Gaelic, and English for many centuries. In Central Africa some 285 languages are spoken in Cameroon and 212 in Zaire; the empires of Islam and France led to Algeria having French, Arabic, and Berber speakers; the consequences of the British Empire and trade led to Malaysia having speakers of Bahasa Malaysia, Chinese, Indian languages, and various indigenous languages. Recent changes in such groups have sometimes consisted of people going back to their homeland; ethnic Germans returning to West Germany from the Soviet Union and Poland, Turkish-speaking Bulgarians returning to Turkey, and so on. A balance between the languages in one country has often been arrived at, though not necessarily with the consent or approval of the speakers of the minority languages — children were forbidden to speak Basque in Spain, Navajo in the USA, or Kurdish in Turkey; Koreans in Japanese-occupied territories had to adopt Japanese names, the Turkish minority in Bulgaria had to use Bulgarian names. Indeed deaf children have often been made to sit on their hands in class to prevent them using sign language.

But the past few decades have also seen massive movements of people from one country to another, as refugees such as the Vietnamese, as immigrants such as Algerians in France, or as migrant workers such as the Turks in Germany. This has created a vast new multilingualism. New York is said to be the biggest Gujerati-speaking city outside the Indian sub-continent, Melbourne the largest Maltese-speaking city in the world. An Indian student of mine born in Uganda said that the first Indian city she had lived in was the London suburb of Southall. A wealth of languages are spoken in every European town today regardless of the official language of the country; Turkish is spoken in London or in Berlin or in Amsterdam, Arabic can be heard from Paris to Brussels to Berlin. In some cases these people are temporary birds of passage intending to return to their country once the political or economic situation changes, for instance many migrant workers in West Germany. In other cases they are permanent citizens of the country with the same rights as any other citizen, like Finnish-speaking citizens of Sweden or Bengali-speaking citizens of England.

In many cases such multilingualism is short-lived. Paulston (1986) describes how immigrants to the United States from Greece and Italy become native speakers of English over three or four generations. She feels that such a shift from minority to majority language is prevented only when there are strong boundaries around the group, whether social or geographical (Gaelic in the Hebrides) or self-imposed (the Amish in the USA), or when there is a clear separation in social use of the two languages ('diglossia'), as in Standard Arabic versus local versions of Arabic in North Africa. Having one's own ethnic culture as a minority group means speaking the language of that culture, usually different from the majority language, but not necessarily so — as in the use of English by many Scottish nationalists. Language is then often part of ethnicity, and hence associated with political movements for the rights of particular groups.

Internationalism and second languages

But for many students the L2 has no real role within the society itself; English is not learnt in China because it is used inside China. Instead the L2 is taught in the educational system because of the benefits it brings from outside the home country. Any language may of course be taught with the aim of promoting relationships with other countries that use it. Most obviously this applies to languages used for international purposes across many countries. Historically such international languages have been the legacy of empires; the Roman Empire bequeathed Latin as an international language of scholarship so that Marvell, Milton, and Newton would use it well over a thousand years after the Romans left England. French, English and Spanish similarly functioned as the languages of colonialism but continued as languages of international communication.

So a particular country, or indeed a particular individual, may decide to learn a second language for a purpose outside their own society, whether to be able to do business with other countries, to gain access to a scientific literature or to a cultural heritage, or to be able to work in other countries. In Israel, English is taught in schools as the language for wider communication and for access to world commerce and culture, although it also serves as the language of English-speaking immigrants and for communicating with English-speaking tourists. Such use of an international language does not necessarily entail any acceptance of the values of the society from which it originates. Steve Biko justified English as the language of the Black People's Convention in South Africa because it acted as a lingua franca and it was 'analytical' (Biko, 1978). Anti-British graffiti in Belfast are written in English not Irish. The speaker's attitudes to the target culture are marginal to such uses.

Sometimes as a legacy of colonialism the original speakers of an international language feel that they have the right to say what it should be or how it should be taught. The best French is still thought of as spoken in France; the Alliance Française in London advertises its courses with the slogan "Learn French from the French". The aims of the UK GCSE syllabus for French (Southern Examining Group, 1986) refer to 'French-speaking countries' but the rest of the document takes this to be France — as a student from the Ivory Coast bitterly pointed out to me. The vocabulary list of nationalities includes only "French" and "Canadian" out of the 17 French unilingual and 9 multilingual states listed in Laponce (1987). French is also often presented as the language of civilisation and culture. Tougas is quoted in Wardhaugh (1987) as saying 'La culture française . . . répond aux aspirations profondes de l'âme noire' (French culture . . . respond to the deep aspirations of the black soul).

English has been treated more as a commercial property to be sold to particular countries as a means of communication and development (Wardhaugh, 1987). However, setting aside political or commercial motivations, the responsibility for international languages has passed out of the hands of the original owners. An Englishman or an American has no more right to tell a Tanzanian how to teach English than does a Chinese; the only one who can say what is right for Tanzania is the Tanzanian. Whether an idea or an approach in language teaching is useful does not intrinsically depend on which country it comes from. Its merits have to be accepted or rejected by the experts on the situation — the teachers and students who live and work there.

2. The goals of language teaching

Keywords

>   ***assimilationist teaching:*** teaching that expects people to give up their native languages and to become speakers of the majority language of the country

transitional L2 teaching: teaching that allows people to function in a majority language, without necessarily losing or devaluing the first language

language maintenance and bilingual language teaching: these teach or maintain the minority language within its group

submersion teaching: extreme sink-or-swim form of assimilationist teaching in which minority language children are simply put in majority language classes

What does this mean for L2 learning and teaching? Let us make a broad division between local goals which foster the L2 within the country, international goals which foster it for use outside the country, and individual goals which aim at developing the potential of the individual learner.

1. Local goals of teaching

Local goals can be seen as having three broad divisions, drawing on the distinctions made in *Bilingualism or Not* (Skutnabb-Kangas, 1981) — *assimilationist, transitional,* and *language maintenance.* All of these are concerned with the position of minority language children relative to the majority language.

a) Assimilationist language teaching

Assimilationist teaching accepts that society has the right to expect people to give up their native languages and to become speakers of the majority language of the country. An example has been the five-month courses teaching Hebrew to new immigrants to Israel. Here the motivation was to unify people coming from many parts of the world within a single cultural heritage, though this is now changing more into vocationally-relevant teaching of the type described below. An extreme form of assimilationist teaching is so-called 'submersion' teaching — the 'sink or swim' method of putting minority-language children in a majority-language classroom and usually forbidding them to use their own language. According to Skutnabb-Kangas (1981), 'This model is used almost exclusively in Denmark, Norway, France, Great Britain, Holland etc'.

b) Transitional language teaching

The aim of transitional L2 teaching is to allow people to function in a majority language, without necessarily losing or devaluing their first language. While resembling assimilationist teaching, the motivation is different. To use Lambert's terms, assimilationist teaching is 'subtractive' in that the learners feel their first language is being taken away from them; transitional teaching is 'additive' in that it adds the ability to function in the majority language without displacing the first language. With transitional language teaching the minority language speaker still has the right to function in his or her own language except when communicating with the majority groups.

Education is one side to this. In many countries education takes place almost exclusively through the main official language — English in England, French in France. Hence those who do not speak the language of the school need help in acquiring it. Often there are special classes to enable children to acquire the majority language for the classroom. The Bilingual Education Act in the United States for example required the child to have English teaching as an aid in the transition to the ordinary classroom. Grosjean (1982) says of such classes, 'For a few years at least the children can be in a transitory haven before being "swallowed up" by the regular system'. Ironically such schemes may now be difficult in the UK following the Calderale report finding that separate provision may contravene laws against racial discrimination (Commission for Racial Equality, 1986).

Employment is another side to this. Schemes are set up to help the worker who does not know the language of the workplace; adult immigrants to Sweden for example are entitled to 600–700 hours of instruction in Swedish. Or the needs of the new adult immigrant are sometimes taken care of by special initial programs. The aim of such transitional teaching is not to suppress the first language in the minority language speakers but to enable them to use the majority language sufficiently for their own educational or employment needs. They still keep the values of their first language for all functions except those directly involving speakers of the majority language.

c) Language maintenance and bilingual language teaching

The aim of language maintenance or 'heritage' teaching is to teach minority languages to speakers of the minority language. Many ethnic groups want to keep their own language alive in their children. One possibility is the bilingualism by choice of bringing up children with two languages in the home. Many groups also collectively organize language maintenance classes outside the official educational system; in London classes can be found in Chinese, Polish, and Greek among other languages, taking place for children after normal school hours or at weekends. The Linguistic Minorities survey (1983) found that in Bradford 13 mother tongues were taught in maintenance classes to 3000 children for between 1 and 14 hours a week, only about a third of the classes being supported by the education authorities in any way.

The mainstream educational equivalent is educating minority children through their first language. At one extreme is the notion that children should be taught solely through the minority language — Bantustans in South Africa, or Turkish migrants' children in Bavaria — keeping the minority speakers as a segregated enclave. More common perhaps is the notion that children have the right to access to their first language through the educational system. In Sweden for example there are playgroups run in minority languages for pre-school children and summer camps using minority languages for older children (Arnberg, 1987). Denmark has German schools in its German-speaking areas (Byram, 1986). The position of Maori in New Zealand has been revitalised in part through the provision of 'language nests' — pre-school playgroups in which Maori is used (Spolsky,

1989b). In Sweden in 1981, 10.6% of immigrant children in primary schools were educated through their mother tongues, ranging from Polish to Assyrian (Skutnabb-Kangas, 1981).

The assumption of maintenance classes is that minority language speakers have the right to continue with their own language and heritage, regardless of the official language. To quote Tove Skutnabb-Kangas (1981), 'Bilingualism is no longer seen as a passing phase, but rather as something good and permanent, something to be striven for.' Transitional language teaching is neutral about the value of the minority language; bilingual teaching actively encourages a multilingual society. In England the 60s talked of 'English for Immigrants', the 70s of 'Multicultural Education', the 80s of 'Bilingual Teaching'. Such changes in slogans do not of course necessarily reflect changes in reality.

One form this emphasis on bilingualism takes is the propagation of other official languages through the school system. 10% of children in Indonesia speak Malay as a first language but 75% learn it at school (Laponce, 1987). Canada has been famous for the experiment of 'immersion' schools where English-speaking children are educated through the medium of French. Whatever the hotly debated merits or demerits of immersion, it resembles bilingualism by choice where parents opt for the advantages that knowing a second language can bestow on their children rather than most minority language situations. Lambert (1990) indeed opposes its use with minority children as 'it fuels the subtractive process and places the minority child into another form of psycholinguistic limbo . . .'

2. International goals of teaching

Let us now turn to international goals, where language teaching has goals that go outside the society itself. The students are assumed to be speakers of the majority language, possibly quite wrongly, say when teaching French in London. There are many types of international goals. Some illustrations will be taken from English syllabuses for Japan (Ministry of Science, Education, and Culture, 1983), where English has no official role, and Malaysia (Kementerian Pendidikan Malaysia, 1987), where it still has some residual value in the society, and from the UK National Criteria for modern languages (cited in Southern Examining Board, 1986, and many sources).

a) Careers that require a second language

Without taking into account the situation facing immigrants practising their profession in another country, such as Polish doctors in England, there are many careers in which knowledge of another language is important. 29% of young people in the EC want to learn second languages to increase their career prospects (Commission of the EC, 1987). For certain professions a particular language is necessary, for example English for air traffic controllers. The *Angol Nyelv alapfoken* English textbook in Hungary (Edina *et al.*, 1987) has a plot line about travel agents and tourist guides, one kind of career that uses international languages. An important function of language teaching is indeed to train people for the international business world. The Malaysian syllabus points to English as 'an important language to enable Malaysia to engage meaningfully in local and international trade and commerce'. Degrees in Japanese are popular among London University students because they lead to jobs in the City of London, as it is allegedly easier to teach a Japanese graduate finance than a finance graduate Japanese. Societies will always need individuals who are capable of bridging the gap between two countries for economic or political purposes, or for the purposes of war, as in the American crash program in foreign languages in World War Two, which led to the audiolingual teaching method. But we should remember that this type of goal is not turning the student into an imitation native speaker. It preserves the L1 alongside the L2 so that the student can mediate between them — preparing an L1 report on a meeting held in the L2 for example.

b) Higher education

In many countries access to higher education is through another language or another country. This may be via universities sited in particular countries that use another language for higher education, say English in the National University of Singapore. Or it may be via universities in Britain or the United States or other English-speaking countries. The importance for the student is not the L2 itself but the information that is gained via the L2. Again the L1 is an important part of the situation.

c) Access to research and information

In schools the Malaysian syllabus encourages the students to 'read factual prose and fiction for information and enjoyment'. At a different level is the need for English to support various careers that are not primarily based on language — for scientists, doctors, or journalists. To keep up-to-date or to be well-informed, it may be necessary to use English. To quote the Malaysian syllabus, English 'also provides an additional means of access to academic, professional, and recreational materials.'

d) Travel

The motivation behind many students' L2 learning is to travel abroad. At one level this is the leisure activity of tourism — two weeks by the sea in Turkey does not require much Turkish. The assumption underlying much of the GCSE syllabus for French in England is that children will visit with families; 'communication is envisaged as taking place . . . in a country where French is spoken (as short-stay visitors, family guests or tourists . . . in the candidate's own country (as host to exchange parties or conversation with a French-speaking tourist etc)' (Southern Examining Group, 1986) One goal for my own beginners book *People and Places* (Cook, 1980) was international travel through English. Again the status of English makes this peculiar in that travel could be assumed in most places in the world to be possible through English. This assumption has still to let me down, whether in Latin America, North Africa, or Eastern Europe. The goal of travel is included under international goals here as it involves contact with other countries, though in a sense it is an individual goal belonging in the next section.

3. Individual goals of language teaching

Let us now briefly look at goals that are not related to the society itself or its external relations. Some of these have already appeared in earlier chapters, where we saw that 51% of young people in the EC survey wanted to learn a second language for personal interest rather than for overtly instrumental or integrative reasons. Several goals can be recognised.

a) Understanding of foreign cultures

The Japanese syllabus for English sets as its goals 'to understand the daily life and way of thinking of foreign people' and 'to develop the basis for international understanding'. The UK National Criteria for modern languages include 'To offer insights into the culture and civilisation of the countries where the language is spoken'. Regardless of the actual language that is being learnt, it is often held to be beneficial for the students to understand a foreign culture for its own sake.

b) Understanding language itself

An educated person should know something of how language itself works as part both of the human mind and of society. The UK National Criteria include 'To develop an awareness of the nature of language and language learning'. The Japanese syllabus puts it as 'to deepen their interests in a language'. This can be gained through foreign language study, or through language awareness training.

c) Cognitive training

The virtue of learning a classical language was held to be that it trained the brain. The logical and reasoning powers of the mind were enhanced through a second language. This has received support from psychological work that shows that children who speak two languages are more flexible at problem-solving (Ben Zeev, 1977), and are better able to distinguish form from meaning (Lanco-Worrall, 1972). It has emerged as one of the UK National Criteria: 'To promote learning of skills of a more general application (e.g. analysis, memory, drawing of inferences)'. One aspect of this is indeed the beneficial effects of L2 learning on using the first language. If children are deficient at listening for information or at taking 'long' turns at speaking, the skills involved can be developed through L2 teaching.

d) General educational values

Just as sport is held to train children how to work in a team and to promote leadership qualities, so L2 teaching can enculcate moral values — Form 1 in Malaysia covers 'courage, honesty, charity and unity' — and the virtues of 'good citizenship, moral values and the Malaysian way of life'. From another angle many support 'autonomous' language learning

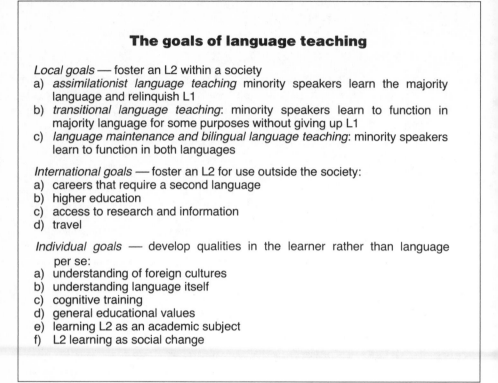

The goals of language teaching

Local goals — foster an L2 within a society
a) *assimilationist language teaching* minority speakers learn the majority language and relinquish L1
b) *transitional language teaching*: minority speakers learn to function in majority language for some purposes without giving up L1
c) *language maintenance and bilingual language teaching*: minority speakers learn to function in both languages

International goals — foster an L2 for use outside the society:
a) careers that require a second language
b) higher education
c) access to research and information
d) travel

Individual goals — develop qualities in the learner rather than language per se:
a) understanding of foreign cultures
b) understanding language itself
c) cognitive training
d) general educational values
e) learning L2 as an academic subject
f) L2 learning as social change

where the learners take on the responsibility for themselves because this is in tune with democracy. As Leslie Dickinson (1987) puts it, 'A democratic society protects its democratic ideals through an educational process leading to independent individuals able to think for themselves.' Another general value that is often cited is the insight that L2 learning provides into the L1 and its culture, or in the words of the UK National Criteria, developing 'the pupil's understanding of themselves and their own culture'.

e) Learning L2 as an academic subject

Language can also be learnt simply as another subject on the curriculum, another examination to be passed. Japanese teachers are not alone in complaining that they are in thrall to the examination system and cannot teach the English the students really need. The very learning of a second language can be an important mark of education. Traditionally it has been a mark of an educated person in some countries to know another language, another facet of 'elite' bilingualism. French had this kind of status in Western Europe, German in Eastern Europe. Skuttnab-Kangas (1981) paraphrases Fishman's account of bilingualism in the US as: 'If you have learnt French at university, preferably in France and even better at the Sorbonne, then bilingualism is something very positive. But if you have learnt French from your old grandmother in Maine then bilingualism is something rather to be ashamed of.'

f) L2 learning as social change

The goals seen so far either accept the world as it is, or benefit the student as an individual. But education and L2 teaching can also be seen as a vehicle of social change. According to Freire (1972) the way out of the perpetual conflict between oppressor and oppressed is through problem-posing dialogues between teachers and students which make both more aware of the issues in their lives and their solutions. Language teaching on a Freireian model would accept that 'authentic education is not carried out by A for B or by A about B, but rather by A with B, mediated by the world, giving rise to views or opinions about it.' Language teaching can go beyond accepting the values of the existing world to making it better (Wallerstein, 1983). While the Freireian approach is included here under individual goals because of its liberating effect on the individual, it may well deserve a category all of its own of goals for changing society.

This discussion has illustrated some of the oversimplifications involved in the labels customarily used by the language teaching profession. Teachers are used to the distinction between 'second' and 'foreign' language teaching or learning. But this two-fold distinction does not begin to cope with the complexities of most situations; foreign language teaching includes such different aspects as English as an International Language in Malaysia, and French literature at A level in England; second language teaching covers the teaching of Hebrew in Tel Aviv, the teaching of French in Quebec, and the teaching of English in London or Western Australia.

A second debatable term is 'communication', the buzzword of language teaching in the past twenty years. This has indeed led to a welcome shift in attention towards teaching practical uses of language. The purposes of language teaching described above cover a vast range of activities, from praying to using a telex, from taking an examination to becoming honest, from entering a new society to rebelling against its values to maintaining one's own values within a majority culture. Describing all these as communication tells one little, if anything. The idea of communication has never been far from language teaching in one way or another. Otto Jespersen back in 1904 was claiming that the purpose of L2 learning 'must be in order to get a way of communication with places which our tongue cannot reach', though this led him to something very different from communicative teaching. The word 'communication' is particularly dangerous if it distracts attention away from the individual goals that aim at benefiting the student or the society.

Much of what has been said here about the goals of language teaching seems quite obvious. Yet it is surprising how rarely it is mentioned. Most discussions of language teaching take it for granted that everyone knows why they are teaching the L2. But the reasons for language teaching in a particular situation depend on factors that cannot be summed up just as communication or as foreign versus second language teaching. Even if teachers themselves are powerless to change such reasons, an understanding of the varying roles for language teaching in different societies and for different individuals is an important aid in teaching.

One practical way in which this affects the classroom is through the actual content of the language lesson or textbook. I have argued elsewhere (Cook, 1983) that too much time is spent teaching 'imaginary' content about fictional people and places rather than 'real' content that tells the students something about the real world and real people. 'Real' content can vary from another academic subject taught through English to facts about English-speaking culture, from information about the English language to information about the other students, and many other varieties. Two solutions to this can be seen in the titles of two EFL textbooks, *South Africa — the Privileged and the Dispossessed,* a collection of annotated texts dealing with a deliberately controversial area, (Davies & Senior, 1983) and *How to Improve Your Memory* (Wright, 1987), one of a series aiming to improve students' reading by teaching them a particular skill through English. In some places information about England or the USA will be specifically ruled out, for example in Israel. In others it will be the most natural content of any lesson. We should not unthinkingly trivialise the content of teaching, when so much else is available. The choice of what the language of the lesson shall be about is as crucial as the choice of the language forms in which it is expressed, and both depend on the whole educational setting. Communication implies something to communicate and that is where the teacher's control of the lesson is crucial.

Teachers should be clear in their minds that they are usually teaching people how to use two languages, not how to use one in isolation. I sometimes call this ability to function in both languages 'multicompetence' to distinguish it from 'communicative competence' that is specific to one language at a time. The person who can speak two languages has the special ability to communicate in two ways. The aim is not to produce L2 speakers who can only use the language when speaking to each other; Mayhill (1990) for instance points to the problems in using English materials for Aboriginals in Australia, such as *Tracks* (Northern Territory, 1979) that reflect their own life style rather than that of the English speaking community. Nor is it to produce imitation native speakers, unless they are training to be spies. Rather the aim is people who can stand between two viewpoints and two cultures. Much language teaching has tried to duplicate the skills of the native speaker in the non-native speaker. Thus the functions of language or the rules of grammar known by the native speaker are taught to the students. The point should not be to manufacture ersatz native speakers but to equip people to use two languages without losing their own identity. The model for language teaching should be the fluent L2 user, not the native speaker what Michael Begram (1990) calls 'intercultural communicative competence'. This enables language teaching to have goals that students can see as relevant and achievable rather than the distant chimera of native speaker competence.

This chapter has drawn on a different type of research to the others, often known as 'bilingualism' rather than 'L2 learning'. To apply SLA research properly to the classroom, this area is as vital as any of the others that have been dealt with. L2 learning varies according to the situation in which the L2 learner is placed. Teaching an L2 is tied in to the political and ethical values of a society. At a practical level students will prosper when their teacher understands the multiple goals they are able to fulfil through the second language. At a more general level teachers should be aware of the depth and range of the values embodied in their teaching and see what function L2 learning has for the individual students they teach and for the society in which they are placed.

In one sense, all of this chapter has been relevant to teachers, in another sense none of it. For the vital issues that are involved are seldom left to teachers to decide. The casting vote for or against bilingual education is more likely to be President Reagan's: 'It is absolutely wrong and against American concepts to have a bilingual education program that is now openly, admittedly dedicated to preserving their native language . . .' (cited in Wardhaugh, 1987). Vital as such decisions about language teaching are, they are not in the hands of teachers. Nevertheless it is important for teachers to be informed about the different alternatives that are available for the aims and goals of language teaching so that they can contribute properly to the debate.

References

Apart from specific references in the text this chapter draws on ideas and examples chiefly from: Grosjean, F. (1982). *Life with Two Languages*, Harvard U.P.; Skutnabb-Kangas, T. (1981). *Bilingualism or not: The Education of Minorities*, Multilingual Matters, Cleveland; Romaine, S. (1989). *Bilingualism*. Blackwell, Oxford; Wardhaugh, R. (1987). *Languages in Competition*. Blackwell, Oxford.

8

General Models of L2 learning

So far this book has illustrated the complexity and diversity of L2 learning and teaching, not from the heights of an overall theory that explains everything and therefore has mammoth global consequences for language teaching, but from the lowlands of particular areas of research and particular conclusions that apply to limited aspects of the language teaching operation. However some general models of L2 learning have nevertheless been proposed. The following discussion tries to give a flavour of these but cannot give them full justice, partly because many are offshoots of theories of linguistics, psychology, or sociology which cannot be treated at length here. This chapter highlights some of the general ideas underlying some of the more specific research looked at so far and relates them to language teaching. Rarely will the models correspond neatly to teaching methods. Nor, as we shall see, is any of them sufficiently powerful to act as the sole basis for teaching.

This chapter recognises four overall types of learning model that represent extreme tendencies. The first type is knowledge models that emphasize the importance of the individual mind in L2 learning, such as the *Universal Grammar* (UG) *Model*, which stresses language as part of the mind and sees learning as setting parameters from the actual sentences the learner encounters. The second type is language processing models, such as the *Competition Model*, which sees language learning as acquiring ways of processing. The third type are mixed models that recognize two sides to L2 learning, either permanently, such as the *Monitor Model*, or as a conversion from one side to another, as in the *Competence/Control Model*. The last type are social models that stress the social aspects of L2 learning, such as the *Socio-Educational Model* and the *Acculturation Model*.

1. Models of knowledge: Universal Grammar

The Universal Grammar (UG) model, proposed by Chomsky in the 1980s, for example in Chomsky (1988), is a development of his earlier ideas into a new form called by him 'the second conceptual revolution'. UG has increasingly been used to explain how second languages are learnt, chiefly by those who approach L2 learning from a linguistics perspective. Its general claims about learning are based on a complex form of linguistics known as Government-Binding (GB) Theory, alias the principles and parameters grammar encountered in chapter Two. A person who knows a language such as English has acquired a grammar which consists of the universal principles of language, such as structure-dependency, as they apply to English, and of the English settings for the parameters such as pro-drop on which languages can vary.

Learning as setting parameters from evidence

The Universal Grammar model claims that principles and parameters are built-in to the mind. Learners do not need to learn structure-dependency because their minds automatically provide it for any language they meet, whether it is English, Chinese, or Arabic. However they do need to learn that English is non-pro-drop, while Chinese is pro-drop. It is the parameter settings that have to be learnt. All the learner needs in order to set the values for parameters is examples of the language. Hearing "There are some books on the table" a learner discovers English is non-pro-drop because 'dummy' subjects only occur in non-pro-drop languages.

Learning in the UG model is a straightforward matter of getting the right input. In this theory language input is the evidence out of which the learner constructs knowledge of language. Such evidence can be either positive or negative.

Positive evidence consists of actual sentences that learners hear, such as "The train leaves London at five". The information in the sentence allows them to construct a grammar that fits the word order 'facts' of English that Subjects come before Verbs, Verbs come before Objects, and Prepositions come before Nouns. The positive evidence of the position of words in a few sentences they hear is sufficient to show them the rules of English.

Negative evidence has two types. Because learners never hear certain kinds of sentence, say sentences without subjects in English such as "Leaves", they deduce that English sentences must have Subjects — the same evidence as that advanced for curved bananas in the song "I have never seen a straight banana". The other type of negative evidence is correction: "No you mustn't say 'You was here' you must say 'You were here.' "

Many linguists are convinced that the child learns the first language by encountering actual sentences of the language. But second language learning is different. The bulk of the evidence indeed comes from sentences the learner hears — positive evidence from linguistic input. But the learner also has the first language available. Negative evidence can be used to work out what does not occur in the second language but might be expected to occur if it were like the first. A Spanish student listening to English will eventually notice that English does not have the subjectless sentences that happen in Spanish. The basis for the expectation is not just sheer speculation but the concrete knowledge of the first language the learners have in their heads.

Negative evidence by correction is also different in L2 learning. In the first language it is not so much that it is ineffective as that it does not occur. In the second language it can, and often does, occur with high frequency. The L2 learner has an additional source of evidence not available to the L1 learner. Furthermore the L2 learner often has grammatical explanation available as another source of evidence. The usefulness and success of this can be debated. Nevertheless it reflects an entirely different type of evidence for the learner that is absent from first language acquisition, at least up to the school years. Finally the input to the L2 learner could be made more learnable by highlighting various aspects of it. James Morgan (1986) has talked of the need for 'bracketted input' — sentences that make clear the phrase structure of the language. L2 teaching could try many ways of highlighting input in this fashion, again an opportunity unique to L2 learning.

L2 setting of parameters

The L2 learner listens to input and sets the parameters accordingly. The question is whether *re*setting parameters is the same as setting parameters. Does the fact that there is already one setting in the L2 learner's mind affect learning? If L2 learning is the same as L1, Japanese learners of English will learn word order in the same way as French learners of English. On the other hand, if the L1 settings influence L2 learning, Japanese learners will differ from other learners wherever their L1 parameter settings are different.

Lydia White (1986) used the pro-drop parameter concerning the presence or absence of a Subject in the sentence to investigate this issue, as outlined in chapter Two. She found that the first language setting for the parameter was indeed carried over to the second. That is to say, Spanish learners of English initially assume that Subjects are not needed, French learners assume that they are. Research on other areas of syntax has often produced similar conclusions. The acquisition of L2 word order is influenced by the L1, as is the acquisition of movement of elements within the sentence. There is some variation according to the area being tested. My own research into 'binding' — the relationship between "John" and himself" in sentences such as "Peter reported John's criticisms of himself" - found similar levels of difficulty and speeds of response between L2 learners of English who spoke Japanese, Norwegian, and Romance languages (Cook, 1990). Nevertheless mostly L2 learners seem to start from their L1 setting rather than from scratch. This does not of course contradict the UG model. The learners still have access to the system of principles and parameters via their L1.

L2 learners need to spend comparatively little effort on grammatical structure, since it results from the setting of a handful of parameters. They do however need to acquire an immense amount of detail about how individual words are used. The comparative simplicity of syntax learning in the UG model is achieved by increasing the burden of vocabulary learning. The learner needs to acquire large numbers of words, not only in the conventional way of knowing their dictionary meaning or pronunciation, but also in knowing how they behave in sentences. It is not just a matter of the beginner in English learning the syntax, function, and meaning of "He plays football", it is learning that in English the Verb "play" needs to be followed by a Noun Phrase. It has often been reported that learners themselves feel vocabulary to be particularly important. A questionnaire I gave to 351 students of English found that they placed the statement "I want to learn more English words and phrases" second out of ten possible aims for their English course, after "I want to practise English so that I can use it outside the classroom", and some way above structures, functions, or life in England. A major learning component according to the UG theory will indeed be vocabulary, if not perhaps in the way that either learners or teachers presently conceive of it. The future may see the reorganization of the role of vocabulary teaching, partly taking account of this, partly utilising other notions presented in chapter Three.

The UG model and language teaching

What do parameters mean for teaching? In the case of the pro-drop parameter UG theory suggests that teachers provide language input that allows the student to find out whether the setting should be pro-drop or non-pro-drop. Let us take *The Cambridge English Course* (Swan & Walter, 1984) as an example. The input for setting the value for the pro-drop parameter is partly the absence of subjectless sentences, which is shared by all EFL course books as well as the *Cambridge Course*, and partly the presence of Subjects such as "it" and "there". Unit 5 has "There's an armchair in the living room". Unit 7 has "There's some water in the big field". Unit 9 introduces 'weather' "it" in "It rains from January to March" and "It'll cloud over tomorrow", together with "there" as in "There will be snow". Unit 10 teaches dummy "it" in "It's a man". Everything necessary to set the parameter is introduced within the first weeks of the course. It is hard to imagine language teaching not reflecting these two aspects of the pro-drop parameter, just as it is hard for any small sample of speech not to use all the phonemes of English. Almost any language input should provide the information on which the parameter setting depends fairly rapidly.

As the Universal Grammar in the student's mind is so powerful there is comparatively little for the teacher to do. Few mistakes occur with the aspects of word order covered by the head parameter; I have never heard a student saying things like "I live London in" for instance. Nevertheless some effects of the first language linger on. Quite advanced L2 learners still differ from native speakers when the L1 and the L2 have different settings for the pro-drop parameter. Thus the teacher's awareness of parameter resetting can be helpful. The useful book *Learner English* (Swan and Smith, 1987) provides examples of mistakes from students with L1s ranging from Italian to Chinese to Thai that linguists would attribute to the pro-drop parameter. Similarly syllabuses for language teaching that use grammar need to accommodate such basic syntactic ideas, if only to indicate to teachers areas that they can refrain from teaching.

Many feel that the UG model is the most powerful account of L2 learning. Its attraction is that it links L2 learning to current ideas about language and language learning. It has brought to light a number of apparently simple phenomena like the pro-drop parameter that appear to be relevant to L2 learning. Yet it would be wrong to draw conclusions from UG theory for anything other than the central area that is its proper domain — the core aspects of syntax. The UG model tackles the most profound areas of L2 acquisition, which are central to language and to the human mind. But there is rather little to say about them for language teaching. The UG principles are not learnt, the parameter settings probably need little attention. Any view of the whole L2 learning system has to take on board more than the UG model. Classroom L2 teaching must include many aspects of language that are not covered by the model. Nevertheless the UG model firmly reminds us that learners have minds and that one crucial question is the form that language knowledge takes in the human mind.

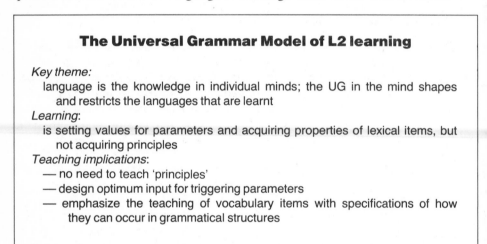

The Universal Grammar Model of L2 learning

Key theme:
  language is the knowledge in individual minds; the UG in the mind shapes and restricts the languages that are learnt
Learning:
  is setting values for parameters and acquiring properties of lexical items, but not acquiring principles
Teaching implications:
  — no need to teach 'principles'
  — design optimum input for triggering parameters
  — emphasize the teaching of vocabulary items with specifications of how they can occur in grammatical structures

2. Processing models: the competition model and the information processing model

The Competition Model

At the opposite pole from UG come models which see language in terms of dynamic processing and of communication rather than as static knowledge. These are interested in what happens in an actual language situation and in how people use language, rather than in knowledge in the mind. One model of this type is the Competition Model developed by Brian MacWhinney and his associates (Bates and MacWhinney, 1981; MacWhinney, 1987). This forms part of a psychological theory of language in which L2 learning forms only one component. The main key to language is communication; 'the surface connections of natural languages are created, governed, constrained, acquired, and used in the service of communicative functions'. Language has four main aspects; word order, vocabulary, word forms (morphology) and intonation.

Whatever the speaker wants to communicate has to be achieved through these four. But the speaker can do only a limited number of things at the same time. So the more a language uses intonation, the less it can rely on word order, the more emphasis it has on word-forms, the less on word order; and so on. The amount of 'space' the mind has for using language is limited. The different aspects of language 'compete' with each other for the same space. The results of this competition for space favour one or other of these aspects in different languages. A language, such as Chinese, that has complicated intonation has no variation in morphology. English with complicated word order puts little emphasis on morphology. Latin with a complicated case system for nouns has little use for word order, and so on. The Competition Model suggests that there is a payoff between the four aspects of intonation, vocabulary, word order, and word forms (morphology). No language can pay equal attention to all of them because they would use up too much of the speaker's processing space.

The part of language that has been most investigated by the Competition Model is the Subject of the sentence. Although Subjects probably exist in all languages, there is a difference in what the Subject actually consists of. Take the sentence "He likes to drink Laphroaig". What are the clues that give away the Subject?

i. *word order*. In many languages the Subject occurs in a definite place in the sentence. In English it usually comes before the verb, — "he" comes before "likes"; hence English is a Subject Verb Object (SVO) language. Arabic and Berber are VSO languages and so the Subject usually comes after the verb. In languages such as Baure and Tzeltal the Subject comes after the object (VOS). Though they differ as to whether the Subject comes in the beginning, the middle or the end, in all these languages word order is a good guide as to which noun phrase is the Subject. The competition for space is being won by word order.

ii. *agreement*. The Subject often agrees with the Verb in Number — "she" and "plays" are both singular in "She plays golf", as are "il" and "aime" in the French "Il aime Paris" (He loves Paris). In some languages then the competition is won by agreement, which plays a subsidiary role in English.

iii. *case*. In other languages the Subject Noun has to be in the Nominative case — "He likes Laphroaig" rather than "Him likes Laphroaig" in English: "Ich liebe Bier" (I love beer) rather than "Mich liebe Bier" in German. In some languages the competition is won by word forms, which play a lesser role in English.

iv. *animacy*. In languages like Japanese the Subject of the sentence must be animate, that is to say, refer to someone or something that is alive. The sentence "The typhoon broke the window" is impossible in Japanese because typhoons are not alive and so "typhoon" cannot be the Subject. However in English it does not matter whether the Subject refers to something alive or not. It is possible to say both "Peter broke the glass" and "The glass broke". The competition is won in some languages by the factor of animacy.

At least four clues potentially signal the Subject of the sentence — word order, case, agreement between words, and animacy. The Competition Model claims that all four compete for space amongst themselves. The different clues to the Subject are not equally important in each language. Rather the competition between them ends up with one dominating the others.

Children learning their first language are therefore discovering which clues are important for that language and learning to pay less attention to the others. Each of the four competing clues has a 'weighting' that affects how each sentence is processed. Experiments have shown that speakers of English depend chiefly on word order; speakers of Dutch depend on agreement (Kilborn & Cooreman, 1987; McDonald, 1987); Japanese and Italian depend most on animacy (Harrington, 1987; Bates & MacWhinney, 1981). Learning how to process a second language means adjusting the weightings for each of the clues. L2 learners of English transfer the weightings from their L1. Thus Japanese and Italian learners select the Subject because it is animate, and Dutch learners because it agrees with the verb. While their processes are not weighted so heavily as in their first languages, even at advanced stages they are still different. On the surface there need not be any sign of this in their normal language use. After all they will still choose the Subject correctly most of the time whichever aspect they are relying on. Nevertheless their actual speech processing uses different weightings.

Processing models and cognitivism

The Competition Model addresses some of the performance processes discussed in chapter Four. The model seems related to the behaviourist tradition which claims that language learning comes from outside — from input from others and from interaction and correction — rather than from inside the mind. An early version was Bloomfield's ideas that language learning is a matter of associating words with things (Bloomfield, 1932). The child who imitates an adult saying "doll" is favourably reinforced by adults whenever a doll is seen and unfavourably reinforced when a doll is absent. The most sophisticated behaviourist account was provided by B.F. Skinner (1957) in the book *Verbal Behaviour* that was savaged in a review by Chomsky (1959). Language to Skinner was learnt though 'verbal operants' that are controlled by the situation, which includes the social context, the individual's past history and the complex stimuli in the actual situation. One type of operant is the *mand*, which is the equivalent to a command and is reinforced by someone carrying it out; another is the *tact*, which is equivalent to a declarative (contact), and which is reinforced by social approval, etc. The child builds up the complex use of language by interacting with people in a situation for a purpose.

Other contemporary psychological theories of language learning are also affiliated to behaviourism. John Anderson (1983) has proposed a 'cognitive behaviourist' model called ACT*, which sees learning as building up response strengths through a twofold division into procedural memory (procedures for doing things) and declarative memory (what has here been called 'knowledge'). As declarative facts get better known they are gradually turned into procedures, and several procedures are combined into one, thus cutting down on the amount of memory involved. This model underlies the work of O'Malley and Chamot (1990) with learning strategies described in chapter Five.

Rumelhart and others (1986) have been developing the similar theory of 'connectionism', which sees learning as establishing the strengths between the vast numbers of connections in the mind and claims that language processing does not take place in a step by step fashion but that many things are being processed simultaneously. So far this model has not been much developed in an L2 context, though it is being increasingly mentioned (Gasser, 1990).

The main L2 model in this tradition is called the information- processing model (McLaughlin *et al.*, 1983). In this learning starts from controlled processes, which gradually become automatic over time. When you first start to drive a car, you control the process of driving very consciously — turning the wheel, using the accelerator, and so on. Soon it becomes automatic and for much of the time you have no awareness of the controls you are using. To quote McLaughlin (1987) 'Thus controlled processing can be said to lay down the 'stepping stones' for automatic processing as the learner moves to more and more difficult levels.' This is not necessarily the same as being conscious of language rules. A learner who starts by communicating hesitantly and gradually becomes more fluent is just as much going from controlled to automatic processes as is one who starts from grammatical rules and then tries to use them in ordinary speech.

Clearly some of the research discussed in chapter Five can be taken to support this model, for instance the increasing quickness of reaction time as learners make the language more and more automatic. However the evidence for the information-processing model is mostly based upon ideas taken from general psychological theory or on experiments with the learning of vocabulary, rather than on L2 learning itself. It requires a continuum from 'higher' to 'lower' skills. Students who do not progress in the L2 are not making the lower level skills sufficiently automatic. Thus children learning to read an L2 may be held back by not having mastered the low-level skill of predicting what words come next. The information-processing model resembles the other processing models in assuming that language learning is the same as the learning of any other skill such as car-driving. All of them claim language is learnt by the same general principles of learning as everything else. They do not separate the mind into language faculties and non-language faculties but adopt the non-uniqueness position.

The main application to teaching is the emphasis on practice as the key to L2 learning. Practice builds up the weightings, response strengths and so on that determine how language is processed and stored. The UG model sets minimal store by practice; in principle a parameter can be set by a single example for ever more. Processing models see language as the gradual accumulation of preferred ways of doing things. Much language teaching has of course always insisted on this whether it is the practice of the audiolingual structure drill or the communicative information gap game. The processing models remind us then that language is also behaviour and skill. As well as the aspects of language that are abstract or under conscious control, there are skills learnt by doing them over and over again.

Processing Models

Key theme:
   language is processing at different levels

Learning:
   learning involves practising to build up the proper weightings, etc.

Teaching uses:
   exercises that build up appropriate strengths of response in student:
      classroom should maximise practice by the students

---

3. Multi-component models: the competence/control model and the monitor model

Models with two components

So far the learning models have been at the two poles of those that emphasize language knowledge and those that emphasize language processing. UG and processing models reduce everything to variations on the same theme, whether abstract parameter settings or response weightings. Many current models within L2 learning research itself can be called 'mixed' because they try to accommodate both sides of this division. This is achieved either by keeping both sides separate, or by seeing one side as converting into the other — 'conversion' models.

Let us start with the Competence/Control Model developed by Ellen Bialystok and Mike Sharwood-Smith (1985), and named after its two main dimensions. This model can be approached through the metaphor of a library. On the one hand the books in the library are set out on the shelves according to a definite system, on the other the user needs to know how to find a particular book. The arrangement of books is the learner's competence in the language ('the way in which the language system is represented in the mind of the learner'), the ways of finding them are control procedures ('the processing system for controlling that knowledge in actual performance').

Learning a second language involves two things — the knowledge that makes up competence and the control that is used in producing speech. The L2 learner may have problems with control procedures or with L2 knowledge. Inadequate procedures taken from the L1 will distort newly learnt L2 knowledge, or the L2 procedures may be adequate but the L2 knowledge is missing. For example English learners of German often have difficulty with the fact that German has SVO order in main clauses but SOV in subordinate clauses. This might be because their English SVO *procedures* are still controlling their L2 *competence* and so leading to mistakes. Or it might be that their German L2 *competence* has incorrectly transferred the word order from English and their L2 procedures are perfectly adequate. Their interlanguage develops either because their underlying knowledge of the language improves or because their processes improve. Control is important also to variation. The reason why an L2 learner produces language that is not appropriate to the situation could be lack of control procedures — of knowing when to use what — rather than because they are not part of competence.

The question of variation was incorporated by Elaine Tarone (1988) into the concept of the interlanguage continuum. She suggests that learners vary their interlanguage for formal and informal situations. Japanese learners of English are better at pronouncing /z/ in more formal situations such as reading word lists than in less formal situations such as speaking spontaneously (Dickerson, 1975). Though they improve with time, nevertheless there is still a gap between their success in these two types of situation, the classroom and the informal. This observation will ring true for many language teachers. It can be interpreted in terms of the Competence/Control Model as showing that the learners' control procedures are not working properly and are holding back their performance. However Tarone's explanation is more consoling for teachers. She believes that the formal and informal varieties of speech are not equally important in L2 learning. Newly learnt items are mastered in the formal situation before they are carried over to informal situations. So it is not just that the learner possesses a range of ways of speaking but that the learner progresses through them from day-to-day along a continuum.

The chief difference between the formal and informal varieties on this continuum is in how much 'attention' speakers pay to their speech. Tarone claims that the formal variety is the most 'attended', in a sense the same as saying the one in which the speaker is most self-conscious. The informal variety is the least 'attended'. So the new elements of the L2 are first acquired in the language variety in which the speaker pays most attention, and then slowly transferred to the variety which is less attended. The interlanguage continuum goes from most-attended speech to least-attended. Learners acquire aspects of the L2 in formal situations before they transfer them to less formal. The classroom is usually a formal attended situation. The teacher is doing the students a disservice to pretend otherwise since the point of entry for new information is only through this situation. Of course there are problems with this analysis in one sense. If the students' only encounter with the L2 is in the classroom, it is hardly surprising that new forms first manifest themselves in their classroom speech as they are not encountered outside.

Attention is one form of control; the more attention paid to speech the more the speaker controls it. Much use of conscious understanding in L2 learning represents a type of conversion model in which one kind of information is turned into another. Is being conscious of the L2 structures and rules a help or a hindrance? The reader now knows from information supplied in the last section that Dutch is an SVO language in main clauses in which the subject of the sentence agrees with the verb. If given a Dutch noun "vogel" (bird), a verb "vliegen" (fly), and a singular ending for verbs "-zt", you could construct a Dutch sentence about a bird flying. You could consciously use explicit knowledge of language to construct a sentence, which might even be acceptable Dutch. But is consciousness-raising of this type useful in learning to actually speak Dutch? Consciousness is excluded from both the UG type models and the Competition Model. The models described in this section all take consciousness into account to some extent. The interlanguage continuum relies on attention, which at an extreme may be awareness of actual rules.

The Monitor Model

The model that was however specifically developed to cover consciousness was the ***Monitor Model of*** Krashen (1981b). This started as an account of some aspects of language processing in the 1970s, and became an all-embracing theory in the early 1980s. However it met with an extremely hostile reception from other researchers, mostly because it seemed too great a leap from a small base of evidence. The relevant aspects here are its attitudes to conscious use of grammatical rules. Krashen claims that there are two possible types of linguistic knowledge, acquired knowledge and learnt knowledge

i. *acquired knowledge*. One type of knowledge is that which is acquired by natural means in informal situations, a process termed acquisition. This is the form of all L1 knowledge and potentially of some L2 knowledge. It consists of rules, principles, etc, that are not available to conscious attention.

ii. *learnt knowledge*. The other type of knowledge is that which is learnt by conscious understanding of rules, a process termed learning. This is the form of much L2 knowledge acquired in formal classroom situations. It consists of explicit linguistic information that is consciously available to the speaker.

In one sense this division between acquisition and learning is obvious and familiar. The UG model for instance makes a distinction between the natural knowledge acquired through the faculty of language and the knowledge of language that could have been learnt by other faculties of the mind, say the reasoning faculty. Krashen's Monitor Model differs over the relationship between the two types of knowledge. The diagram on the facing page is found in the variations in many books by Krashen (e.g. 1981a).

The process of speaking a second language depends primarily on acquired knowledge for all learners. Those who have a conscious learnt knowledge of the L2 are able to use it only as a Monitor of what they have already acquired. Thus someone who wants to say something in a second language will be able to Monitor what they are saying via the conscious grammatical

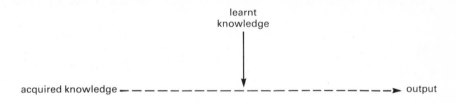

The Monitor Model of L2 production

rules they know — checking whether the tense is right for instance. Krashen is not just saying that this is one of the uses of learnt knowledge. After all everyone probably checks out their knowledge from time to time by muttering, say, "The mites go up and the tights come down" as a mnemonic for "stalagmite" versus "stalactite". Rather Krashen is saying this is the *only* use of learnt conscious knowledge. Consciously learnt rules are never turned into acquired knowledge. Conscious learning *never* leads to anything more than the ability to Monitor what you want to say or write when the circumstances allow. His is the extreme non-conversion model in which the two sides do not mix. Hence it is sometimes called the 'dual competence' model.

Such models remind us of the range of language use. Different aspects of language are prominent in different situations. The L2 learner's speech is no more a single uniform variety than is the native speaker's. The conversion models in particular are the justification for giving explicit rules of language to the students. Teaching that asks the learner to convert conscious knowledge, for example, "To be polite you use past tense auxiliaries in requests", into appropriate use of requests in real situations relies on a conversion model. Krashen emphasizes the development of both sides. Acquisition in his terms is fostered by communicative 'natural' activities. Learning in his sense can be helped to some limited extent by the provision of appropriate 'rules of thumb'. Similarly, according to Bialystok (1990), L2 learning requires knowledge such as rules of grammar for the development of competence in her terms and needs practice in speaking etc to develop control processes.

Conversion Models and Mixed Models

Key theme:
   L2 learning has more than one side to it, both skills and knowledge
Learning:
   the two sides are either learnt separately or one leads into the other
Teaching uses:
   exercises which exploit different aspects of learning, whether by conversion or
      separately

4. Social models: the socio – educational model and the acculturation model

But many would say all the models described so far neglect the most important part of language — its social aspect. There are two interpretations of this. One is that L2 learning usually takes place in a social situation where people interact with each other, whether in the classroom or outside. The discourse and strategy elements in this have already been covered in earlier chapters. The second interpretation is that L2 learning takes place within a society and has a function within that society. This relates to the local and international goals of language teaching discussed in chapter Seven.

The Socio-Educational Model

A complex view of L2 learning called the Socio-Educational Model has been put forward by Gardner (1985) to explain how individual factors and general features of society interact in L2 learning. He sees two main ingredients in the learners' success — motivation, and aptitude — both of which were examined briefly in chapter Five. Motivation consists of two chief factors: attitudes to the learning situation — i.e. to the teacher and the course — and integrativeness, which is a complex of factors about how the learner regards the culture reflected in the L2. These elements are put together to yield the following model:

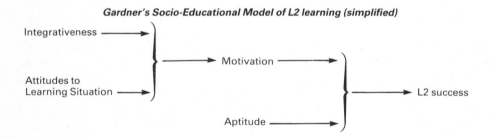

Gardner's Socio-Educational Model of L2 learning (simplified)

Success depends on motivation and aptitude; motivation depends on integrativeness and attitudes. Or, to put it another way, according to Gardner integrativeness and attitudes lead to motivation; motivation and aptitude lead to success. Each causes the other.

But where do attitudes and integrativeness come from? The answer according to Gardner is the social milieu in which the students are placed. The society sets a particular store by L2 learning; it has particular stereotyped views of foreigners and of particular nationalities, and it sees the classroom in a particular way. Hence one way of predicting if students will be successful at L2 learning is to look, not at the attitudes of the students themselves, but at those of their parents. The crucial factors are how the learner thinks of the speakers of a second language and how highly he or she values L2 learning in the classroom. The socio-educational model chiefly applies to language teaching for local goals, where the students have definite views on the L2 group whose language they are learning through everyday contact with them within the society, say the position of Japanese learners of English in Toronto. In teaching for international goals they may not have such definite opinions. For example French teaching in England involves little contact with French-speaking groups.

The Acculturation Model

John Schumann (1978a) has proposed a complementary approach called the *Acculturation Model*. The most important influence on L2 learning is for him the relationship between the social group of the L2 learners and the social group of the speakers of the target language. Successful learning means *acculturation* — becoming part of the target culture. If the group of L2 learners thinks of itself as superior or inferior to the target language speakers, they will not learn the language very well. So in a colonial situation the rulers do not learn the language of their supposed inferiors as this would be 'going native'; the indigenous people on the other hand do not learn the language of their supposed superiors very well as this would be 'collaborationist'. An example from English history is that after 200 years when French was the official language of the ruling Normans in England and English was almost invisible, English re-emerged with hardly any effects of disuse. The Normans and the Anglo-Saxons were not very good at learning each other's languages. In more modern days English, Russian, and French have all failed to be learnt successfully in various parts of the world because of their political overtones.

The relationship between the learner and the target group exists on many different levels — social, artistic, political, technological, religious. Football is given as a reason by some English boys for preferring to learn German rather than French. Again it is hard to use the second/foreign language distinction. English learnt in South Africa is very different from English learnt in Canada though both can be called 'second' languages. English learnt in Argentina is very different from English in Italy though both might be 'foreign' languages. It is the unique relationship between the learner's group and the target group that is crucial. One problem with this analysis is that international languages to some extent do not fit Schumann's scheme. The international use of languages such as English for example is often detached from the English-speaking peoples. Schumann does however have a further term *'enculturation'* to cover circumstances in which it is desirable to speak a second language within one's own culture, a form of elite bilingualism.

One interesting insight from such theories is the similarity between L2 learning and the development of pidgin languages. A pidgin comes into being as a solution to the problems of two groups trying to communicate with each other without a shared language. As the contact is maintained so the pidgin gets more developed; eventually children learn it as their first language and it becomes a creole language. Examples of pidgins are

Tok Pisin spoken in Papua New Guinea, Hongkong Pidgin, and Cameroon Pidgin English. Creoles are found everywhere from the English-based Krio of Sierra Leone, to French-based Louisiana creole, to Portuguese-based creole in Macao. Pidgins have certain characteristics in common regardless of the combinations of language involved, particularly their 'simplified' grammars. Schumann (1978b) originally drew people's attention to this through his study of a Spanish learner of English called Alberto whose speech had many of the simplified characteristics of pidgin, e.g. negation was expressed as "no" + verb. Roger Andersen (1983) has developed the concepts of *nativization* and *denativization*. Nativization is progress towards universal underlying forms. This consists of adapting the language that is being acquired to built-in universal tendencies. Denativatization on the other hand is movement in the opposite direction and involves changing the internal system to suit the language that is being learnt.

Oddly the consideration of society has led back to the discussion of aspects of language built-in to the mind. Thus the sociological equivalent of Chomsky's Universal Grammar is Derek Bickerton's **Bioprogram** (Bickerton, 1981). Creole languages are created by children out of the pidgins spoken by their parents. The characteristics of creole languages may tell us about the essential features of the human language capacity.

The implications for teaching hark back to the discussion in the last chapter of the roles of language teaching in society. The total situation in which the students are located plays a crucial part in their learning. If the goals of teaching are incompatible with their perceptions of the world and the social milieu in which they are placed, teaching has little point. Teachers have to fit their teaching to the roles of language teaching for the person or the society, or attempt to reform the social preconceptions of their students. If they do not, the students will not succeed. These models also remind the teacher of the nature of the L2-using situation. The goal of teaching is to enable a non-native speaker to communicate adequately, not

---

Social Models

Key theme:
   learning takes place in society

Learning:
   learning depends upon motivation and aptitude, which in turn depend on integrativeness and attitudes (The Socio-Educational Model)
   learning depends upon the perceived relationships between the target and the L2 groups (The Acculturation Model)
   L2 learning is related to processes in pidginization

Teaching use:
   — match the teaching with the social and personal roles of language teaching
   — remember L2 use is a multilingual situation

to enable him or her to pass as native. Hence pidgins and so on make us think once again of the central cross-linguistic nature of L2 use.

Each of these models of learning accounts persuasively for what it considers the crucial aspects of L2 learning. What is wrong with them is not their claims about their own front yard so much as their tendency to claim that the whole street belongs to them. Each of them is at best a piece of the jigsaw. Do the pieces add up to a single picture? Can a teacher believe that language is mental knowledge gained by assigning weightings to factors by those with good attitudes towards the target culture without committing Orwellian doublethink? The answer is probably yes. The differences between the areas of L2 learning dealt with by each model mean that they are by no means irreconcilable. UG applies only to 'core' grammar; response weightings apply to speech processing; attitudes to behaviour in academic classrooms. Only if the models dealt with the same areas would they come into conflict. At the moment there is no overall framework for all the models. When they are fitted together, an overall model of L2 learning will one day emerge. At the moment there are many area-specific models, each of them providing some useful insights into its own province of L2 learning. For the sake of their students, teachers have to deal with L2 learning as a whole, as we shall see in the next chapter. It is premature for any one of these models to be adopted as the sole basis for teaching, because, however right or wrong they may be, none of them covers more than a small fraction of what the students need. As Spolsky (1989a) wisely remarks, 'any theory of second language learning that leads to a single method must be wrong'.

Reading

The UG model is introduced in Cook, V.J., 1988a. *Chomsky's Universal Grammar: An Introduction*, Blackwell, and White, L., 1989. *Universal Grammar and Second Language Acquisition*, John Benjamins. An overall account of some L2 models by a psychologist can be found in McLaughlin, B. (1987). *Theories of Second-Language Learning*. Edward Arnold, London. A synthesizing overview of L2 learning can be found in Spolsky, B. (1989a). *Conditions for Second Language Learning*. OUP. For other models such as the Competition Model there is nothing but the original articles and books mentioned in the text.

9

Second Language Learning and Language Teaching Styles

This chapter looks at some general questions of teaching methodology in the light of L2 learning research. It connects established methods of teaching to the research that has already been outlined, in a sense, reversing the direction of the last chapter in going from teaching to L2 learning. 'Teaching method' has been used in this book as a broad cover term for the diverse activities that go on in language teaching. Various suggestions have been put forward over the years for making the term 'method' more precise or for abandoning it. The traditional distinction is between overall approaches, such as the oral approach, methods, say the audiolingual method, and teaching techniques, such as drills (Anthony, 1963). More recently Richards and Rodgers (1986) see approaches as related through design to procedures. Marton (1988) on the other hand talks about four overall teaching 'strategies' — the receptive strategy which relies primarily on listening, the communicative strategy in which students learn by attempting to communicate, the reconstructive strategy in which the student participates in reconstructive activities based on a text, and the eclectic strategy which combines two or more of the others. Allen *et al.*, (1990) distinguish experiential activities which rely on language use within a situation from analytic activities which use language study and practise.

To avoid the various associations that these terms convey, let us use the more neutral terms 'teaching technique' and 'teaching style'. The actual point of contact with the students is the teaching technique. Thus a structure drill in which students intensively practise a structure is one technique; dictation is another, information-gap exercises another, and so on. A technique, as Clark (1984) puts it, is a 'label for what we do as teachers'. Teachers combine these techniques in various ways within a particular teaching style. Put a structure-drill with a repetition dialogue and a role-play and you get the audiolingual style with its dependence on the spoken language, on practise, and on structure. Put a functional drill with an information gap exercise and a role-play and you get the social communicative style with its broad assumptions about the importance of communication in the classroom. A teaching style is a loosely connected set of teaching techniques believed to share the same goals of language teaching and the same views of language and of L2 learning. The word 'style' partly refers to the element of fashion and changeability in teaching. A teacher who might feel guilty switching from one method to another or in mixing 'methods' within one lesson has less compunction about changing 'styles'. It is rare to encounter a classroom that is a pure version of one or other of these teaching styles as none of them fully satisfy all the needs of any real class of students.

This chapter relates six teaching styles to L2 learning research: the academic teaching style common in academic classrooms, the audiolingual style that emphasizes structured oral practise, the social communicative style that aims at interaction between people, the information communicative style that stresses information transfer from one person to another, the mainstream EFL style which combines aspects of the first three, and finally, other styles that look beyond language itself.

The academic style

An advanced foreign language lesson in an academic context often consists of a reading text taken from a newspaper or similar source, for example the lead story on the front page of today's newspaper under the headline "PM seeks new curbs on strikes". The teacher leads the students through the text sentence by sentence. Some of the cultural background is elucidated — for example, the context of legislation about strikes in England. Words that give problems are explained or translated into the students' first language by the teacher or via the students' dictionaries — "closed shop" or "stoppage" say. Grammatical points of interest are discussed with the students, such as the use of the passive voice in "A similar proposal in the Conservative election manifesto in 1983 was also shelved". The students go on to a fill-in grammatical exercise on the passive. Perhaps for homework they translate the passage into their L1.

The academic teaching style then is characterized by teaching techniques of grammatical explanation and translation, and by its reliance on texts. Hence the style is similar in concept to Marton's reconstructive strategy or Allen *et al.*'s analytic activities. The academic style is a time-honoured way of teaching foreign languages, popular in secondary schools till quite recently and widespread in the teaching of advanced students in university systems around the world. The academic style occurs even when the teacher is ostensibly using other styles. A teacher explains how to apologize in the target language, a teacher gives a quick grammatical explanation of the present perfect tense, a teacher describes where to put the tongue to make the sound /θ / — all of these are slipping into an academic style.

The academic style does not directly teach people to use the language for some purpose outside the classroom. Ostensibly it is language teaching with individual goals aimed primarily at the learning of the L2 as an academic subject, in other words at the creation of linguistic competence in the students' minds. It often tries in addition to train the students to think better, to appreciate other cultures, and to foster other educational values. But the academic style is also frequently intended as preparation for the actual use of language. By developing academic knowledge the student eventually becomes able to use the L2 in real-life situations outside the classroom. While the style does not directly practise communication in the classroom, nevertheless it can provide a basis for communication when the student requires it.

Its view of learning emphasizes the teaching of grammatical competence as rules of a traditional type and as lists of vocabulary. It values what people know about the language rather than what they comprehend or produce. Students are seen as acquiring knowledge of language rather than communicative ability directly. It uses a conversion model of L2 learning that sees the learner progressing from controlled conscious understanding to automatic processing. The classroom is similar to classrooms in other school subjects, with the teacher as a fount of knowledge and advice.

The academic style is appropriate for a society or an individual that treats academic knowledge of the L2 as a desirable objective and that holds a traditional view of the classroom and of the teacher's role. One weakness is its description of language. On the one hand the linguistic content is usually traditional grammar, rather than more recent or more comprehensive approaches. On the other hand, while the treatment of vocabulary in text exercises like those above is far-ranging, it is also unsystematic. Though the academic style laudably strives to build up relationships between vocabulary items encountered in texts, it has no principled way of doing so. Despite being concerned with linguistic forms, it pays little attention to components of language other than grammar and vocabulary and, occasionally, pronunciation. The same techniques could be applied systematically to other areas, say listening comprehension.

The academic teaching style caters for academically-gifted students, who will supplement it with their own Good Language Learner strategies, and who will probably not be young children — in other words, they are Skehan's analytic learners. But, while the style has often succeeded with such students, they represent the tip of an iceberg. Those who are learning language as an academic subject — the linguistics students of the future — may be properly served by an academic style. Indeed at Essex University, a descriptive grammar course is compulsory for all students learning modern languages. But such academic students form a small fraction of those in most educational settings. Those who wish to use the L2 for real-life purposes may not be academically gifted or may not be prepared for the long journey from academic knowledge to practical use that the style requires.

When should the academic style be used? If the society and the students treat individual goals as primary, language use as secondary, and the students are academically-gifted, then the academic style is appropriate. But the teacher has to recognize its narrow base. For the academic style to be adequate, it needs to include on the one hand descriptions of language that are linguistically sound, on the other, descriptions that can be converted by the students into actual use. The academic style would be more viable as a way of L2 teaching within its stated goals if it changed the grammatical and vocabulary core to something that better reflects how language is described today and something that relates better to the processes of conversion on which it relies.

While the individual goals of the academic style are potentially profound, there is a danger that teachers can lose sight of them and see grammatical explanations as having no other role than imparting factual knowledge. The goals of language awareness, mental training, and the appreciation of other cultures may not be achieved spontaneously if the teacher does not give them particular attention in planning lessons and in carrying them out.

The academic style of language teaching

Typical teaching techniques:
   grammatical explanation, translation etc

Goals:
   — directly individual learning of the L2 as an academic subject, sometimes
      leading to communicative ability
   — indirectly ability to use language

Type of student:
   academically-gifted, not young children

Learning assumptions:
   acquisition of conscious grammatical knowledge, conversion of knowledge
      to use

Processing assumptions:
   none

Weaknesses from L2 research perspective:
   — inadequate use of grammar
   — no position on other components of language knowledge or use
   — inefficiency as a way of teaching use

Suggestions for teaching:
   — use it with academic students with individual goals
   — supplement it with other components of language and processes
   — remember its individual goals

The audiolingual style

The name 'audiolingual' is attached to a teaching style that reached its peak in the 1960s, best conveyed in Robert Lado's thoughtful book ***Language Teaching: A Scientific Approach*** (Lado, 1964). Its emphasis is on teaching the spoken language through dialogues and drills. A typical lesson in an audiolingual style starts with a dialogue, say about buying food in a shop. The language in the dialogue is controlled so that it introduces only a few new vocabulary items, and includes several examples of any new structural point. The students listen to the dialogue as a whole, either played back from a tape or read by the teacher; they repeat it sentence by sentence, and they act it out. Then they drill grammatical points connected with the dialogue, such as the polite questions used in requests; the drills practise a structure repeatedly with some variation of vocabulary. Finally there are expansion activities to make the students incorporate the language in their own use. As Wilga Rivers (1964) put it, 'Some provision will be made for the student to apply what he has learnt in a structured communication situation'. Instead of homework, the students go to the language laboratory to practise dialogues and drills individually. Language is divided into the four skills of listening, speaking, reading, and writing, which have to be *taught* in that order. Hence the audiolingual style stresses the spoken language rather than the written and the so-called 'active' skills of speaking and writing rather than the 'passive' skills of listening and reading.

Though few teachers employ a 'pure' audiolingual style, many of the ingredients are nevertheless common in today's classrooms — the use of short dialogues, the emphasis on spoken language, the value attached to practice, the emphasis on the student speaking, the division into four skills, the importance of vocabulary control, the step-by-step progression, and so on. Virtually all pronunciation teaching uses the audiolingual techniques of repetition and drill when it does not employ the academic style. Many teachers clearly feel comfortable with the audiolingual style and use it at one time or another in their teaching, even if most would challenge its assumptions about learning.

The audiolingual style most blatantly reflects a particular set of beliefs about L2 learning, often referred to as 'habit-formation'. Language is a set of habits, just like driving a car. Each habit is learnt by doing it time and again. The dialogues concentrate on unconscious 'structures' rather than the conscious 'rules' of the academic style. Instead of understanding every word or structure, students learn the text more or less by heart. Learning sentences means learning structures and vocabulary, which means learning the language. Like the academic style, language is seen as form, though its basis is more in structural than traditional grammar.

The goal of the audiolingual style is to get the students to 'behave' in common L2 situations, such as the station or the supermarket. In one sense it is practical and communication-oriented. The audiolingual style is not learning language for its own sake but learning it for actual use, either within the society or without. The appropriate student type is not defined but the style is not restricted to the academically gifted. Indeed its stress on practice can disadvantage those with an analytical bias. Nor is the audiolingual style obviously restricted to students of a particular age.

Its views of L2 learning are closest to the processing models described in the last chapter. Partly this comes across in its emphasis on the physical situation. Most importance is attached to building up the strength of the student's response through practice. Little weight is given to the understanding of linguistic structure or to the creation of knowledge. It is not a conversion model in which knowledge of one type is turned into another. Rather the ability to use language is built up piece by piece using the same type of learning. Grammar is seen in terms of 'structures' within which items of vocabulary are substituted. Courses are graded around structures; drills practise particular structures, dialogues introduce and exemplify structures and vocabulary in context. The style has no particular views on language processing, apart from its interest in the production and comprehension of phonemes. It requires a classroom where the students are teacher-controlled except for the final exploitation phase when, as Lado puts it, the student 'has the patterns ready as habits but he must practice using them with full attention on purposeful communication'. Until the expansion phase of the cycle students repeat, answer, or drill at the teacher's behest. Though they work individually in the language laboratory, they still use the same activities and teaching materials. The style demands students who do not expect to take the initiative. All responsibility is in the teacher's hands.

One virtue of the academic style was that, if it didn't achieve its secondary goal of allowing the student to communicate, it still might have educational value via its goals of improving thinking, promoting cross-cultural understanding, and so on. The audiolingual style has no fall-back position. If it doesn't succeed in getting the student to function in the L2, there is nothing else to be gained from it — no academic knowledge or problem-solving ability. Lado does however claim that it teaches a positive attitude of identification with the target culture. Furthermore its insistence on L2 learning as the creation of habits is an oversimplification of behaviourist models of learning. And of course many would deny that the distinctive elements of language are in fact learnable by these means. The principles of Universal Grammar for example are impossible to acquire through practice and reinforcement.

Syllabuses and textbooks in the audiolingual style see structures, phonemes, and vocabulary items as the sum total of language. Though based on the four skills of listening, speaking, reading, and writing, it pays surprisingly little attention to the distinctive features of each skill. The skill of listening for example is not usually broken up into levels or stages that resemble those seen earlier. More crucially, its view of language use now seems naive. The communication situation is far more complex than the style implies. If communication is the goal of language teaching, its content needs to be based on an analysis of communication itself, which is not covered properly by structures and vocabulary. Even if students totally master the content of an audiolingual course, they need much more to function in a real-life situation.

Yet many teachers fall back on the audiolingual style. One reason may be that it provides a clear framework for teachers to work within. Teachers always know what they are supposed to be doing, unlike more flexible or improvisational styles. Certain aspects of language may lend themselves best to audiolingual teaching. Pronunciation teaching has hardly developed in the past thirty years, perhaps because of lack of imagination by teachers, perhaps because the audiolingual style is indeed the most effective in this area. Lado's 1964 pronunciation techniques of 'demonstration, imitation, props, contrast, and practice' seem as comprehensive as anything that has come since. The style reminds us that language is in part physical behaviour and the total language teaching operation must take this into account.

The teacher should be aware of the audiolingual source of many familiar teaching techniques. Though ostensibly out of fashion, its influence is still pervasive. Take for instance the emphasis on spoken language and on practice in speaking, which are found in many contemporary techniques. Where do they come from if not the audiolingual style? It is important for teachers to be aware that they are based on a particular view of language — which may well not be the one they consciously favour.

The audiolingual style of language teaching

Typical teaching techniques:
  dialogues, structure drills, etc.

Goal:
  getting students to 'behave' in appropriate situations

Type of student:
  non-analytical, non-academic

Learning assumptions:
  'habit-formation' behaviourist theory

Processing assumptions:
  none

Classroom assumptions:
  teacher-controlled classroom

Weaknesses from L2 research perspective:
  — inadequate form of grammar
  — no position on other aspects of language knowledge or use
  — inefficiency of habit-formation as way of teaching use

Suggestions for teachers:
  — use for teaching certain aspects of language only
  — be aware of audiolingual basis for many everyday techniques

---

The social communicative style

The beginning of the 1970s saw a shift towards teaching methods that emphasized communication. Initially this was largely a matter of redefining what the student had to learn in terms of communicative competence rather than linguistic competence — ability to use the language appropriately rather than knowledge of grammatical rules. The behaviour of native speakers was analysed and developed into syllabuses incorporating ideas of language functions and notions which were more sophisticated than those possible with the limited concepts of structure and situation of the audiolingual style. Recently, communication is often seen more in terms of the processes that people use to carry out specific communicative tasks.

The elaboration of communicative competence affected the specification of the teaching target but did not at first have direct consequences for teaching. The fact that the teaching point of a lesson is the function 'asking directions' rather than the structure 'yes-no questions' does not prevent it being taught through any teaching style, just as grammar can be taught in any style. Even a communicative function can be taught through academic style explanation or audiolingual style drills. The course *Function in English* (Blundell *et al.*, 1982) displays a list of alternatives for each function categorized as neutral, informal, and formal, and linked by codes to a structural index — clearly academic style. The textbook *Opening Strategies* (Abbs and Freebairn, 1982) for example makes students substitute "bank", "post office", "restaurant" and so on into the sentence "Is there a —— near here?" — clearly audiolingual.

To many people however the end dictates the means: a goal expressed in terms of communication means classroom teaching based on communication. Hence a number of techniques developed that evolved into two distinct styles, which we shall call here 'social communicative' style and 'information communicative' style. The social communicative style has its main emphasis on the joint functioning of two people in a situation, what Halliday (1975) terms the 'interpersonal' function of language. The archetypal social communicative techniques are information gap exercises teaching how to give locations of people and places. Take an example from the textbook *Coast to Coast* (Harmer and Surguine, 1987). The students divide into pairs; one has a map of a street showing where Jim, Kathleen, and so on live, the other has a map of the same street showing where Kristy, Ben, and others live. They have to "ask and answer questions to find where the people live" following a model exchange, and then write the names on the map. The students are given the vocabulary on the map and have an example question and answer. But they have to improvise the dialogue themselves to solve their communicative task. The second standard technique of the social communicative style is guided roleplay. The students improvise conversations around an issue but do not have the same contrived information gap. *Blueprint 1* (Abbs & Freebairn, 1990) for instance has a roleplay about Hong Kong that asks the students in pairs to act out conversations such as "You are vegetarian. Phone the airline and tell them where you are travelling to, when and what you would like for lunch and dinner on the flight".

In the social communicative style language is defined as communication between people, rather than as texts or grammatical rules or patterns. Language is for forming relationships with people and for interrelating with them. Using language means meeting people and talking to them. Language is not so much rules or structures or texts as ways of talking to people. It aims to give the students the ability to engage in conversations with people. The teaching syllabus is primarily a way of listing the aspects of communication the students will find most useful, whether functions, notions, or processes. It tries to develop the students' ability to communicate fluently rather than in grammatically flawless sentences.

The goals of the social communicative style are most often towards international use of the second language with people in another country rather than locally in multilingual societies. In general purpose language teaching the overall goals of the social communicative style have not usually been specified in great detail; they usually aim at the generalized situation of visitors to the target country with the accent on tourism and travel, without specific goals for careers, for education, or for access to information, as in the GCSE syllabuses cited in chapter Seven. In more specialized circumstances of course language been taught for specific careers and for higher education. In practice many communicative textbooks for beginners adopt what might be called 'travel agent communication' centred upon tourist activities, with the coursebook resembling a glossy holiday brochure and the teacher a jolly package-tour representative organizing fun activities.

The classroom is a very different place in the social communicative style. The teacher is no longer a dominant figure continuously controlling and guiding the students. Rather the teacher takes one step back and lets the students take over the activities, making up their own conversations in pairs and groups, learning language by doing. A key difference is that the students are not required to produce substantially errorless speech in native terms, as in the other styles. Instead they use whatever forms and strategies they can devise to solve their communication problem, ending up with sentences that are entirely appropriate to their task but are often highly deviant from a native perspective. So, while the teacher provides some feedback and correction, this plays a much less central part in his or her classroom duties. This cofigurative role for the teacher is a jump in cultural terms from the traditional teacher-led class and hence disconcerts or indeed alienates those from cultures who see education differently. The adoption of a social communicative style, however ideal on other grounds, always has to recognize this cultural problem. The style also is potentially limited to certain types of student. For instance it might benefit field-independent students rather than field-dependent students, extroverts rather than introverts, and less academic students rather than academic students. Its cofigurative implications can also go against students' expectations of the classroom more than other styles.

Language learning in this style is the same as language using. Information gap and roleplay techniques imitate what happens in the world outside the classroom in a controlled form, rather than being activities peculiar to language learning. Students will later be asking the way or requesting vegetarian meals in a foreign language environment just as they are now doing in the classroom. Learning language means practising communication within the four walls of the classroom. You learn to talk to people by actually talking to them. L2 learning arises from meaningful use. This has been emphasized in recent developments which use the idea of communication as dynamic process to stimulate communication in the classroom through task-based activities.

The social communicative style does not hold a view about L2 learning as such but believes it happens automatically provided the student interacts with other people in the proper way. Many of its techniques carry on the audiolingual style's preoccupations with active practice by the students, and with spoken language, in a sense elaborating the expansion phase of the audiolingual style. Indeed like the audiolingual style it often resembles behaviourist views of learning. I have sometimes introduced the ideas of mands and tacts mentioned in the last chapter to teachers without telling them they are verbal operants within Skinner's behaviourist model. Their reaction is normally that they sound a useful basis for a communicative syllabus! The main difference between the audiolingual style and the social communicative style is the latter's emphasis on spontaneous production and comprehension in pursuit of interpersonal communication.

In general, there is surprisingly little connection between this style and L2 learning research. It resembles to some extent the Conversational Analysis model described in chapter Three but differs in specifying abstract elements of communicative competence such as language functions and processes rather than the moves of discourse. Its nearest relations are functional theories of L1 acquisition, rather than many of the models of L2 learning described in the last chapter. As always, this is not to say that it is wrong — perhaps L2 learning research should pay more attention to this side of learning. It can be called a black box model of L2 learning because it assumes little about the learning process, apart from claiming that, if the right circumstances are provided to the students, something will happen inside their minds.

Historically there is a link between the social communicative style and the idea of interlanguage, which means that teachers should respect the developing language systems of the students rather than seeing them as defective. The style uses techniques that change the teacher's roles to those of organization and support rather than direction and control, because it does not set the same store on the students consistently producing near-native sentences. One element in this comes from ideas of Universal Grammar. If the students are using natural processes of learning built-in to their minds, the teacher can step back and let them get on with it by providing activities and language examples to get these natural processes going. This is related to the view of language learning as hypothesis-testing, an early version of the Universal Grammar theory, in which the learner makes a guess at the rules of the language, tries it out by producing sentences, and accepts or revises the rules in the light of the feedback that is provided. However hypothesis-testing in this sense has been abandoned as it requires types of correction that L1 children never get and most L2 learners seldom encounter, particularly in a communicative classroom. Elsewhere I have called this *laissez-faire* teaching (Cook, 1988a); learning takes place in the students' minds in ways over which teachers have no control, and so the students should be trusted to learn without the teacher's interference. It can lead to the dangerous assumption that any activity is justified that gives students the opportunity to test out 'hypotheses' in the classroom, with no criteria applied other than getting the students talking.

Chapter Seven suggested that the word 'communication' can blind us to individual goals of language teaching. The social communicative style covers only some of the relevant aspects of L2 learning, however desirable they may be in themselves, and has no techniques of its own for teaching pronunciation or vocabulary, little connection with speech processing or memory, and little systematic recognition of the possibilities available to the learner through the L1. Pairwork and groupwork among students with the same L1 for example often leads to frequent codeswitching between L1 and L2, perhaps something to be developed systematically rather than seen as undesirable. In so far as the style recognizes grammar, it is often of a structuralist kind reminiscent of audiolingualism, for instance, the substitution tables seen in many communicative textbooks.

The social communicative style is highly appropriate for students and societies that value international goals of a non-specific kind. The teacher using it with a particular class has to remember that it will not appeal to students with other types of goal, say an interest in language structure or a desire for personal liberation. The unexpectedness of the classroom situation it employs may need selling to the students. It needs balancing with other styles to make certain that the coverage of language components is adequate even to achieve its own goal of communicative competence. But at least it sees communication as a dynamic social activity to be acquired by active participation by the students, marking a clear break in this respect from the academic and audiolingual styles.

The social communicative style of language teaching

Typical teaching techniques:
  information gap, roleplays

Goal:
  getting students to interact with other people in the L2

Type of student:
  any

Learning assumptions:
  learning by communicating with other students in the classroom: "laissez-faire"

Processing assumptions:
  none

Classroom assumptions:
  teacher as organiser, not fount of wisdom

Weaknesses from L2 research perspective:
  — lack of views on discourse processes, communication strategies, etc.
  — black-box model of learning
  — lack of role for L1
  — possible cultural conflicts because of its cofigurative basis

Suggestions for teachers:
  — use with appropriate students in appropriate circumstances
  — supplement with other components of language
  — avoid trivialisation of content and aims

The information communicative style

The social communicative and information communicative styles are in a sense two sides of the same coin. A conversation requires not only someone to talk to but also something to talk about. As de Saussure (1916) said, 'Speech has both an individual and a social side and we cannot conceive of one without the other'. Nevertheless communication can be seen as an exchange of ideas rather than as relationships with people, what Halliday (1975) calls the 'ideational' function of language, since these result in rather different teaching styles. Teaching that emphasizes the information that is transferred rather than the social interaction between the participants can be called the information communicative style, equivalent to Marton's receptive strategy. A typical technique in this style is Asher's Total Physical Response (TPR) method, described along with other listening-based techniques in chapter Three.

The information communicative style is hard to illustrate from teaching materials because it mostly depends on the individual teacher's preparation and improvisation during the class. Gary and Gary (1981a) have, however, published a specimen lesson from their materials *More English Now!*, which are designed for hotel staff in Egypt. The lesson starts with a 'Preview' section in which the language content of the lesson is explained and in which 'important words' are translated into Arabic. In the next section, 'Let's Listen', students hear a tape giving the bookings for a hotel for next week and carry out a task-listening exercise, first filling in a form with the guests' names and details and then answering questions such as, "Who was in room 104?" in writing. Finally a 'Let's Read' section gives them the same tasks with a written text. Such 'listening-first' teaching requires the students to listen actively but not to produce sentences until they are ready. The point here is the information transfer. TPR students are listening to discover what actions to carry out; their social interaction with the teacher is quite unlike that found in any normal language exchange, except perhaps for the military drill square. Students following *More English Now!* are listening to get specific information to be written down in various forms. While this partly resembles their real-life hotel duties, it deliberately minimizes spoken production and natural social interaction, vital to their actual conversation with guests. The concentration is in both cases on the information to be obtained from language, not on the social relationship between listener and speaker. Working out information is the key factor: take care of the message and the learning will take care of itself. Hence the style is compatible with a large range of teaching techniques, united only by their emphasis on information.

The overall goal is to get students to use the language, first by comprehending, then by producing. Comprehension of information is not seen as a goal in its own right, but as a way -in to fuller command of the language in use. Sometimes the overall goal is more specific, as with the Cairo hotel staff. Mostly however it has a non-specific communicative goal, similar to that in the social communicative model. The information communicative style is used in both local and international circumstances. It implicitly plays down the individual goals of language teaching, making few claims to general educational values. In terms of classrooms, it is teacher-dominated, with the teacher supplying, in person or through materials, the language input and the organization of the students' activities and classroom strategies. The social communicative style is limited by physical factors in the classroom in that it becomes progressively more difficult to organize its activities with larger groups. The information communicative style lends itself to classes of any size. Some versions of the style are more compatible with the traditional teacher-dominated classroom than is the social communicative style. It caters for a range of student types, provided they do not mind having to listen rather than speak in the classroom. Hence again the students need to be prepared for what the style is trying to do, since it differs from their expectations of the classroom.

The style makes two assumptions about learning. One that was already encountered in chapter Three is the equation of decoding with codebreaking. Getting people to comprehend in the classroom is getting them to learn. Comprehending *is* learning. This shelves the issue of learning to some extent. The processes of learning are less important than the conditions for successful learning. The style again uses a black box model that does not concern itself with specific processes of L2 learning, but with the nature of the input. While the black box of the social communicative style draws on social interaction, the black box of the information communicative style draws on information exchange. It is another form of laissez-faire.

The style links listening and speaking in a conversion model. Listening is not just a separate skill from speaking, but forms the foundation for speaking. Learning how to listen helps the person with other skills as well as listening. Knowledge acquired by listening converts into knowledge of speaking. This ignores the distinctive features, memory systems and processes involved in each skill. The problem is also the obverse of the social communicative model in that it provides no guidance how to construct discourse by putting sentences together for a particular purpose. It is hard to see how TPR gets the student to build up natural exchanges in the world outside the classroom since they are experiencing a particular style of classroom interaction rather than any simulation of non-classroom exchanges. TPR ignores the twofold nature of classroom language mentioned in chapter Six. Listening tasks often train people to do listening tasks rather than to engage in interaction in the world outside.

As with the other teaching styles, L2 research points to the partial coverage of language content, components of language, and processes of language. The information communicative style also has little connection with multilingual use of language but assumes an imitation monolingual speaker. The suggestions for the teacher are as usual to balance it against other demands of teaching. The style may be made more relevant to the students' goal by adapting the techniques in various ways. In particular the listening tasks it employs can be chosen to correspond to those the students will meet in the world outside the classroom, rather than being arbitrary tasks in which anything goes provided it carries a message. This step is a useful preparation for the later transition to non-classroom use of language, without sacrificing the principles of the style. Indeed the nature of listening itself could be built upon; systematic attention to teaching the listening processes of access to vocabulary, parsing, and relating the text to prior knowledge might be useful.

The information communicative style of language teaching

Typical teaching techniques:
  information gap, roleplays

Goals:
  getting students to comprehend information in the L2

Type of student:
  any that don't want necessarily to speak

Learning assumptions:
  learning by comprehending information in the classroom leads to full ability to use language

Processing assumptions:
  blackbox — decoding is the same as codebreaking

Classroom assumptions:
  teacher-dominated; classroom type exchanges

Weaknesses from L2 research perspective:
  — failure to specify the nature of learning itself
  — narrowness of components and processes covered

Suggestions for the teacher
  — adapt to goals of students and to less classroom-based language
  — develop specific processes of listening

The mainstream EFL style

The mainstream EFL style has developed in British-influenced EFL from the 1930s up to the present day. Till the early 1970s, it mostly reflected a compromise between the academic and the audiolingual styles. Another name for this style in India was the Structural-Oral-Situational (SOS) method, an acronym that captures several of its main features (Prabhu, 1987). Recently it has taken on aspects of the social communicative style. Palmer in the 1920s saw classroom L2 learning as a balance between the 'studial' capacities by which people learnt a language by studying it like any content subject, that is to say what we have called here an academic style, and the 'spontaneous' capacities through which people learn language naturally and without thinking, seen by him in similar terms to the audiolingual style (Palmer, 1922). Until the seventies this early mainstream style was characterized by the term 'situation' in two senses. In one sense language was to be taught though demonstration in the real classroom situation. In the other sense language teaching was to be organized around the language of the real-life situations the students would encounter — the railway station, the hotel, etc. A lesson using the mainstream EFL style starts with a presentation phase in which the teacher introduces new structures and vocabulary. In the Australian course *Situational English* (Commonwealth Office, 1967) for example the teacher demonstrates the use of "can" for ability 'situationally' to the students by touching the floor and trying unsuccessfully to touch the ceiling to illustrate "can" versus "can't", until there are clear signs that the students understand them.

The next stage of the lesson usually involves a short dialogue. In this case it might be a job interview which includes several examples of "can" — "Can you drive a car?", or "I can speak three languages". The students listen to the dialogue, they repeat parts of it, they are asked questions about it, and so on. Then they might see a substitution table from which they have to make sentences with "can" by combining words from different columns — "John can speak French", "Helen can ride a bicycle". Both types of L2 learning capacity mentioned by Palmer are included. The studial capacities are involved in the conscious understanding of structures such as "can", while the repetition and substitution activities use the spontaneous capacities.

Since around 1970, the mainstream EFL style has incorporated aspects of the social communicative style. A typical modern coursebook such as *Headway* (Soares & Soares, 1987) for instance has elements of the academic style in that it explains structures such as the passive; "Passive sentences move the focus of a sentence from the subject to the object of an active sentence". It has elements of the audiolingual style in that it is graded around structures and the 'four skills'. It has elements of the social communicative style in pairwork exercises such as acting out conversations about choosing Christmas presents. A typical lesson such as Unit 9 focuses on conditional sentences. First it presents conditionals in a short dialogue; this develops into pairwork on 'imaginary fears'; then the three types of conditional sentence are explained, followed by a questionnaire on your life expectancy ("If you finished university add 1"); it goes on to an exercise of converting proverbs into conditionals and finishes with a task-listening exercise and a reading passage.

The pivot around which the lesson revolves is the grammatical point, couched in terms of structural or traditional grammar. The main difference from the early mainstream style is the use of group and pairwork and the information orientation to the exercises. A mainstream EFL method is implied every time a teacher goes through the classic progression from presentation of the function through teaching the dialogue to controlled practice. It is the central style described in such TEFL manuals as *A Training Course for English* (Hubbard *et al.*, 1983), or *The Practice of English Language Teaching* (Harmer, 1983). It represents the mainstream EFL teaching of the past thirty years, if not longer.

The goals are in a sense updated versions of audiolingualism. What counts is how students use language in the eventual real-world situation rather than their academic knowledge or the spin-off in general educational values. The version of learning involved is similarly a compromise, suggesting that students learn by conscious understanding, by sheer practice, and by attempting to talk to each other. Some aspects of the knowledge models seen in the last chapter are reflected here, as are aspects of the processing models. Mainstream EFL teaching tries to have its cake and eat it by saying if the student doesn't benefit from one part of the lesson, then another part will help. In terms of student types as well, this broadens the coverage. One student benefits from the grammatical explanation, another from structure practice, another from roleplay. Perhaps combining these together will suit more of the students more of the time than relying on a purer style. It does not usually encompass the information communicative style with its emphasis on listening, preferring to see listening and speaking as more or less inseparable.

It has the drawbacks common to the other styles — the concentration on certain types of grammar and discourse at the expense of others. Is such a combination of styles into one mainstream style to be praised or blamed? In terms of teaching methods, this has been discussed in terms of 'eclecticism'.

The mainstream EFL style of language teaching

Typical teaching techniques:
  presentation, substitution, roleplay

Goal:
  getting students to know and use language

Type of student:
  any

Learning assumptions:
  understanding, practice, and use

Processing assumptions:
  none

Classroom assumptions:
  both teacher-controlled and groups

Weaknesses from L2 research perspective:
  — combination of other styles
  — lack of L1 role
  — drawbacks of mixture of styles

Suggestions for teacher
  — do not worry about the mixture of different sources
  — remember that it still does not cover all aspects relevant to L2 teaching

Some have argued that there is nothing wrong with eclectic mixing of methods provided the mixing is rationally based. Others have claimed that it is impossible for the students to learn in so many different ways simultaneously; the teacher is irresponsible to combine incompatible models of language learning. Marton (1988) argues that only certain sequences between methods are possible. His receptive strategy for instance may precede, but not follow, the reconstructive or communicative strategies.

This book has illustrated some of the complexities of L2 learning. Each of the teaching styles captures some aspects of this complexity and misses out on others. None of the teaching styles is complete, just as none of the models of L2 learning is complete. Eclecticism is only an issue if two styles concern the same area of L2 learning rather than different areas. Hence it is, at the moment, unnecessary to speculate about the good or bad consequences of eclecticism. When there is a choice between competing styles of language teaching, each with a coverage ranging from grammar to classroom language, from memory to pronunciation, from motivation to the roles of the L2 in society, then eclecticism becomes an issue. At the moment all teaching methods are partial in L2 learning terms. Some areas of language are only covered by one type of teaching technique. Some methods conversely deal with only a fraction of the totality of L2 learning. Hence the mainstream EFL style cannot be dismissed simply because of its eclecticism, as it is neither more nor less eclectic than any other overall teaching style in terms of L2 learning.

Other styles

Other teaching styles have been proposed in recent years that mark a radical departure from those outlined earlier, either in their goals or in their execution. It is difficult to assign these a single name. Some have been called 'alternative methods', but this suggests there is a common conventional method to which they provide an alternative and that they are themselves united in their approach. Some are referred to as 'humanistic methods' because of their links to 'humanistic psychology', but this label suggests religious or philosophical connections that are mostly inappropriate. Others are called 'self-access' or 'self-directed learning'. In England the practice of these styles is still so rare that they are difficult to observe in a full-blooded form, although every EFL or modern language teaching class probably shows some influence from communicative teaching.

Let us start with Community Language Learning (CLL), derived from the work of Curran (1976). Picture a beginners class in which the students sit in a circle from which the teacher is excluded. One student starts a conversation by remarking "Weren't the buses terrible this morning?" in his L1. The teacher translates this into the language the students are learning and the student repeats it. Another student answers "When do the buses ever run on time?" in her L1, which is translated once again by the teacher, and repeated by the student. And the conversation between the students proceeds in this way. The teacher records the translations said by the students and later uses them for conventional practice of an audiolingual or academic kind. But the core element of the class is spontaneous conversation following the student's lead, with the teacher offering the support facility of instant translation. As the students progress to later stages they become increasingly independent of the teacher's support. CLL is one of the 'humanistic' methods that include Suggestopedia with its aim of relaxing the student (Lozanov, 1978), the Silent Way with its concentration on the expression of meaning through coloured rods (Gattegno, 1972), and Confluent Language Teaching with its emphasis on the classroom experience as a whole (Galyean, 1977).

In general CLL subordinates language to the self-expression of emotions and ideas. If anything, language gets in the way of the clear expression of the student's feelings. The aim is not at the end of the day to be able to do anything with language in the world outside. It is to do something here and now in the classroom, so that the student, in Curran's words, 'arrives at a more positive view of himself, of his situation, of what he wishes to do and to become' (Curran, 1976). A logical extension is the use of language teaching for psychotherapy in mental hospitals. Speaking in a second language about their problems is easier for some people than in the first language.

The goal of teaching is to develop the students' potential and to enable them to 'come alive' through L2 learning, not to help them directly to communicate with others outside the group. Hence it sees language teaching in terms of individual goals. It stresses the general educational value for the individual rather than any local or international benefits. The student in some way becomes a better person through language teaching. The concept of 'better' is usually defined as greater insight into one's self, one's feelings and one's relationships with others. Learning a language through a humanistic style has the same virtues as jogging; it does you good and it is worthy at the same time. This type of goal partly accounts for the comparative lack of impact of CLL on the mainstream educational system, where language teaching is often thought of as having more benefit outside the classroom, and where self-fulfilment through the classroom has been seen more as a product of lessons in the mother tongue and its literature, as the film *Dead Poets' Society* demonstrated. Hence the humanistic styles are often the preserve of part-time education or self-improvement classes. The goals of realizing the individual's potential are perhaps coincidentally attached to L2 teaching; they might be achieved as well through mother-tongue teaching, aerobics, Zen, assertiveness training, or motor-cycle maintenance. Curran says indeed that CLL 'can be readily adapted to the learning of other subjects'; Suggestopedia similarly is supposed to apply to all education; the Silent Way comes out of an approach to teaching mathematics.

A strong similarity between humanistic styles is that they see a 'true' method of L2 learning that can be unveiled by freeing the learner from inhibiting factors. L2 learning takes place if the learner's inner self is set free by providing the right circumstances for learning. If teachers provide stress-free, non-dependent, value-respecting teaching, students will learn.

Hence a black box model of learning is again invoked. While no-one knows what mechanisms exist in the students' minds, we know what conditions will help them work. So the CLL model of learning is not dissimilar to the communicative learning-by-doing. If you're expressing yourself, you're learning the language, even if such expression takes place through the teacher's mediating translation.

The other humanistic styles are equally unlinked to mainstream L2 learning research. Suggestopedia is based on an overall theory of learning and education. The conditions of learning are tightly controlled in order to overcome the learner's resistance to the new language. Lozanov, its inventor, has indeed carried out numerous psychological experiments, mostly unavailable in English, which make particular claims for the effective learning of vocabulary (Lozanov, 1978). Again, where the outlines of an L2 learning model can be discerned, it resembles the processing models seen in the last chapter.

Oddly enough, while the fringe humanistic styles take pride in their learner centredness, they take little account of the variation between learners. CLL would clearly appeal to extrovert students rather than introverts. Their primary motivation would have to be neither instrumental nor integrative, since both of these lead away from the group. Instead it would have to be self-related or teaching-group related. What happens within the group itself and what the students get out of it are what matters, not what they can do with the language outside. Nor, despite their psychological overtones, do methods such as CLL and Suggestopedia pay much attention to the performance processes of speech production and comprehension.

An opposing trend in teaching styles is the move towards learner autonomy. Let us look at a student called Mr D, described by Henner-Stanchina (1985). Mr D is a brewery engineer who went to the CRAPEL in France to develop his reading skills in English. He chose, out of a set of options, to have the services of a 'helper', to have personal teaching materials, and to use the sound library. The first session with the helper revealed that his difficulties were, *inter alia*, with complex noun phrases and with the meanings of verb forms. Later sessions dealt with specific points from this, using the helper as a check on the hypotheses he was forming from the texts he read. The helper's role faded out as he was able to progress through technical documents with increasing ease.

The aim above all is to hand over responsibility for learning to the student. The teacher is a helper who assists with choice of materials and advises what to do but does not teach directly. As Holec (1985a) from the CRAPEL (Centre de Reserches et d'Applications Pédagogiques en Langues) puts it, 'By becoming autonomous, that is by gradually and individually acquiring the capacity to conduct his own learning programme, the learner progressively becomes his own teacher and constructs and evaluates his learning programme himself'. Using autonomous learning depends on devising a system through which students have the choice of learning in their own way. To quote Holec (1987) again, 'Learners gradually replace the belief that they are "consumers" of language courses . . . with the belief that they can be "producers" of their own learning program and that this is their right.'

At North-East London Polytechnic in the 1970s, we had a simple system in which students could make use of language teaching material of their own choice from the selection provided in a language laboratory at any time. One afternoon per week, helpers were available in all the languages on offer. These could be used by the students in any way they liked, say discussion of which materials to use, or assessment of progress, or straightforward conversation practice. Dickinson (1987) describes more sophisticated systems in operation at the Language Laboratory in Cambridge University, at Moray House in Edinburgh, and the system encountered by Mr D at the CRAPEL in Nancy. But self-direction can also be offered to children within the secondary school classroom. Leni Dam in Copenhagen uses a system of group-based tasks chosen by the students to suit their own needs and interests, what they want to learn, and how they want to learn.

Autonomous learning is not yet widely used, nor is it clear that it would fit in with many mainstream educational systems. One reason is the incompatibility between the individual nature of the instruction and the collective nature of most classrooms and assessment. Autonomous learning takes the learner-centredness of the humanistic styles a stage further in refusing to prescribe a patent method that all learners have to follow. It is up to the student to decide on goals, on methods, and on assessment. That is what freedom is all about. Hence in a sense autonomous learning is free of many of the criticisms levelled against other styles. No teaching technique, no type of learner, no area of language is excluded in principle. Nevertheless much depends upon the role of the helper and the support system. Without suitable guidance, students may not be aware of the possibilities. The helper has the difficult job of turning the student's initial preconceptions of language and of language learning into those attitudes that are most effective for that student. L2 learning research can assist autonomous learning by ensuring that the support systems for the learner reflect a genuine range of choices with an adequate coverage of the diverse nature of L2 learning.

The diversity of L2 teaching styles seen in this chapter may seem confusing: how can students really be learning language in so many ways? However, such diversity reflects the complexity of language and the range of student needs; why should one expect that a system as complex as language could be mastered in a single way? Even adding these teaching styles together gives an inadequate account of the totality of L2 learning. Second language learning means learning in all of these ways and in many more. This chapter has continually been drawing attention to the gaps in the coverage of each teaching style. As teachers and methodologists become more aware of L2 learning research, so teaching methods will alter to take them into account and cover a wider range of learning. Much L2 learning is concealed behind such global terms as 'communication' or such two-way

---

Other styles of language teaching

Typical teaching techniques:
   CLL, Suggestopedia, Confluent Language Teaching, self-directed learning

Goals:
   individual: development of the potential; self-selected
   type of student: those with individual motivation etc.

Learning assumptions:
   diverse, mostly learning by doing, or a processing model

Processing assumptions:
   none

Classroom assumptions:
   usually small groups with cofigurative or even prefigurative aims

Weaknesses from L2 research perspective:
   — black box view of learning or partial idiosyncratic views
   — little attention to learner variation in humanistic styles
   — difficulties in generalising to many educational situations

Suggestions for teachers:
   — importance of students feelings and involvement
   — provision of student choice throughout

---

oppositions as 'experiential/analytic' or indeed such simplistic divisions into six teaching styles. To improve teaching we need to appreciate learning in all its complexity

But teachers live in the present. They have to teach now rather than wait for a whole new L2 learning framework to emerge. They must get on with meeting the needs of the students, even if they still don't know enough about L2 learning. A psychoanalyst treating an individual patient has to set aside theories in order to respond to the uniqueness of that particular person. Teachers also have the duty to respond to their students. To serve the unique needs of actual students, the teacher needs to do whatever is necessary, not just that which is scientifically proven and based on abstract theory.

And the teacher needs to take into account far more than the area of L2 learning research; in the present state of knowledge L2 learning research has no warrant to suggest that any current teaching is more than partially justified. This book has therefore made suggestions and comments rather than asserted dogmatic axioms. Practising teachers should weigh them against all the other factors in their unique teaching situation before deciding how seriously to take them. Considering teaching from an L2 learning perspective in such a way will, it is hoped, lead in the future to a more comprehensive, scientifically-based view of language teaching.

References

An overall discussion from a slightly American perspective (i.e. no discussion of audiovisual methods, graded objectives, and other European movements) is Richards, J.C. and Rodgers, T.S. (1986). *Approaches and Methods in Language Teaching*. CUP; the balance is slightly redressed by Marton, W. (1988). *Methods in English Language Teaching*. Hemel Hempstead, Prentice Hall. Other useful books: for the audiolingual style, Lado, R. (1964). *Language Teaching: A Scientific Approach*. McGraw-Hill; for self-directed learning, Dickinson, L. (1987). *Self-instruction in Language Learning*. CUP

EFL Course books mentioned in text

Abbs, B. and Freebairn, I. (1982). *Opening Strategies*. Longman, Harlow

Abbs, B. and Freebairn, I. (1990). *Blueprint One*. Longman, Harlow

Baker, A. (1981). *Ship or Sheep?*. CUP

Blundell, J., Higgins, J. and Middlemiss, N. (1982). *Function in English*. OUP

Bosewitz, R. (1987). *The Penguin English Grammar*, Penguin, Harmondsworth

Capelle, G. Pavik, C. and Segal M.K (1985). *I Love English, Level 1*. Regents, New York

Carrier, M., Haines, S. and Christie, D. (1985). *Break Into English*, Hodder and Stoughton, Sevenoaks

Commonwealth Office of Education (1967). *Situational English*, Longman, London

Cook, V.J. (1968). *Active Intonation*, Longman, London

Cook, V.J. (1975). *English Topics*, OUP

Cook, V.J. (1979). *Using Intonation*, Longman, Harlow

Cook, V.J. (1980). *People and Places*, Pergamon. Polish edition, Polish Scientific Publishers 1987

Cook, V.J. (1982). *Meeting People*, Pergamon. Polish edition, Polish Scientific Publishers, 1987

Dalzell, S. and Edgar, I. (1988). *English in Perspective*, OUP

Davies, E. and Whitney, N. (1979). *Reasons for Reading*. Heinemann, London

Davies, G. and Senior, M. (1983). *South Africa — the Privileged and the Dispossessed*, Fredinand Schoningh, Paderborn

Despotova, V., Shopov, T. and Stoyanka, V. (1988). *English for the Fifth Class*, Narodna Prosveta, Sofia

Edina, B.A. and Ivanne, S. (1987). *Angol Nyelv Alapfoken*, Tankonyvkiado, Budapest

Ellis, G. and Sinclair, B. (1989). *Learning to Learn English*, CUP

Garton-Sprenger, J. and Greenall, S. (1990). *Flying Colours 1*, Heinemann, London

Graf, G. (1983). *English for You*. Volk and Wissen Volkseigener Verlag, Berlin

Harmer, J. and Surguine, H. (1987). *Coast to Coast*, Longman, Harlow
Klippel, F. (1984). *Keep Talking*, CUP
Molinsky, S.J. and Bliss, B. (1989). *Side by Side*, Prentice-Hall, New Jersey
Northern Territory Dept. of Education (1979). *Tracks*, Northern Territory
  Dept. of Education, Australia
Oxford, R.L. (1990). *Language Learning Strategies*, Newbury House
Rudzka, B. Channell, J. Putseys, Y. and Ostyn, P. (1981). *The Words You
  Need*, Macmillan, London
Soares, J. and Soares, M. (1987). *Headway*, OUP.
Swan, M. and Walters, C. (1984). *The Cambridge English Course*, CUP
Willis, J. and Willis, D. (1987). *The COBUILD English Course I*, Collins,
  London
Willis, J. and Willis, D. (1989). *The COBUILD English Course II*, Collins,
  London
Wright, A. (1987). *How to Improve Your Memory*, CUP

References

Adams, S.J. (1983), 'Scripts and Second Language Reading Skills', in Oller, J.W., Jr., and Ricard-Amato, P.A. (eds.) (1983), *Methods that Work*, Newbury House

Allen, P., Swain, M., Harley, B., and Cummins, J. (1990), 'Aspects of classroom treatment: toward a more comprehensive view of second language education', in Harley, B., Allen, P., Cummins, J., and Swain, M. (eds.) (1990), *The Development of Second Language Proficiency*, CUP

Allwright, D. (1988), *Observation in the Language Classroom,* Harlow, Longman

Alptekin, C. and Atakan, S. (1990), 'Field-dependence — independence and hemisphericity as variables in L2 achievements', *Second Language Research,* 6,2, 135–149

Altenberg, E.P., and Cairns, H.S. (1983), 'The effects of phonotactic constraints on lexical processing in bilingual and monolingual subjects', *JVLVB*, 22, 174-188

Andersen, R.W. (ed.) (1983), *Pidginisation and Creolisation as Language Acquisition*, Newbury House

Anderson, J. (1983), *The Architecture of Cognition*, Harvard University Press

Anthony, E.M. (1963), 'Approach, method and technique', *English Language Teaching*, 17, 63-7

Arnberg, L. (1987), *Raising Children Bilingually: The Pre-school Years*, Multilingual Matters, Clevedon

Asher. J. (1986), *Learning Another Language Through Actions: the Complete Teacher's Guidebook*, Sky Oaks Productions, Los Gatos, CA

Asher, J., and Garcia, G. (1969), 'The optimal age to learn a foreign language', *Modern Language Journal*, 38, 334-341

Asher, J., and Price, B. (1967), 'The learning strategy of total physical response: some age differences', *Child Development*, 38, 1219-1227

Assessment of Performance Unit (1986), *Foreign Language Performance in Schools: Report on 1984 Survey of French*, Dept. of Education and Science, UK

Bacon, S. (1987), 'Differentiated cognitive style and oral performance', in VanPatten, B., Dvorak, T.R., and Lee, J.F. (eds.) (1987) *Foreign Language Learning: A Research Perspective*, Newbury House

Baddeley, A.D. (1986), *Working Memory*, Clarendon Press, Oxford

Bahrick, H.P. (1984), 'Semantic memory content in permastore: fifty years of memory for Spanish learned in school', *J. Exp. Psychol.:General*, 113, 1, 1-30

Bahrick, H.P., and Phelps, E. (1987), 'Retention of Spanish vocabulary over eight years', *J. Exp. Psychol.: Learning, Memory and Cognition*, 13, 2, 344-349

Bates, E., and MacWhinney, B. (1981), 'Second language acquisition from a functionalist perspective', in H. Winitz (ed.), *Native Language and Foreign Language Acquisition*, Annals of the NY Academy of Sciences, Vol. 379

Ben Zeev, S. (1977), 'The influence of bilingualiism on cognitive strategies and cognitive development', *Child Development*, 48, 1009-18

Bialystok, E. (1990), *Communication Strategies*, Blackwell, Oxford

Bialystok, E., and Sharwood-Smith, M. (1985), 'Interlanguage is not a state of mind: an evaluation of the construct for second-language acquisition', *Applied Linguistics*, 6, 1, 101-117

Bickerton, D. (1981), *Roots of Language*, Karoma, Ann Arbor

Biko, S. (1978), *I Write What I Like*, The Bowerdan Press. Reprinted in Penguin, 1988

Bloomfield, L. (1933), *Language*, New York, Holt

Bransford, J.D., and Johnson, M.K. (1982), 'Contextual prerequisites for understanding: some investigations of comprehension and recall', *JVLVB*, 11, 717-726

Broselow, E. (1988), 'Prosodic Phonology and the Acquisition of a Second Language', in S. Flynn and W. O'Neil (eds.), *Linguistic Theory in Second Language Acquisition*, Kluwer, Dordrecht

Brown, G., Anderson, A., Shillcock, R., and Yule, G. (1984), *Teaching Talk: Strategies for Production and Assessment*, CUP

Brown, G., and Yule, G. (1983), *Teaching the Spoken Language*, CUP

Brown, R. (1973), *A First Language: The Early Stages*, London, Allen and Unwin

Bruner, J. (1983), *Child's Talk*, Oxford University Press

Byram, M. (1986), *Minority Education and Ethnic Survival*, Multilingual Matters, Clevedon

Byram, M. (1990), 'Foreign language teaching and young people's perceptions of other cultures', *ELT Documents*, 132

Call, M. (1985), 'Auditory Short-Term Memory, listening comprehension and the Input Hypothesis', *TESOL Quarterly*, 19, 4, 765-781

Cancino, H., Rosansky, E. and Schumann, J. (1978) 'The acquisition of English negative and interrogatives by native Spanish speakers', in E. Hatch (ed.). *Second Language Acquisition*, Newbury House

Caramazza, A, and Brones, I. (1980), 'Semantic classification by bilinguals', *Canad. J. Psychol.*, 34, 1, 77-81

Carrell, P.L. (1983), 'Three components of background knowledge in reading comprehension', *Language Learning*, 33, 2, 183-207

Carrell, P.L. (1984), 'Evidence of a formal schema in second language comprehension', *Language Learning*, 34, 87-111

Carroll, J.B. (1981), 'Twenty-five years of research on foreign language aptitude', in Diller, K.C. (ed.) (1981), *Individual Differences and Universals in Language Learning*, Newbury House, 83-118

Carter, R. (1988), 'Vocabulary, cloze, and discourse', in R. Carter and M. McCarthy (eds.), *Vocabulary and Language Teaching*, Longman

Caskey-Sirmons, L.A., and Hickerson, N.P. (1977), 'Semantic shift and bilingualism: variation in the color terms of five languages', *Anthropological Linguistics*, 19/8, 358-367

Chamot, A. (1987), 'The learning strategies of ESl students', in Wendon, A., and Rubin, J. (ed.) (1987), *Learner Strategies in Language Learning*, Prentice-Hall, New Jersey

Chaudron, C. (1983), 'Research on metalinguistic judgements: a review of theory, methods, and results', *Language Learning*, 33, 3, 343-377

Chaudron, C. (1988), *Second Language Classrooms: Research on Teaching and Learning*, CUP.

Chomsky, N. (1959), 'Review of B.F. Skinner Verbal Behavior', *Language*, 35, pp. 26-58

Chomsky, N. (1986), *Knowledge of Language:Its Nature, Origin and Use*, New York, Praeger

Chomsky, N. (1988), *Language and Problems of Knowledge: The Managua Lectures*, MIT Press

Clark E. (1971), 'On the acquisition of "before" and "after"', *JVLVB*, 10, 266-275

Clark, M.A. (1984), 'On the nature of techniques; what do we owe the gurus?', *TESOL Quarterly*, 18 (4), 577-584

Clement, R., and Kruidenier, B.G. (1983), 'Orientations in second language acquisition:

I. the effects of ethnicity, milieu, and target language on their emergence', *Language Learning*, 33, 3, 274-291

Collin, A., and Holec, H. (1985), 'Foreign language acquisition processes in a secondary school setting: negation', in P. Riley (ed.) (1985)

Commission of the European Communities (1987), *Young Europeans in 1987*, EC Commission

Commission for Racial Equality (1986), *Teaching English as a Second Language: Report of a Formal Investigation in Calderdale Education Authority*

Cook, V.J. (1973), 'The comparison of language development in native children and foreign adults,' *IRAL*, XI/1, 13-28, 1973

Cook, V.J. (1977), 'Cognitive processes in second language learning', *IRAL*, XV/1, 73-90

Cook, V.J. (1979), 'Aspects of memory in secondary school language learners', *Interlanguage Studies Bulletin — Utrecht*, 4, 2, 161-172

Cook, V.J. (1981a), 'Some uses for second language learning research', *Annals of the New York Academy of Sciences*, 379, 251-258

Cook, V.J. (1981b), 'Using authentic materials in the classroom,' *Modern English Teacher*, 9, 2

Cook, V.J. (1982), 'Kategorisierung und Fremdsprachenerwerb', *Gegenwartige Probleme and Aufgaben der Fremdsprachen-psychologie*, Karl Marx University, Leipzig

Cook, V.J. (1983), 'What should language teaching be about?', *English Language Teaching Journal*, 37, 3

Cook, V.J. (1985), 'Language functions, social factors, and second language teaching', *IRAL*, 13, 3, 177-196,

Cook, V.J. (1986), 'Experimental approaches applied to two areas of second language learning research: age and listening-based teaching methods', in Cook, V. (ed.), *Experimental Approaches to Second Language Learning*, Pergamon, Oxford

Cook, V.J. (1988a), *Chomsky's Universal Grammar: An Introduction*, Oxford, Blackwell

Cook, V.J. (1988b), 'Language learners' extrapolation of word order in phrases of Micro-Artificial Languages,' *Language Learning*, 38, 4, 497-529

Cook, V.J. (1989a) 'The relevance of grammar to the applied linguistics of language teaching', *Trinity College Dublin Occasional Papers*, 22

Cook, V.J. (1989b), 'Reciprocal language teaching: another alternative', *Modern English Teacher*, 16, 3/4, 48-53

Cook, V.J. (1990), 'Timed comprehension of binding in advanced learners of English', *Language Learning*, 40, 4, 557–599

Cruz-Ferreira, M. (1986), 'Non-native interpretive strategies for intonational meaning: an experimental study', in James and Leather (1986)

Cummins, J. (1981), 'Age on arrival and immigrant second language learning in Canada: a reassessment', *Applied Linguistics*, 2, 132-49

Curran, C.A. (1976), *Counselling-Learning in Second Languages*, Apple River Press, Apple River Illinois

de Jong, E. (1986), *The Bilingual Experience: A Book For Parents*, CUP

de Saussure, F. (1916), Cours de Linguistique Generale, ed by C.Bally, A., Sechehaye, and A. Reidlinger, Paris, Payot

Dickerson, L. (1975), 'The learner's language as a system of variable rules', *TESOL Quarterly*, 9

Dickerson, W. (1987), 'Explicit rules and the developing interlanguage phonology', in James and Leather (1987)

Dickinson, L. (1987), *Self-instruction in Language Learning*, CUP

Dollerup, C., Glahn, E., and Hansen, C.R. (1989), 'Vocabularies in the reading process', *AILA Review*, 6, 21-33

Dornic, S. (1969), 'Verbal factor in number perception', *Acta Psychologica*, 29, 393-399

Dulay, H.C., and Burt, M.K. (1973), 'Should we teach children syntax?' *Language Learning*, 23/2, 245-258

Dulay, H.C., and Burt, M.K. (1980), 'On acquisition orders', in S. Felix, (ed.), *Second Language Development: Trends and Issues*, Narr, Tubingen

Dulay, H., Burt, M., and Krashen, S. (1983), *Language Two*, Newbury House

Eastern Examining Board (1986), *French*, Eastern Examining Board, Colchester, UK

Eckman, F.R., Bell, L., and Nelson, D. (1988), 'On the generalization of relative clause instruction in the acquisition of English as a Second Language', *Applied Linguistics*, 9, 1, 1-20

Eckstrand, L. (1978), 'Age and length of residence as variables related to the adjustment of migrant children with special reference to second language learning', in G. Nickel (ed.), *Proceedings of the Fourth International Congress of Applied Linguistics*, Stuttgart, Hochschulverlag, 3, 179-197

Ellis, R. (1985), *Understanding Second Language Acquisition*, Oxford University Press

Ellis, R. (1986), *Classroom Second Language Development*, Pergamon

Ellis, R. (1990), *Instructed Second Language Acquisition*, Blackwell, Oxford

Faerch, C., and Kasper, G. (1984), 'Two ways of defining communication strategies', *Language Learning*, 34, 45-63

Faltis, C.J. (1989), 'Codeswitching and bilingual schooling: an examination of Jacobson's new concurrent approach', *Journal of Multilingual and Multicultural Development*, 10, 2, 117-127

Favreau, M., and Segalowitz, N.S. (1982), 'Second language reading in fluent bilinguals', *Applied Psycholinguistics*, 3, 329-341

Felix, S.W. (1981), 'The effect of formal instruction of language acquisition', *Language Learning*, 31, 87-112

Flege, J.E. (1986), 'Effects of equivalence classification on the production of foreign language speech sounds', in James and Leather (1986)

Flege, J.E. (1987), 'The production of "new" and "similar" phones in a foreign language: evidence for the effect of equivalence classification', *Journal of Phonetics*, 15, 47-65

Flege, J.E., and Hillenbrand (1984), 'Limits on phonetic accuracy in foreign language speech production', *J. Acoustical Society of America*, 76, 708-721

Freed, B. (1980), 'Talking to foreigners versus talking to children; similarities and differences', in S.D. Krashen and R.C. Scarcella (eds.), *Issues in Second Language Research*, Newbury House, 19-27

Freire, P. (1972), *Pedagogy of the Oppressed*, Penguin

Frohlich, M., Spada, N., and Allen, P. (1985), 'Differences in the communicative orientation of L2 classrooms', *TESOL Quarterly*, 19, 1, 27-56

Gaies, S.J. (1979), 'Linguistic input in first and second language learning', in Eckman, F.R., and Hastings, A.J. (1979), *Studies in First and Second Language Acquisition*, Newbury House

Galyean, B. (1977), 'A confluent design for language teaching', *TESOL* Quarterly, 11/2

Gardner, R. (1985), *Social Psychology and Second Language Learning*, London, Edward Arnold

Gardner, R.C., and Lambert, W.E. (1972), *Attitudes and Motivation in Second Language Learning*, Rowley, Mass., Newbury House

Gary, J. and Gary, N. (1981a), 'Comprehension-based language instruction: practice,' in H. Winitz (ed.), *Native and Foreign Language Acquisition*, N.Y. Academy of Sciences

Gary, J. and Gary. N. (1981b), 'Caution: talking may be dangerous to your linguistic health', *IRAL*, XIX/1

Gass, S. (1979), 'Language transfer and universal grammatical relations', *Language Learning*, 29/2, 327-344

Gasser, M. (1990), 'Correctionism and universals of second language acquisition', *Studies in Second Language Acquisition*, 12, 2, 179–200

Gattegno, C. (1972), *Teaching Foreign Languages in Schools: the Silent Way*, NY, Educational Solutions

Genesee, F. (1976), 'The role of intelligence in second language learning, *Language Learning*, 26/2, 267–280

Glicksberg, D.H. (1963), 'A study of the span of immediate memory among adult students of English as a Foreign Language', Ph.D., University of Michigan

Grosjean, F. (1982), *Life with Two Languages*, Harvard U.P.

Grosjean, F. (1989), 'Neurolinguists, beware! The bilingual is not two monolinguals in one person', *Brain and Language*, 36, 3-15

Gross M (1990), 'Lexique — Grammaire LADL', paper given at the AILA Congress, Thessaloniki, April

Gruneberg, M. (1987), *The Linkword Language System: French*, London, Corgi

Guiora, A.Z., Brannan, R.C.L., and Dull, C.Y. (1972), 'Empathy and second language learning', *Language Learning*, 22, 2, 111-130

Hakuta, K. (1974), 'A preliminary report on the development of grammatical mor-phemes in a Japanese girl learning English as a second language, *Working Papers on Bilingualism*, 3, 18–38

Halliday, M.A.K. (1975), *Learning How to Mean*, Edward Arnold, London

Hansen, J., and Stansfield, C. (1981), 'The relationship of Field Dependent-Independent cognitive styles to Foreign Language Achievement', *Language Learning*, 31, 2, 349-368

Hansen, L. (1984), 'Field Dependence-Independence and language testing: evidence from six Pacific Island cultures', *TESOL Quarterly*, 18/2, 311-324

Harding, A., Page, B., and Rowell, S. (1981), *Graded Objectives in Modern Languages*, CILTR, London

Harding, E., and Riley, P. (1986), *The Bilingual Family: A Handbook for Parents*, C.U.P.

Harley, B. (1986), *Age in Second Language Acquisition*, Multilingual Matters

Harley, B., Allen, P., Cummins, J., and Swain, M. (eds.) (1990), *The Development of Second Language Proficiency*, CUP

Harmer, J. (1983), *The Practice of English Language Teaching*, Longman

Harrington, M. (1987), 'Processing transfer: language specific processing strategies as a source of interlanguage variation', *Applied Psycholinguistics*, 8, 351-377

Hatch, E. (1978), 'Discourse Analysis and Second Language Acquisition', in E. Hatch (ed.), *Second Language Acquisition: A Book of Readings*, Newbury House

Hatch, E., and Hawkins, B. (1987), 'Second language acquisition: an experiential approach', in S. Rosenberg (ed.), *Advances in Applied Psycholinguistics*, Volume 2, C.U.P.

Hawkins, E. (1984), *Awareness of Language*, C.U.P.

Hawkins, J.A. (1983), *Word Order Universals*, New York, Academic Press

Henner-Stanchina, C. (1986), 'From reading to writing acts', in Riley (ed.) 1986, 91-104

Holec, H. (1985a), 'On autonomy: some elementary concepts', in Riley (1985)

Holec, H. (1985b), 'You did say 'oral interactive discourse'?', in Riley (1985)

Holec, H. (1987), 'The learner as manager: managing learning or managing to learn?', in Wendon and Rubin (1987)

Hooton, A.B., and Hooton, C. (1977), 'The influence of syntax on visual perception', *Anthropological Linguistics*, 19/8. 355-357

Horwitz, E.K. (1986), 'Surveying student beliefs about language learning', in Wendon and Rubin (1987)

Howatt, A. (1984), *A History of English Language Teaching*, Oxford University Press

Hubbard, P., Jones. H., Thornton, B. and Wheeler, R. (1983), *A Training Course for TEFL*, OUP

Hullen, W. (1989), 'Investigations into classroom discourse', in Dechert, H. (ed.) *Current Trends in European Second Language Acquisition Research*, Clevedon, Multilingual Matters

Hyams, N. (1986), *Language Acquisition and the Theory of Parameters*, Reidel, Dordrecht

Hymes, D. (1972), 'Competence and performance in linguistic theory', in R. Huxley and E. Ingram (eds.), *Language Acquisition: Models and Methods*, New York, Academic Press

Ianco-Worrall, A. (1972), 'Bilingualism and cognitive development', *Child Development*, 43, 1390-1400

Ioup, G., and Tansomboon, A. (1987), 'The acquisition of tone: a maturational perspective', in Ioup, G., and Weinberger, S.H. (eds.) (1987), *Interlanguage Phonology*, Newbury House

Institute of Linguists (1988), *Examinations in Languages for International Communication*, Institute of Linguists, London

James, A., and Leather, J. (eds.) (1986), *Sound Patterns In Second Language Acquisition*, Dordrecht, Foris

Jespersen, O. (1904), *How to Teach a Foreign Language*, London, Allen and Unwin

Keenan, E. and Comrie,B. (1977), 'Noun phrase accessibility and universal grammar', *Linguistic Inquiry*, 8, 63-100

Kellerman, E. (1986), 'An eye for an eye: constraints of the L2 lexicon', in Kellerman, E., and Sharwood-Smith, M. (eds.), *Crosslinguistic Influences in Second Language Acquisition*, Pergamon

Kellerman, E., Bongaerts, T., and Poulisse, N. (1987), 'Strategy and system in L2 referential communication', in Ellis, R. (ed.) *Second Language Acquisition in Context*, London, Prentice-Hall

Kellerman, E., Ammerlaan, T., Bongaerts, T., and Poulisse, N. (1990), 'System and hierarchy in L2 compensatory strategies', in Scarcella, R.C., Andersen, E.S., and Krashen, S.D. (eds.) *Developing Communicative Competence in a Second Language*, NY, Newbury House

Kementerian Pendidikan Malaysia (1987), *Sukatan Pelajaran Sekolah Menengah: Bahasa Inggeris*, PPK, Malaysia

Kenworthy, J. (1987), *Teaching English Pronunciation*, Longman

Kilborn, K., and Cooreman, A. (1987), 'Sentence interpretation strategies in adult Dutch-English bilinguals', *Applied Psycholinguistics*, 8, 415-431

Kirsner, K., Brown, H.L., Abrol, S., Chadha, N.K., and Sharma, N.K. (1980), 'Bilingualism and lexical representation', *Q. J. Exp. Psychol.*, 32, 585-594

Krashen, S. (1981a), *Second Language Acquisition and Second Language Learning*, Oxford, Pergamon

Krashen, S. (1981b), 'The Fundamental Pedagogical Principle in Second Language Teaching,' in B. Sigurd and J. Svartvik (eds.), *AILA 1981*, CWK Gleerup,

Krashen, S., Scarcella, R., and Long, M. (eds.) (1982), *Child-Adult Differences in Second Language Acquisition*, Newbury House

Krashen, S., Sferlazza, V., Feldman, L., and Fathman, A. (1976), 'Adult performance on the SLOPE test: more evidence for a natural sequence in adult second language acquisition', *Language Learning*, 26, 1, 145-151

Krashen, S. and Terrell, T.D. (1983), *The Natural Approach*, Pergamon

Lado, R. (1964), *Language Teaching: A Scientific Approach*, McGraw-Hill

Lambert, W. (1981), 'Bilingualism and language acquisition', in H. Winitz (ed.), *Native and Foreign Language Acquisition*, N.Y. Academy of Sciences

Lambert, W.E. (1990), 'Persistent issues in bilingualism', in Harley et al (eds).

Landry, R.G. (1974), 'A comparison of second language learners and monolinguals on divergent thinking tasks at the elementary school level', *MLJ*, 58, 10-15

Laponce, J.A. (1987), *Languages and their Territories*, University of Toronto Press

Larsen-Freeman, D. (1976), 'An explanation for the morpheme order of second language learners', *Language Learning*, 26, 125-34

Leather, J. (1987), 'F_0 pattern inferences in the perceptual acquisition of second language tone', in James and Leather (1987)

Lee, D.J. (1981), 'Interpretation of morpheme rank ordering in L2 research', in P. Dale and D. Ingram (eds.)

Lenneberg, E. (1967), *Biological Foundations of Language*, New York, Wiley

Levenston, E.A. (1979), 'Second Language Acquisition: Issues and Problems', *Interlanguage Studies Bulletin-Utrecht*, 4, 2, 147-160

Lightbown, P.M. (1987), 'Classroom language as input to second language acquisition', in C.W. Pfaff (ed.) *First and Second Language Acquisition Processes*, Newbury House

Linguistic Minorities Project (1983), *Linguistic Minorities in England*, University of London Institute of Education, distributed by Tinga Tonga

Little, D., Devitt, S., and Singleton, D. (1988), *Authentic Texts in Foreign Language Teaching: Theory and Practice*, Dublin, Authentik

Littlewood, W. (1981), *Communicative Language Teaching*, C.U.P.

Long, J., and Harding-Esch, E. (1977), 'Summary and recall of text in first and second languages: some factors contributing to performance difficulties', in H. Sinmaiko and D. Gerver (eds.), *Proceedings of the NATO Symposium on Language Interpretation and Communication*, Plenum Press

Long, M.H. (1983), 'Does second language instruction make a difference? A review of the research', *TESOL Quarterly*, 17, 359-82

Lozanov, G. (1978), *Suggestology and Outlines of Suggestopedia*, New York, Gordon and Breach

MacWhinney, B. (1987), 'Applying the Competition Model to bilingualism', *Applied Psycholinguistics*, 8, 315-327

Mackey, W.F. (1967), *Bilingualism as a World Problem*, Montreal, Harvest House

Magiste, E. (1979), 'The competing linguistic systems of the multilingual: a developmental study of decoding and encoding processes', *JVLVB*, 18, 79-89

Major, R. (1986), 'The natural phonology of second language acqusition', in James and Leather (1986)

Makino, T. (1980), 'Acquisition order of English morphemes by Japanese secondary school students', *Journal of Hokkaido University of Education*, 30, 2, 101-148

Marsh, L.G. and Maki, R.H. (1978), 'Efficiency of arithmetic operations in bilinguals as a function of language', *Memory and Cognition*, 4/4, 459-464

Marton, W. (1988), *Methods in English Language Teaching*, Hemel Hempstead, Prentice Hall

McDonald, J. (1987), 'Sentence interpretation in bilingual speakers of English and Dutch', *Applied Psycholinguistics*, 8, 379-413

McLaughlin, B. (1987), *Theories of Second-Language Learning*, Edward Arnold, London

McLaughlin, B., Rossman, R., and McLeod, B. (1983), 'Second language learning: an information-processing perspective', *Language Learning*, 33, 135-158

Mead, M. (1970), *Culture and Commitment*, London, Bodley Head

Milon, J.P. (1974), 'The development of negation in English by a second language learner', *TESOL Quarterly*, 8, 2, 137-143

Ministry of Education, Science and Culture (Japan) (1983), *Course of Study for Upper Secondary Schools in Japan*

Morgan, J.L. (1986), *From Simple Input to Complex Grammar*, MIT Press

Myhill, M. (1990),'Socio-cultural content in ESL programmes for newly arrived and NESB and Aboriginal school children in Western Australia, *English Language Teaching Documents*, 132, 117–131

Naiman, N., Frohlich, M., Stern, H.H., and Todesco, A. (1978), *The Good Language Learner*, Toronto, OISE

Nathan, G.S. (1987), 'On second-language acquisition of voiced stops', *Journal of Phonetics*, 15, 313-322

Neufeld, G. (1978), 'On the acquisition of prosodic and articulatory features in adult language learning', *Canadian Modern Language Review*, 34, 163-174

Nunan, D. (1989), *Designing Tasks for the Communicative Classroom*, C.U.P.

Odlin, T. (1989), *Language Transfer*, CUP

O'Mahoney, M., and Muhiudeen, H. (1977), 'A preliminary study of alternative taste languages using qualitative description of sodium chloride solutions: Malay versus English', *British Journal of Psychology*, 68, 275-278

O'Malley, J.M., and Chamot, A.U. (1990), *Learning Strategies in Second Language Acquisition*, CUP

O'Malley, J.M., Chamot, A.U., Stewner-Manzares, G., Kupper, L., and Russo, R.P. (1985a), 'Learning strategies used by beginning and intermediate ESL students', *Language Learning*, 35, 21-46

O'Malley, J.M., Chamot, A.U., Stewner-Manzares, G., Russo, R.P. and Kupper, L. (1985b), 'Learning strategy applications with students of English as a Second Language', *TESOL Quarterly*, 19, 3, 557-584

O'Malley, J.M., Chamot, A.U., and Kupper, L. (1989), 'Listening comprehension strategies in second language acquisition', *Applied Linguistics*, 10, 4, 418-437

Ornstein, P.A., and Naus, M.J. (1978), 'Rehearsal processes in children's memory', in Ornstein, P. (ed.), *Memory Development*, Hillsdale N.J., Lawrence Erlbaum

Palmer, H.E. (1926), *The Principles of Language Study*, London, Harrap

Paulston, C.B. (1986), 'Linguistic consequences of ethnicity and nationalism in multilingual settings', in Spolsky, B. (ed.) (1986), *Language and Education in Multilingual Settings*, Clevedon, Multilingual Matters

Pienemann, M. (1986), 'Psychological constraints on the teachability of language', in Pfaff, C.W. (ed.), *First and Second Language Acquisition Processes*, Rowley MA, Newbury House

Pienemann, M., and Johnston, M., (1987), 'Factors influencing the development of language proficiency', in D. Nunan (ed.), *Applying Second Language Research*, NCRC, Adelaide, Australia, 45-141

Pittenger, R.E., Hockett, C.F., and Danbury, J.J. (1960), *The First Five Minutes: A Sample of Microscopic Interview Analysis*, Ithaca, Paul Marteneau

Poplack, S. (1980), 'Sometimes I'll start a sentence in English y termino en espanol', *Linguistics*, 18, 581-616

Porter, P.A. (1986), 'How learners talk to each other: input and interaction in task-centered discussions', in Day, R.R. (ed.) *Talking to Learn: Conversation in Second Language Acquisition*, Newbury House

Postovsky. V. (1974), 'Effects of delay in oral practice at the beginning of second language learning', *MLJ*, 58

Poulisse, N. (1987), 'Classification of compensatory strategies', *Second Language Research*, 3, 2, 141-153

Prabhu, N.S. (1987), *Second Language Pedagogy*, OUP

Prodromou, L. (1989), 'English as cultural action', *English Language Teaching Journal*, 43

Ramsey, C., and Wright, C. (1974), 'Age and second language learning', *Journal of Social Psychology*, 94, 115-21

Richards, J.C., and Rodgers, T.S. (1986), *Approaches and Methods in Language Teaching*, Cambridge University Press

Riley, P. (1985), 'Mud and stars: personal constructs, sensitization, and learning', in Riley, P. (ed.) (1985), *Discourse and Learning*, Longman, London

Riley, P. (ed.) (1985), *Discourse and Learning*, Longman, London

Rivers, W.M. (1964), *The Psychologist and the Foreign Language Teacher*, Chicago University Press

Romaine, S. (1989), *Bilingualism*, Oxford, Blackwell

Rosch, E. (1977), 'Human categorisation', in N. Warren (ed.), *Studies in Cross-Cultural Psychology*, New York, Academic Press

Rossier, R. (1976), 'Extroversion-introversion as a significant variable in the learning of oral English as a second language', Ph.D., USC

Rumelhart, D.E., and McClelland, J.L. (1986), 'On learning the past tenses of English verbs,' in J.L. McLelland, D.E. Rumelhart, and the PDP Research Group, *Parallel Distributed Processing: Volume 2 Psychological and Biological Models*, Cambridge Ma; MIT, 216-271

Rutherford, W.E. (1987), *Second Language Grammar: Learning and Teaching*, Harlow, Longman

Sampson, G.P. (1984), 'Exporting language teaching methods from Canada to China', *TESL Canada Journal*, 1, 1

Saunders, G. (1982), *Bilingual Children: Guidance for the Family*, Clevedon, Multilingual Matters

Schank, R., and Abelson. R. (1977), *Scripts, Plans, Goals, and Understanding*, New Jersey, Lawrence Erlbaum

Schumann, J. (1978a), 'The acculturation model of second language acquisition' in R.C. Gingras (ed.) *Second Language Acquisition and Foreign Language Teaching*, CAL

Schumann, J. (1978b), *The Pidginisation Process: A Model for Second Language Acquisition*, Rowley MA, Newbury House

Selinker, L. (1972), 'Interlanguage', *IRAL*, X/3

Service, E. (1989), *Phonological Coding in Working Memory and Foreign-Language Learning*, General Psychology Monographs B9, Dept. of Psychology, University of Helsinki

Sinclair, J., and Coulthard, M. (1975), *Towards an Analysis of Discourse*, OUP

Singleton, D. (1989), *Language Acquisition: The Age Factor*, Multilingual Matters, Clevedon.

Skehan, P. (1986), 'Cluster Analysis and the identification of learner types', in Cook, V. (ed.), *Experimental Approaches to Second Language Learning*, Oxford, Pergamon

Skehan, P. (1988), 'Early lexical development and the prediction of foreign language learning success, *polyglot*, 9, fiche 2

Skehan, P. (1989), *Individual Differences in Second-Language Learning*, London, Edward Arnold

Skinner, B.F. (1957), *Verbal Behavior*, New York, Appleton-Century-Crofts

Skutnabb-Kangas, T. (1981), *Bilingualism or not: The Education of Minorities*, Cleveland, Multilingual Matters

Snow, C., and Hoefnagel-Hohle, M. (1977), 'Age differences in the pronunciation of foreign sounds', *Language and Speech*, 20, 357-365

Snow, C., and Hoefnagel-Hohle, M. (1978), 'The critical period for language acquisition: evidence from second language learning', *Child Development*, 49, 1114-1128

Southern Examining Group (1986), *French*, South-East Regional Examinations Board, Tunbridge Wells, UK

Spolsky, B. (1989a), *Conditions for Second Language Learning*, OUP

Spolsky, B. (1989b), 'Maori Bilingual education and language revitalisation', *J. Multilingual and Multicultural Development*, 10, 2, 89-106

Swan, M., and Smith, B. (1987), *Learner English*, CUP

Tarone, E. (1980), 'Communication strategies, foreigner talk, and repair in interlanguage', *Language Learning*, 30/2, 417–431

Tarone, E. (1988), *Variation in Interlanguage*, London, Edward Arnold

Underwood, M. (1989), *Teaching Listening*, Longman, Harlow

Valdman, A. (1976), *Introduction to French Phonology and Morphology*, Newbury House

Wallerstein, N. (1983), 'The teaching approach of Paolo Freire', in Oller, J.W., Jr., and Ricard-Amato, P.A. (eds.) (1983), *Methods that Work*, Newbury House

Wardhaugh, R. (1987), *Languages in Competition*, Oxford, Blackwell

Wendon, A and Rubin, J. (eds.) (1987), *Learner Strategies in Language Learning*, New Jersey, Prentice–Hall

Werker, J.F., Gilbert, J.H.V., Humphrey, K., and Tees, R.C. (1981), 'Developmental aspects of crosslanguage speech perception', *Child Development*, 52, 349-355

Wesche, M.B. (1981), 'Language aptitude measures in streaming, matching students with methods, and diagnosis of learning problems' in Diller, K. (ed.) (1981), *Individual Differences and Universals in Language Learning*, Newbury House, 83-118

Wesche, M.B., and Ready, D. (1985), 'Foreigner talk in the university classroom', in Gass, S.M., and Madden, C.G. (eds.), *Input in Second Language Acquisition*, Rowley, Mass; Newbury House

White, L. (1986), 'Implications of parametric variation for adult second language acquisition: an investigation of the pro-drop parameter', in V.J. Cook (ed.), *Experimental Approaches to Second Language Acquisition*, Oxford, Pergamon

White, L. (1989), *Universal Grammar and Second Language Acquisition*, John Benjamins

Winitz, H. (1981) (ed.), *The Comprehension Approach to Foreign Language Instruction*, Newbury House

Williams, L. (1977), 'The perception of consonant voicing by Spanish English bilinguals', *Perception and Psychophysics*, 21, 4, 289-297

Wode, H. (1981), *Learning a Second Language*, Tubingen: Narr

Index

Numbers in **bold** refer to pages where a word is glossed.